DECEIT OF JUDGMENT

GUY K. GRIFFIN

NEWMAN SPRINGS PUBLISHING
320 Broad Street
Red Bank, NJ 07701

First originally published by Newman Springs Publishing 2021

ISBN 978-1-63692-691-9 (Paperback)
ISBN 978-1-63692-692-6 (Digital)

Printed in the United States of America

To Stephanie Merkel; special thanks

PROLOGUE

You kick my cat,
I'll kill your dog.

—Bubba

The morning's dawn was just beginning to filter the sun's rays through the east Texas woods as the two assailants drove the back-country roads toward Kaufman. Since gearing up and setting off for their destination, they had sat in silence, each lost in their own thoughts. But neither of them held doubts about what lay ahead; both were committed to the task at hand. This morning's long-planned execution had them both anxious with nervous anticipation.

The man riding shotgun removed the pistol from his hoodie's kangaroo pocket, doing so for his own amusement. He liked the heft of the revolver and the caliber, 357 magnum. Flicking his wrist, the cylinder snapped open. He extracted one of the bullets from the chamber, turning the shell to look at the hollow point. A small smile creased his lips as he thought of the design...manufactured for mayhem. Lightly bouncing it in his palm, feeling the weight, he held it up toward the driver. They exchanged glances and smiled. "Bada bing...bada boom," he said, laughing. The driver joined in, laughing at the quip.

Chambering the shell, he returned the pistol to the pouch pocket and pulled the hood up to cover his head. He slouched down in the car's seat as they began to enter Kaufman's city limits. The driver navigated the small town's side streets as planned, following a route to avoid having the car picked up on CCTV from a gas station or some other place. Within a few minutes, they reached their destination, pulling up to the curb on East Grove Street that ran alongside the Kaufman courthouse. The passenger looked at his watch...one minute ahead of schedule. Perfect. The driver put the car in park, letting it idle. Both of them knew the wait would be short. Their target was very punctual.

Sure enough, within just a few minutes there was his car, heading toward them. Slumped down in the front seat, with the driver peering under a ball cap and passenger under the hoodie, they watched as he drove right past their car. The passenger used the side mirror to watch as he turned to park just across the street, a mere hundred feet away. His walk to work from where he parked would bring him back their way along the sidewalk right across the street. The passenger had to cover a few short steps to confront him. The plan was for the driver to not exit the car, just drive.

The passenger slowly rose up in the front seat intently watching the car's side mirror. The target exited his car, putting on his sports coat before opening the door to his back seat and retrieving his briefcase. For him, this was just like any other morning. He had followed this routine hundreds of times, having no idea that in a few moments, he would never walk the earth again. Briefcase in hand, he turned toward the sidewalk and headed to work.

"Here he comes," said the assassin as he reached for the door handle.

CHAPTER 1

THE EARLY MORNING HAD TYLER following his routine of fifty crunches. Kano, his pit bull mix, was doing his morning ritual—watching Tyler. Finishing his six-pack maintenance, Tyler shit, showered, and shaved, dressing into his slacks, shirt, and tie. Sitting on the bed pulling on his boots, Kano was giving him the look, the *what's in store for me today* look.

"Sorry, Kano, this is the 'no way, Jose' day. I'm going to the office." Cocking his head in a vain attempt to decipher human lingo, the dog's tail was going a mile a minute. If anything, he was ever hopeful. Tyler smiled to himself as he gazed at the dog, knowing how much Kano loved going with him. They were truly close friends. As he stood and walked to the closet to get his jacket, his cell phone began to ring. The screen read "Russ."

"Morning, Russ, what's up?"

"Shit's hit the fan big-time, Tex. Mark Hasse has been gunned down outside the Kaufman courthouse this morning. Happened less than an hour ago." A comatose person could have sensed the tension in Major Wilson's voice. "The assailant killed him in the street. I'm on my way there now. Can't tell you any more than that...hell, I don't have any more than that except that the gunman fled the scene and disappeared. Get your ass to Kaufman. I've got to take these calls. My phone's blowing up." The line went dead.

Tyler stood there for a moment, dumbfounded. It wasn't like Major Wilson hadn't contacted him many a time over the years with some terrible news, but what the hell? Mark Hasse, the chief assistant district attorney for Kaufman County, murdered. Outside his court-house, no less!

Pocketing his cell phone, Tyler put on his jacket and then went to his nightstand, retrieving his pistols from the drawer, putting his .380 auto in his ankle holster and inserting the .357 SIG auto into his shoulder holster. He lifted his light-gray Stetson from the peg by the bedroom door and put it on. Walking into the kitchen, he grabbed a banana from the fruit tray on the counter. Kano was right on his heels. Tyler opened the door to the garage he had converted into a kennel. Kano knew the drill. "Go on, Kano, get in there," Tyler said firmly. Kano lowered his head and skulked slowly down the steps. Tyler did a visual for food and water, switched on the thermostat, and hauled ass to the back door to his truck parked in the driveway.

The route to Kaufman would take Tyler roughly an hour if the traffic cooperated. The Dallas / Fort Worth metropolitan traffic had a way of bogging down, especially early in the morning. Kaufman is some forty miles from Dallas with the county bearing the same name having a population of about six thousand people. The small Texas city was not exactly known as a hotbed for people being gunned down in the street, much less prominent prosecutors.

His thoughts turned to Mark Hasse. Tyler knew him fairly well. Hasse had worked in Dallas before transferring to Kaufman. He was one of the most respected prosecutors in North Texas. Hell, the whole damn state, reasoned Tyler. All members of law enforcement knew that their jobs created enemies, with prosecutors being at the top of the enemy-creating food chain. They were the men and women who stood front and center in the courtrooms and declared, "The evidence will show that the person sitting here before you is guilty as sin and should be sent to the penitentiary," or something along those lines. Their job did have a way of leaving a lasting impression on criminals. Now just who the hell did Hasse piss off enough for them to blast his ass off in the street?

Knowing he wouldn't have a clue until he got there, Tyler pulled his phone from his pocket and hit the name on the top of his contact list: girlfriend. "Good morning, Tyler," answered Priscilla. "These early-morning phone calls usually come with some sort of surprise," she said, sounding slightly disappointed.

"Yeah, babe, I know, and this one is no different," said Tyler. "I've got some bad news and some bad news. Which do you want first?"

"Oh, well…since I get a choice, give me the bad news first." Her voice was flat as a pancake. "But I'm sure it will have a negative effect on our plans for Lee Harvey's tonight. So I just can't wait to hear it."

Lee Harvey's is a popular bar in Dallas named after you-know-who. The residents of Big D aren't cold SOBs, but hey, they have a sense of humor and it's been long enough. Well, they think so anyway, and this night the Graceland Ninjaz band was playing there. With them being one of the metroplex's most popular party bands, having a signature nod to Elvis, Tyler and Priscilla had been looking forward to seeing them for several weeks.

"There was a murder in Kaufman this morning…" Tyler paused before going on. "A prominent prosecutor was shot in the street outside the courthouse downtown."

"Oh…my…word!" gasped Priscilla.

"Yeah, it doesn't get any worse than this," continued Tyler. "I knew this prosecutor fairly well. We've worked some cases together."

"Tyler, I'm sorry for sounding so disappointed about tonight. I thought it might have been something more trivial." The concern was evident in her voice. He knew she worried for his safety, especially working murder cases. "We can see the Ninjaz any time. I just want you to be careful. And, my god…who would have done such a thing?"

"That exact thought has been on my mind since Russ called me this morning with the news. I'm on my way to Kaufman now to investigate," replied Tyler. "As of right now, the assailant is smoke. Or that is the last word I got from Russ. The possibilities are endless. Prosecutors piss off a lot of dangerous people. I'm chomping at the bit to get there."

"I'm sure you are. This is what you're so good at," replied Priscilla, attempting to put a positive slant on some very bad news.

"You just be careful. We'll see the Ninjaz this summer at the House of Blues."

He had to hand it to her; she was already thinking ahead. The girl did like to have her fun. "Sorry, Priscilla, I was looking forward to tonight as much as you."

"I know, sweetie, I understand." Tyler could hear the school bell ringing in the background. "I've got to run. The bell just rang for my class."

"I'll call you this evening and give you a what's-up. Love you, babe," said Tyler.

"Love you too, Tyler. Be careful. Bye."

*****

Tyler exited the LBJ freeway loop, taking Highway 175 east to Kaufman. The traffic hadn't been a problem to speak of, and it would only get better now that he was traveling east away from the loop and suburb of Mesquite. His thoughts turned to his conversation with his girlfriend. He couldn't begin to count the number of times he had made such a call to cancel plans. Thank goodness she understood, especially with her background.

She had been married before to her high school sweetheart from her hometown of El Paso. Her husband had joined the Department of Justice right after college, becoming a DEA agent. At one point in their marriage, he was assigned to the American embassy in Mexico City. Priscilla had experienced the life of law enforcement long before meeting Tyler.

She was a beautiful woman of Latin descent, a full-figured senorita with a full mane of chestnut hair. She had a flair for how to dress and an outgoing personality, which Tyler liked. She was game for anything. Tyler had taught her how to snow ski. She went with him to his cabin in east Texas to deer hunt, and they both enjoyed the Texas music scene. They frequented the local nightclubs for dancing, be it rock or country, on a few occasions going to the famous hill country town and clubs around Austin like Luckenbach and Gruene

Hall, the latter being where George Straight got his start before moving to Nashville to become a superstar.

Priscilla's father owned a grocery supply business in El Paso, and her mother was a schoolteacher. Priscilla had followed her mother's footsteps into teaching, as did her two sisters. She was a University of Texas at El Paso alumna, now teaching bilingual elementary education to disabled children in the same suburb of Dallas where Tyler lived. She came from a very close family. Tyler liked them. She was also a mother of two, Jacqueline and Justin. Her children were in high school when she and Tyler met several years back, but now they both attended college. Jacqueline was enrolled at the University of North Texas in Denton, and Justin was at UTEP living with Priscilla's brother in El Paso. Tyler liked her kids; Priscilla had done a good job with them.

Approaching the Kaufman courthouse, Tyler could see exactly where to go. The street was cordoned off with crime tape. A contingent of police and plainclothes officers were gathered behind it. Tyler recognized several of his fellow Rangers even from this distance. Parking his truck, he ducked under the tape and made his way toward Major Wilson, who was on his cell phone with his back to Tyler. As he approached, he could see all the blood pooled in the street. There was no body; Mark Hasse's corpse was gone. All that was left of the murder was a bloody briefcase, number photo markers, and more blood. He caught the eyes of his fellow Rangers, and they in turn nodded to one another. The atmosphere was somber, with a couple of small groups of Kaufman police officers talking quietly among themselves. The Rangers were standing close to Wilson, who was still on his phone. As he turned Tyler's way, his eyebrows rose in recognition while holding the phone to his ear.

"He's here now," said Wilson into his phone. "As soon as I bring him up to speed, we'll be right up there." Wilson dropped the phone into his coat pocket and took the few steps toward Tyler. "There you are, Tex," he said as he walked past Tyler toward the bloody pavement. "Let me tell you what we've got so far, then we are wanted at the courthouse for a meeting with McLelland and the FBI." Tyler followed the Major to the edge of the photo markers surrounding the blood and Hasse's briefcase.

"There was a witness," explained Wilson. "He said it went down like this." He turned around and pointed to the opposite side of the street. "Parked there was a cream-colored Crown Vic, driver and passenger inside. Passenger door street-side." Turning now to the other side of the street, closer to the blood by the curb, Wilson pointed to a car parked between white parking stripes just off the street some one hundred feet away to the right. "That Acura parked down the way is Hasse's car. He's parked there for years. It's his designated spot."

Turning and facing Tyler, the Major continued. "Tex, Hasse exits his car and walks along the sidewalk toward the courthouse. The shooter exits the Vic from the passenger door, crossing the street to confront him. They engage in a very brief conversation, the witness said fifteen seconds or so. The shooter is dressed in black slacks and a black hoodie. The hoodie is pulled up to cover his face. The witness stated that within just seconds of their confrontation on the sidewalk, Hasse raises his right hand as if to show he wants nothing to do with the gunman and begins to back away into the street, dropping his briefcase. As he's doing this, the shooter pulls a pistol and shoots Mark twice in the upper torso. Mark falls into the street, landing on his back. The shooter then steps into the street, standing over Hasse, shooting him three more times point blank in the head. Then he calmly walks back to the Vic, and the two of them drive away."

Wilson pointed down the street to the residential neighborhood behind the courthouse. "Driving that way. It took place just after seven this morning. Hasse was dead at the scene. Large caliber, probably .357. Won't know for sure until autopsy. No bullet casings at the scene, and witness said the killer didn't retrieve any, so it had to be a revolver."

Tyler didn't expect much from his next questions, but he was going to ask them anyway. "Did the witness get the plates or description of the shooter?"

Slightly shaking his head, Wilson replied, "No plates. As for the shooter...all very generic. Five ten to six feet, two hundred pounds to maybe two twenty. White male, possibly Hispanic, but the witness is thinking white dude." Wilson turned to the opposite end of the street from where the killer's car drove away. "Just there at that intersection is where the witness was. He was on his way from breakfast up the street, going to work. Zero on the driver with the Vic facing the other way. So he only had a rear view. Plus, he stated that the driver seemed to be slumped down in the seat, or very short. Thinks driver may have been wearing a ball cap. He knows cars, states that it was a 2005 or 2006 Crown Vic. Chief Burns called in all of his off-duty men to search for it. But shit, Tex, by the time the word got out about the car, over half an hour had passed. They could have been almost to Dallas by then."

Wilson was looking at Tyler intently, his forehead a mass of furrows. "If they went east...then shit fire, they could be deep in the backwoods." With this comment came a sigh of utter frustration. "So we're looking for the fucking needle." The Major reached into his jacket pocket and retrieved his ringing phone. He looked at the screen. "I've got to take this, it's Preston." He turned and walked a few feet away, putting the phone to his ear.

*****

Tyler's fellow Rangers Vasquez, Jamison, and Miles formed a loose circle around him. From the magnitude of this crime, the atmosphere was weird. It was like an evil spirit was lurking in the vicinity, and Tyler could feel it. And it wasn't just the murder; it was who was murdered and how. These kinds of prominent people were rarely killed in Texas. Vasquez was the first to break the silence, looking at Tyler. "What do you think, man?"

"Joe, I think every criminal prosecutor makes more enemies than there are barbs on a barbed wire fence, but it's very rare that they get killed," replied Tyler, looking at each Ranger circled around him. "Now as far as how this went down, I have mucho questions. Like, why does the shooter confront Hasse on the street?"

"I'm thinking to stop him in his tracks," chimed in Jamison. "To be right on top of him for the execution. That's about as point-blank as you can get."

"I'm with you there. The duo seemed to know his routine by where they parked waiting for him," replied Tyler. "But why the confrontation? Why not just walk up behind him and shoot him in the back? Or say, 'excuse me, sir,' and nail him as he turns around? The witness stated that he stopped Hasse for a brief conversation."

"So you're thinking the shooter wanted Hasse to see his face?" asked Vasquez.

"Look at this weather. It's been very mild here the last few days, especially considering it's January in Texas," stated Tyler. "But it's still cool enough that if someone sees a person in a hoodie, they aren't going to think much of it. So it seems to me that the shooter could have pulled this off without a 'by your leave, sir.' No, this shooter wanted a 'by your leave, sir.' I'm thinking he wanted Hasse to see his face. He wanted Hasse to know he was about to die. Probably said it right to his face. To announce, 'the angel of death is here to collect your soul.' He wanted to see Mark's fear."

"You seem pretty convinced," said Miles.

"It just reeks personal to me," replied Tyler. "Say it was a vendetta from a family member Hasse had prosecuted, or a friend. Would they have carried out the hit here? Outside the courthouse? I'm thinking someone is making a statement."

"Damn, Tyler, you've been here ten minutes and you've already got a hypothesis on this murder," exclaimed Vasquez with a slight smile. "You're light-years ahead of me."

"No shit," replied Jamison.

"Hell, y'all heard the same thing Wilson told me. It's just a gut feeling. You could be right, Steve. The shooter might have wanted to be right on top of Hasse for the deed. Maybe Hasse had no idea who this person was. Maybe it was a vendetta," replied Tyler. "Could have said, 'this is for so-and-so.' Hell, we're all a long way from knowing for sure. But I must admit I have another thing that makes me feel that all this adds up to very personal." Several of the Kaufman police officers had now joined the group of Rangers, listening in on their conversation.

"And that is...?" asked Miles, looking at the gathered group using a slight inflection. This caused the Rangers to smile at one another. They all liked Tyler and knew he was a good investigator.

"Who was the driver? It seems to me that Hasse panicked. The witness stated that he held up his hand, backing off the sidewalk before dropping his briefcase into the street," explained Tyler. "Even the best-laid plans can go awry. Say Hasse keeps his cool and takes his briefcase and knocks the shit out of the shooter or at least throws it into him, giving Mark time to make a run for it back to his car and across the parking lot," Tyler continued, "and doing a shuck-and-jive as he's putting as much space as he can between him and the shooter. Yeah, I know his escape would have been a long shot, but after hearing what transpired, at least he would have had a chance. And we all know it's much harder to hit a moving target, especially with a pistol. And even that much harder to make a kill shot. Every few feet of distance makes a big difference. And what if Hasse had got a really good lick in, getting a big head start? Is the shooter going to chase him across the parking lot blasting away even in the early morning? Maybe, but I doubt it."

"That's a lot of could-haves and what-ifs," responded Miles.

"Bear with me here," replied Tyler. "Where I'm going with this is, there wasn't just the shooter—there was a driver! Two fuckers out to do the deed. That's very rare in this kind of murder. Shit, no, not murder...a fucking assassination! Ask yourself, how often are two people totally invested to attempt this kind of crime?"

The Rangers and the Kaufman police officers began to nod and acknowledge by their body language that Tyler was making a good point.

"The shooter is on a mission," continued Tyler. "This location convinces me of that. These were a couple of characters who were both totally committed. It feels so personal to me. Two people all in, no matter the consequences. They took a hell of a chance pulling this off."

One of the Kaufman police officers spoke up. "You've got a good point, Mr. Davis. Besides being the DA here, Mr. Hasse was a licensed police officer in Kaufman. He carried a gun with him at all times. It was on his person when he was killed but found to be still in his holster."

Nodding to acknowledge the officer's input, Tyler responded, "I wouldn't be a bit surprised to learn that the shooter knew that." He glanced around the circle of men. "He was extremely determined, that's for damn sure. He didn't fuck around. He was looking forward to the confrontation. Though the outcome was stacked squarely in their favor, it was very risky. Just who the hell agreed to drive? Who is this pair?"

CHAPTER 2

Major Wilson walked back to his men after finishing the call with Director Preston. "If there ever was a man fit to be tied, I just got off the phone with him," said Wilson, looking intently at his Rangers. "Telling you men this is like telling Santa when it's Christmas, but as you can imagine, the brass in Austin is going apeshit right now. This fucking murder is going to put pressure on all of us like you can't imagine. Anyway…" Wilson paused ever so briefly as though he was thinking about something before he continued. "Tex, I want you and Steve to come with me to the courthouse meeting with the feds. Joe, you and Miles go to the police station and see what is going on at their end. Let's make haste, gentlemen. McLelland has called me twice already."

When the three Rangers entered the conference room, the others were seated and standing around a large conference table. DA McLelland was standing with a large cup of coffee in his hand talking with FBI agent Mike Smith. Tyler had met all the men in the room before, but he had not worked closely with any of them. The Rangers only worked with the FBI on major cases. What's more, people were always being transferred to other locales; an agent from just the year before could be in Chicago now. Police Chief Burns was seated on the opposite side of the table from McLelland and was talking with another FBI agent. They all turned toward the doorway as Wilson, Davis, and Jamison entered the room.

"Have a seat, gentlemen," said McLelland. "I believe we all know one another." Mike McLelland looked haggard. He was a large, robust man, known for wearing his cowboy hats and boots. His black Stetson was on a small table behind him. The men shook hands and said their greetings, and the Rangers took seats at the table. It was a very big room, the table seated about thirty. With the addition of the Rangers, there were now seven people in the room. More FBI agents and detectives would be at the Kaufman police station.

It was so early in this investigation that law enforcement would be fragmented. Each group would work different angles to collect evidence. Later, these men and women would meet and compare information. Solving this murder as quickly as possible was too important to not look at all possible scenarios. The men in this conference room wanted to hear from the Rangers. At the Kaufman police station, the FBI would want to talk with the Kaufman detectives. Right now it was all about fact-finding.

McLelland took a seat close to the Rangers. "As you men know, we have very little to work with. What we do know is that Mark Hasse was prosecuting a case involving an Aryan Brotherhood member. He is locked up in our jail, awaiting trial. Last month, we issued a state-wide bulletin warning that the Brotherhood was planning to inflict death on law enforcement officials involved in cases where members are facing life sentences or the death penalty. We certainly have no intention of getting tunnel vision here, but it has been discussed as a possible motive. The murder does have signs of an organized hit, in its brutality as well as in its brazen planning. Broad daylight at the courthouse. I know it was early morning, but still, it defies logic."

Saying this, McLelland looked exasperated. "The case with the Aryan Brotherhood suspect is an ongoing case, and Hasse prosecuted many cases in the past that could have persons seeking revenge. So therein lies the rub. Mexican cartel, drug gang, Aryan Brotherhood—it's all up in the air. This county has more than its fair share of dirt-bags." McLelland was talking very calmly, but Tyler could detect the slightest tremor in his voice. He was mad as hell that his senior deputy had been brutally slain outside his courthouse earlier that morning.

FBI Special Agent Smith spoke up. "Major Wilson, we would like one of your Rangers to work with Agent Thompson here"—he motioned toward the agent sitting next to him—"to go over the cases Mark Hasse has in the works as well as those going back the last several years. We want to see if anything stands out. This could go anywhere, so it's imperative that we keep an open mind. Sheriff Allbright has his men spread out all over the county trying to locate the getaway car. Right now it's the only big lead. That car is registered to someone, and it needs to be found. Do any of you men have something you want to discuss?"

With the question being directed toward the Rangers, Wilson turned and glanced at Tyler, giving him the floor. Wilson knew Tyler well enough to know that he was thinking outside the box. Tyler looked at McLelland and said, "Mr. McLelland, at this point I only know what you men know, which isn't much." Then turning to Special Agent Smith, he said, "I do have questions about why the shooter confronted Hasse on the street. That baffles me. But I'm with you gentlemen. Right now, with what little we know, it does seem to point to an organized hit. And if it's okay with my Major here, I would like to look over Hasse's case files."

"You're who I had in mind, Tex," said Wilson.

Tyler acknowledged Wilson's statement and then looked at Chief Burns. "Chief, where is the witness?"

"At the police station giving his statement on video. He's with our detectives and the FBI," said Chief Burns.

"First of all, I would like to head that way now. Video or not, I'd like to speak to him in person," said Tyler. "Especially with it being fresh in his mind."

"No problem, Davis," replied Burns. "I'll call over to the station and make sure that they keep him there until you arrive. He hasn't been there long. We had him out at the crime scene for an hour this morning going over with us what he saw." Chief Burns stepped to the back of the conference room to make the call.

"Well, by the time you get back it will probably be only you and Thompson," said McLelland. "Mark's secretary is still here, but she's really shook up. She's down the hall in her and Mark's office with a Kaufman police officer to make her feel safe. But she expressed wanting to leave as soon as possible to go home and compose herself. The courthouse staff in general is very upset with what happened here this morning. It's effectively shut down for the day. Mary did know that we would need her help today, so she's putting together the computer case files as well as pertinent paperwork for you to look over. If she has left by the time you get back, Thompson will be in their office. Chief Burns is going to have police security at the courthouse for as long as anyone needs to stay. I want to catch these sons of bitches more than you can imagine." There was that underlying tremor in his throat; Mike McLelland was acting stoic but inside he was raging.

Chief Burns finished his call and approached Tyler. "Davis, the witness is finishing up his video. We are going to have him stay put to speak with you after he's done."

"Thank you, Chief." Tyler turned to Wilson. "I'm out of here, boss. I'll keep you informed on what comes up."

"All right, Tex," said Wilson.

With an adios to the agents, Chief, and DA, Tyler left for the police station; he was very interested in speaking to the witness. As Tyler was leaving the courthouse, he couldn't help but notice how quiet it was. Yes, it was mostly empty, but the few people there seemed to be dazed. There was also quite a police presence outside the entrance way. Tyler had the feeling that this was just the beginning of things to come; he couldn't shake the notion that it was going to get much worse. Say the Aryan stronghold had to be taken down; they would be armed to the teeth. *Well, this is America*, thought Tyler. *Every police officer understands second amendment rights. You fight fire with fire.* Tyler had no problem with that; he could shoot his ass off. Sheriffs and outlaws; cowboys and Indians. Just get the job done. And the Texas Rangers had been getting the job done since the 1800s.

*****

When Tyler pulled up to the Kaufman police station, he had to park down the street. The station's lot was full of marked and unmarked cars. Tyler saw ATF, FBI, and Homeland Security mixed in among the police vehicles. This was a major crime and it was getting major attention. As Tyler walked to the entrance of the station, he saw FBI Agent Allen Harvey smoking a cigarette.

Harvey greeted Tyler and flipped the cigarette butt into the bushes; Tyler followed him inside. Tyler hoped the video was over; he was ready to interview the witness. Harvey stopped outside interrogation room number one, but this was not going to be an interrogation. This was going to be a simple interview with the eyewitness. Tyler was ready to get started.

"He's in there," said Harvey. "He finished up the video a few minutes ago. The detectives and agents left him alone for a few minutes to gather himself. He's been questioned, videoed, and questioned again. He's been more than cooperative, doing all he can to help. Agents are down the hall reviewing the video. Collins asked me to have you stop by and speak with him after talking to the witness. His name is Hamilton, George Hamilton. We're letting him smoke in there. Is that cool with you?"

"Harvey, you could let him build a fucking campfire, I just want to talk to him," replied Tyler.

Agency Harvey laughed. "Well, Davis, go see what he has to say." The two men smiled at one another; first tension-breaker of the day for both of them. Tyler turned the knob and entered the room.

Mr. Hamilton was seated at a table. In front of him was a cup of coffee, a can of Coke, and a plate with a half-eaten sandwich on it. He was smoking a cigarette and using the coffee cup for an ashtray. Mr. Hamilton was about forty-five years old, average height and build, and clean-shaven. But what stood out were his hands; they were rough. Whatever Mr. Hamilton did for a living, he did it with his hands. Salt-of-the-earth kind of people, thought Tyler; the kind of person he wanted to go to work for each day.

"Hello, Mr. Hamilton, I'm Tyler Davis with the Texas Department of Public Safety. I appreciate you sticking around to meet with me. I know that you've already answered a slew of questions and sat through a video. And I'll probably ask you some of the same questions you've already been asked a dozen times. I'm sure that you're more than ready to be on your way and wondering why I don't just watch the video. But I'm very interested in talking with you in person just in case we might uncover something together."

George Hamilton had made eye contact with Tyler from the moment he entered the room. He stood up to shake Tyler's hand with a good strong grip and replied, "Mr. Davis, it's a pleasure to meet you. Yes, I'm worn-out, it's been quite a morning. I'm here to help any way I can. I was told that after meeting with you I could be on my way. Let's get on with it. By the way, you introduced yourself as a Texas Department of Public Safety officer. What you are is a Texas Ranger. Every Texan worth his salt knows that. I was raised right here in Kaufman. I know my Texas history."

"Thank you, Mr. Hamilton."

"Call me George."

"You got it," replied Tyler. "Now tell me where you were when you witnessed the killing."

George Hamilton took a deep breath and said, "I work at an auto garage just down the street from the courthouse. Most mornings, I eat at a café just a couple of blocks away on the corner. It opens at six each morning, so I park at the garage and walk to the diner, you know, just to get the body moving and the juices flowing. Then I walk the two blocks back to work, which puts me there just before seven thirty. That's starting time. So I'm crossing the East Grove intersection at, say, seven twenty-five, or thereabouts. That put me fifty yards away from where the murder took place, give or take."

George lit another cigarette and leaned on the table. "I'm crossing the street, no cars or people to speak of, when I glance to my right and see this figure—and I say figure because he's wearing a hoodie, dressed in all black. Black slacks, black hoodie. Now it's January, early morning, so it's a little cool out. I don't think a thing about it really. I've got a light jacket on myself."

He took a draw on his cigarette, leaned back in his chair, and said, "A few seconds later, that's when the shit started. I hear raised voices, nothing I could distinguish. Covered that a thousand times already, believe me. So by now I've made it to the corner at the opposite side of the street. I turn, and for the first time I notice the other person on the sidewalk. Didn't see him at first, just the man crossing the street dressed in black. The FBI and Kaufman police showed me where Hasse parked. I guess he sat in his car for a minute before he got out because I didn't see his car pull up. I didn't even see him exit his car. I only noticed him when I saw the two talking on the street and heard their voices. It was brief, Mr. Davis, maybe twenty seconds at most, maybe less.

"The next thing I see is the killer pulling a pistol from his front hoodie pocket and Mr. Hasse raising his hands and backing away. The killer fires two rounds. Mr. Hasse stumbles and falls into the street. No, that's not right—he blows him away into the street. Mr. Hasse had on a sports coat, and I could see blood spewing from his back after the shots. But he's not through. The killer steps forward and stands over him and shoots him three more times at point-blank range. He calmly walks back across the street, gets in the car from the passenger side, and the car drives away. It drove right by the courthouse." Mr. Hamilton put his cigarette out in the coffee cup and looked up at Tyler, waiting for his next question.

"George, think really hard," said Tyler. "Do you think from what you saw that Mr. Hasse and the killer knew each other?"

George lowered his head and rubbed his face with his hands. He sat back up and replied, "Well, now that you mention it, I did think that maybe at first, when I heard the conversation and turned that way to watch them. They seemed to be having a heated conversation, but it was brief, like I said, so I can't be positive."

"And did you catch any of the conversation?" asked Tyler.

"I was asked that a thousand times already," said George. "And every time I told the FBI and Kaufman detectives no, because I couldn't say for sure. I was down the block. But just maybe, when he was pulling out the gun, I heard the killer say, 'you cocksucker.' I hope me telling you that doesn't mean I was holding something back, I'm not sure. I've been trying my best to help y'all find the killer."

"No, George, you're good. Just a couple of more questions. What did the shooter look like?" asked Tyler. "What was his race?"

"Got that one a lot too," said George. "He had the hoodie pulled really far forward to hide his face, and it was early morning, so it was light out but not, you know, really sunny yet. I can only say he was a white dude, maybe a light-skinned Mexican. Definitely not a Black dude. Six foot or so, two hundred, two ten, no facial hair."

"One last question, George, and you're out of here. What about the driver?"

"Not a fucking clue. Just a figure in the driver's seat, a silhouette. I think he had on a ball cap, didn't make out any hair. Plus he stayed in the car, so the inside was dark, especially early in the morning. And when they left, they drove away from me. Just the car. I know cars, being a mechanic. It was a light- or cream-colored Crown Vic, maybe a 2005 or '06. Hell, they look so much alike, and I was in shock. I'm positive on the make, just not the year. When I saw it parked there, I thought, *unmarked police car.* One thing about the driver. He wasn't very tall but he could have been slouching down in the seat to be less conspicuous."

"George, I want to thank you very much. I'm sure most of this was redundant, but you've helped this investigation more than you can imagine. May God bless you and yours. You're free to go."

"No problem, Ranger Davis. Y'all catch this bastard."

"George, you have my word, we'll catch both of the bastards. Thank you again."

They shook hands. George Hamilton took his jacket from the back of the chair and went out the door.

CHAPTER 3

T YLER SAT THERE FOR A moment thinking about what George Hamilton had told him. It was basically the same story he had gotten that morning from Major Wilson. But there were quite a few things creeping into his head. He just couldn't shake the feeling that this murder was personal, and it seemed really thought out. There was the car, a Crown Vic. George Hamilton even said it himself: "unmarked police car." A person would think that, especially by a courthouse. Then there was the location of the hit, outside the Kaufman courthouse. To Tyler, that was the biggest puzzle of them all. Why there?

It seemed to him it would have been easier and safer for the killer to execute Hasse somewhere else. Yeah, it was seven o'clock in the morning, and there were few people around, and he was wearing a hoodie, but he's still outside the frigging courthouse. Any Kaufman police officer, probation officer—hell, fucking janitor in the area could have called it in and given chase; everyone and their dog had a cell phone. Yeah, they did some things that were smart but also did some things that defied logic. It was leading Tyler to believe that the shooter was trying to make a statement by doing it at the courthouse. He had been willing to take that chance, and he got very, very lucky.

Another thing, thought Tyler: the confrontation on the street, especially calling Hasse a cocksucker just before blowing him away. To Tyler, it had "personal" written all over it. Then again, Tyler needed to take a step back. There was the Aryan Brotherhood member in the Kaufman jail. Anything was possible with that gang. Not only were they the most vicious gang in the Texas prison system, they were the most unpredictable. It was possible they could pull off such a murder. But being so early in the investigation, there were some very intelligent and experienced people working on this case; it needed to run its course. Law enforcement had made many a mistake putting blinders on, and that goes for anyone putting on a shield with the very best of intentions. Yes, Tyler was leaning toward this being more personal than a gang or cartel hit, but that didn't mean he was right. He was going to look over the *Hasse* case files and let his gut, his intellect, and the facts direct him.

Agent Harvey had said Collins wanted a word with him after his interview with Hamilton, so he stepped out of the interrogation room and into the hallway. "Tyler, down here." It was FBI Agent Harvey. "We're in here watching the video of Hamilton. Come on in."

Tyler walked down the hallway, and Harvey opened the door for him to enter the police station's conference room, which was much smaller than the one over at the courthouse. The table had been pushed against the wall and all the chairs moved to one side of it. Sitting on the table was a laptop with Hamilton giving his video interview of the morning's events. Gathered around the table were FBI, ATF, Kaufman detectives, and Homeland Security agents. There was a video camera over in the corner, and Tyler deduced that the video was made in here. Some of the people present had probably been here when it was made, but quite a few were probably seeing it for the first time.

It was not yet noon, and some of these agents had probably just arrived within the last hour or so. Many were just now being brought up to speed on what exactly had transpired that morning. This eyewitness video was the best thing that anyone had for now. The agents were sitting in the chairs intensely watching it.

Collins looked over his shoulder at Tyler when he entered the room. He got up from his seat, walked over to Tyler, and extended his hand. "Hello, Davis, long time no see."

"Hello, Agent Collins, good to see you," said Tyler. The two men shook hands.

Chris Collins was special agent in charge of the Dallas FBI office, known in law enforcement circles as the SAC. Tyler had met him several times over the years, but the two didn't know each other all that well. Tyler did know that Collins and Major Wilson were close friends, so Tyler felt like Collins had heard at least one or two good things about him. "Let's step outside the room and let these men watch this video. Some of them are seeing it for the first time," said Collins as he opened the door, the two of them stepping into the hallway. "Wanted to ask you how the interview went with Mr. Hamilton. What are you thinking from what you've learned so far?"

"Well, sir, it's very early, but I'm leaning toward this being a much more personal murder than say a gang or cartel hit," replied Tyler.

"Hmmm...and why is that?"

"Mainly because of the location of the murder. Why would a cartel or, say, the Aryan Brotherhood do the hit at the Kaufman courthouse? Much less a drug gang? Seems to me someone was trying to make a statement with the killing being carried out there. Also the shooter confronted Hasse on the street, face-to-face. Who would do that if it wasn't personal? That's where I'm leaning as of right now."

Special Agent Collins stood contemplating. A moment later, he stated, "You've made some interesting observations. Must admit I wasn't thinking along those lines, but that's exactly why we have you and other agents on this case. We need people thinking outside the box. This is one of the highest profile crimes to ever hit this county— no, let me rephrase that. It is the highest profile case this county has ever seen. I know that you're supposed to go over Mark Hasse's case files with one of my agents this afternoon. Go get some lunch and head that way. I talked to Thompson about fifteen minutes ago. He's already eaten and is at the courthouse now. He said that Hasse's secretary has given him computer files and paperwork for the two of you to examine. Look over those cases and let me know what you come up with. We can't afford any more nine elevens. As of now, there are several agencies involved with this investigation. There has to be complete communication within the agencies. Unilateral action will lead to embarrassment at the very least."

"Yes, sir, I understand completely."

"Fine, I won't keep you, then. Enjoy your lunch."

"Mr. Collins, thank you for letting me have a one-on-one with Mr. Hamilton. I know that could have been shot down, especially under the circumstances."

"Don't thank me, thank Chief Burns. Mr. Hamilton was about to finish the recording and he had been told he could leave afterward. I think he thought he was a suspect. Chief Burns called over here and told his detectives that under no circumstances was he to leave before you had a chance to interview him. It's there on the video. Mr. Tyler 'Tex' Davis, you carry a lot of weight." Collins smiled as he turned and walked back into the conference room.

Tyler did need to eat; he had only had a banana so far that morning, and it was pushing noon. When he left the police station, he saw the media trucks and press vans parked all along the street. They were made to park on the opposite curb so as not to block the police parking lot. As he walked to his truck past the media circus, reporters shouted out to him, asking if he was FBI and would he do an interview. Shaking his head no, he got in his truck and headed to the café George Hamilton had eaten breakfast at earlier that morning.

CHAPTER 4

Tyler sat at the counter at the café. There were a few locals inside, gathered at the tables and booths talking in hushed tones. It was like a pall hung in the air; it was depressing. This town was in mourning. The young lady took his order at the counter, and her voice was flat like the life had been sucked out of her. Tyler ordered a cheeseburger and fries, wolfed them down, got a Coke to go, and got the hell out of there. It was like being at a funeral.

He parked in the front of the courthouse; very few cars were there. Then it hit him. Why didn't Hasse park up here? It was closer to the courthouse main entrance and farther from the street. Then he remembered the large oak tree closer to East Grove Street. Tyler bet Mark had that spot designated for himself so he could park in the shade on the blistering hot Texas summer days. Another thought ran through his mind. Mark Hasse wasn't married. He flew small aircraft as a hobby; that and law enforcement were the two things in his life; that was what he lived for. Tyler strolled into the courthouse to see if his case files held a clue as to whether what he lived for had turned on him and led to his demise.

FBI Agent Thompson was at Hasse's desk when Tyler walked into the office. He looked up. "Hey, Tyler," he said. "Hasse's secretary split up Mark's case files into the last two years and the two years before that. I'm going through the previous two. She left the information for you there on her desk. I was going to let you look over those. I mean we've got to start somewhere, right? Mark has only worked for Kaufman County since 2009. So I thought we would cover those years first. If we don't find something there, we can search further back, but there's plenty here to keep us busy for a while. She's really organized. You'll see the folder there on the desk in front of the computer has each case categorized by month and year in descending order for that time period. Each case has a file number that will bring it up on the computer. It's really simple; you'll figure it out. And inside Mark's office here behind this door is their file cabinet storage for all their paper files. We have complete access to any and all the info in these offices. McLelland doesn't want us to remove anything unless we check with him first. Make yourself at home."

"All right, David, thanks." Tyler went and sat at Mary's desk and opened the folder. Sure enough, there they were, laid out pretty as a picture. Case name, number, year, and month, with a computer file number to bring each case up on the hard drive. There were a lot of cases but at least they were going to be simple enough to access. Tyler looked down at the folder, and sure enough, there was a case pending on an Aryan Brotherhood member sitting in the Kaufman county jail awaiting trial. Tyler kept scanning down the list looking at rape cases, meth cases, murders, and on and on. He was almost at the end of the folder, about two years back, when he stopped and stared.

Eric Williams. He had forgotten about Eric Williams. Tyler knew Eric Williams; he had been a justice of the peace and lawyer here in Kaufman County. Since he presided over minor civil cases, he had never handled any cases for Tyler, but they had met.

Tyler put Williams's case number in the computer and began to read the transcripts. Eric Williams had been convicted of theft of three computer monitors from the county storage locker. The case had been prosecuted by Mark Hasse and Mike McLelland. It said that Williams had been found guilty of the offense but given probation, not jail time. Hasse and McLelland had asked the presiding judge for jail time for Williams because he had "threatened people, scared people, and stolen from the people of Kaufman County." It turns out from the court transcripts that this had been a very contentious trial. A former girlfriend of Williams had come forward and testified that she had been harassed and threatened by Williams. Williams's lawyer contended that this was a "personal and political witch hunt" against

Williams partly because he had opposed the election of McLelland for Kaufman district attorney when he ran back in 2006. This was all very interesting to Tyler.

There was a lot here; many character witnesses had testified positively for Mr. Williams. Some were fellow attorneys; others were college friends who had attended Texas Christian University with Williams. One character witness, a police officer in Collin County, testified that "I put in him the most sacred trust I have." The witness also testified that he and Williams served together in the Texas State Guard, that Williams served as the weapons safety officer and instructor, and that he was proficient with the use of weapons ranging from the M16 to semiautomatic pistols.

Whoa... Tyler had thought all along that this murder was personal, and you don't get any more personal than this. And who would have known Hasse's routine better than someone working as a lawyer and justice of the peace in the very same building for years? *And if you're pissed, and I mean really pissed,* he thought, *what better place to do the deed and make a statement to* everyone *inside this building?* And he could see why Eric Williams would be really pissed. He had lost his job as justice of the peace, lost his law license, essentially lost his means to make a living as he had done for many years. The man had been stripped of what he had spent years educating himself for. Of course, if he felt like it was a vendetta, as his defense lawyer put it, "the whole thing is a witch hunt and anyone in the legal community here knows that," Tyler could see why the man might be just a little pissed. Pissed off enough to murder someone in cold blood on the street by the courthouse? Tyler could see that. Plus he knew how to handle weapons. "Proficient in their use"—direct testimony at his trial. Damn.

This was fitting with what Tyler had been thinking all along. Someone highly intelligent, someone with a personal motive, and someone who would want to confront Mark Hasse on the street so he would know who was about to take his life then and there. This was fitting like a glove. And not like OJ's glove; no, this baby was slipping right on, a perfect fit. But who would have driven the car? Tyler wondered. It's not like you walk up to your next-door neighbor and ask, "Hey, Bob, would you drive a getaway car for me while I knock off somebody?"

Tyler could understand why so many people were thinking it was an organized hit. Doing this kind of murder in broad daylight, a hundred yards or so from the front entrance of a courthouse, wasn't something your average Joe Blow pulls off. Tyler needed to find out more about Mr. Eric Williams. He wanted to talk to someone who worked with him every day, someone at the courthouse who wasn't a lawyer or a judge. He wanted to talk to Williams's secretary. He needed to find out if she still worked at the courthouse.

"David, come in here for a minute," Tyler called into the next room where Agent Thompson was.

Thompson entered the room. "What ya got?"

Tyler stood up from his seat, motioned to his chair, "Sit down here for a minute and look over this case file and transcripts." As Agent Thompson came around the desk to sit, Tyler went to the front desk and picked up a chair that had no rollers and lifted it up and brought it around the desk to sit beside Thompson. The two of them began reading the transcripts.

"Whoa, whoa, back up just a bit, David," Tyler said. "Look there, where the ex-girlfriend testified about what he said to her at the hotel. He told her he had a gun and, quote, 'would use it, he didn't have anything to lose.'"

"Yeah, Tyler, who says and does that kind of shit?"

"Read on, David, there's a lot more good testimony in there."

Agent Thompson read through the case file and transcripts for about ten minutes. "Tyler, a lot of people have some really good things to say about this Williams. One of them is a Collin County police officer. Several are attorneys, not exactly the dregs of society," injected David. "You've got to have some pretty big balls to pull off a hit like what happened this morning. It's not exactly your garden variety."

"Yeah, I don't know how big his balls are, they could be as big as cantaloupes," replied Tyler. "But what about his proficiency with firearms? And his attorney coworker overhearing him saying he was going to kill someone and burn his house down? The testimony of the ex-girlfriend?"

David stood up to head back into Mark Hasse's office. "There is some interesting stuff there for sure. I can see where the guy could hold a grudge. Lots of people say things when they're mad that they never have intention of doing. And it's a big step from being pissed off to blowing someone away on the street. And who would have helped him? There were two of them. Who would he have gotten to drive the car? I don't know, Tyler, it just seems kind of a reach, especially this early in the investigation. I saw you have the pending case of the Aryan Brotherhood dude. Did you read over that one?"

Tyler hid his emotions. He just knew he was on to something big with this Williams. But he knew from experience that he could see something one way and others wouldn't see the same puzzle pieces. Tyler was just elated with excitement inside. He felt like he was on the path to the fabled "aha" moment.

He looked at David and calmly said, "Just wanted you to take a look and get your feedback. And, yeah, I haven't yet, but I'm going to look over the Aryan Brotherhood file, as well as others. Thanks for looking this over with me." Tyler sat back down in Mary's chair and turned his attention back to the computer screen.

"Well, let me know if anything else interesting turns up," said David as he walked back to Hasse's office.

Tyler did read over the pending case file on the Aryan Brotherhood suspect. And he read over case files of rapes, murders, child molestation, all that negative shit that law enforcement dealt with every day. And sure, it could have been any one of those people who had it in for Mark Hasse. But for all the hours he had sat in front of that computer screen and read, none of them fit the overall crime scene scenario like the Eric Williams case. Tyler looked at his watch; it was 6:15. He called Major Wilson.

"Yeah, Tex, find anything?"

"Well, boss, only one case really stands out to me," said Tyler.

"Which one is that?"

"It's the one involving a convicted justice of the peace here in Kaufman County, Eric Williams."

There was a long pause on the other end of the line before Major Wilson spoke. "Good detective work, Tex. Mike McLelland went over that whole case with me this afternoon down here at the courthouse. McLelland thinks that if it isn't an organized gang hit, then it is Eric Williams. There is no love lost between those two. And from what I got from him, there was no love lost between Williams and Hasse either. Tex, go home or get a hotel room. Just be at the courthouse tomorrow morning at eight to meet with me, McLelland, and Police Chief Burns. Special Agent Collins is coming too. They want to look over the case files. Good night, Tex, see you in the morning."

Tyler closed the windows on the computer, stood up, stretched, and thought about how all this sitting really tightened up the body. Thank God he was still working in the field; if he sat at a desk all day, he would go crazy. Tyler stood in the doorway between Mary and Mark's offices and addressed David. "Just talked with Major Wilson. I'm supposed to be back here at eight in the morning to meet with him, McLelland, and Burns. I'm sure you'll get the word to be here too. Collins is also coming. They're wanting to go over the case files with us and, I'm sure, pick our brains." Thompson's phone began to ring; he held up his hand for Tyler to hold on.

"Yes, sir, all right. Eight o'clock. Yes, sir. All right, sir. See you then." He hung up. "Yeah, that was Collins. Go ahead, Tyler. I want to read one last thing and I'll be right behind you. See you in the morning."

"Good night, David," said Tyler. He put on his sports coat and gratefully headed for the parking lot.

CHAPTER 5

I<small>T WAS STILL EARLY, ONLY</small> six thirty on a Thursday evening. If his day hadn't been so stressful, Tyler and Priscilla could still make it to Lee Harvey's and catch the Graceland Ninjaz, but there was no way he was going anywhere but home and staying put. Tyler's mind would be running like a chainsaw; he doubted he would even be able to sleep. Tyler took out his phone and tapped the top contact on his call list.

"Hi, sweetie, how did it go today?" There was concern in Priscilla's voice.

"Not bad under the circumstances. I feel like I made some headway, especially for it being the first day of the investigation. Believe it or not, I'm coming home for the evening. I'm on the highway coming that way."

"Oh, thank God! I was going to meet up with some teacher friends for dinner if you were staying in Kaufman. I'll call and cancel and meet you at your house," said Priscilla. "I'll take Kano for a walk to the park. By that time you should be home, then we can relax and watch some TV."

Tyler knew that Priscilla would not mention going out for the evening, even though it was early. She knew that with the kind of case he was on today, his head just wouldn't be in it. "Thank you, babe, I'm looking forward to seeing you. Just chilling at home will work for me big-time."

"Have you eaten?" she asked.

"I haven't eaten since this afternoon," replied Tyler. "I can stop on the way and pick up something, or we can do pizza. I have one in the freezer at the house. We can keep it simple. I don't feel like a big meal tonight. I've got to be back out here in the morning by eight. It's going to be another busy day."

"Pizza works for me. I know you have wine and beer, so we'll be good. I'll bring some lettuce from home and make a salad. I love you, Tyler. See you in a bit. I need to call my teacher friends and tell them about the change of plans."

"Sounds good. See you in an hour or so. Bye, Priscilla."

"Bye, Tyler."

Priscilla knew that he couldn't tell her much about an ongoing investigation, so she wouldn't ask. This one, though, was going to get a lot of media attention, so he was pretty sure she had already heard quite a bit about it already on the news. All her friends knew he was a Texas Ranger; she had told him about her friends who would ask questions about cases he was on, whether she worried, or whether she could tell them anything that wasn't on the news or in the paper? They had a good laugh about it; people really wanted to dig for the dirt.

*****

Tyler wanted to take his mind off the case on the drive home, so he turned up the radio. There was a really good station in the metroplex called the Range. Its music format was Texas country: "home, home on the range, where the deer and the antelope play." Its call letters were KHYI, 95.3 on the FM dial. The station didn't play that pop country crap like Kenny Chesney or Luke Bryan. They billed themselves as "hard country" radio, playing the likes of Willie, Waylon, Strait, Zac Brown, and Haggard, to name a few. This station rocked; if Tyler wasn't in a blues or rock mood, he had it tuned to the Range.

Tyler knew one of the disc jockeys casually; his name was Brett Dillon. Dillon had been named DJ of the Year in 2011 by the Texas Music Award Association. Tyler had met him at a popular bar-restaurant in Plano called Love & War in Texas. It promoted itself by embracing the ups and downs of Texas culture through food and music and, of course, alcohol. It was a popular place that Tyler and Priscilla frequented to listen to live music and two-step. They had torn up the dance floor there more than a time or two. Tyler knew the owner of Love & War fairly well; he also knew the owner's brother who managed the place. The two brothers were from Kerrville, Texas, and had opened Love & War about fifteen years before. Between the owner, Tye Phelps, and his brother, Tory, they ran one of the most popular live music establishments in the Dallas area.

The bar was well known for its Shiner Sundays, sponsored by the Spoetzl Brewery company located outside Houston. Shiner beer was a very popular bock beer. The brewery was founded in 1909 and brewed its bock beer in the old-world German-Czech tradition, dark and rich-tasting. On the patio of Love & War was the Shiner stage, and on Sundays from four to six, the bands that performed were broadcast on KHYI 95.3 radio for the live sets. Since this was a premium gig due to its free radio airtime, only the most popular bands played on Shiner Sundays. Many a Sunday, Tyler had seen crowds of well over three hundred to see bands like Eleven Hundred Springs, The Tejas Brothers, or Chris Knight. And with Brett Dillon being the most senior and popular disc jockey at the station, he would introduce the acts each Sunday for the live radio broadcast. That was how Tyler and Priscilla came to know Brett Dillon—the disc jockey would interact with his fans during the Sunday shows. It was all good fun, a real Texas hoedown. Tyler loved living in Texas. If his job didn't bring him in contact with so many dirtbags, life would be perfect, but he knew that every state had its share of dirtbags, so he rolled with it.

Brett Dillon wasn't on the Range in the evening; he had the late-morning slot from ten till four on weekdays. But it was all good; the music that the station was playing right now was really good. Dale Watson had sung about trucking, Jason Boland and the Stragglers had done their tune about redemption, and Charlie Robinson had done "Barlight." Again, KHYI was cranking out the great tunes, just the kind of mental distraction Tyler needed after the day he had.

When he pulled up to his house, Priscilla's car was parked out front. When he came up the back steps, he could see her in the kitchen through the glass patio door. As he walked into the house, he could smell the pizza and saw two glasses of wine on the kitchen counter. Tyler could use a drink, and the wine would work fine. He had no intention of drinking anything stronger tonight, but he did plan on having more than one. "Hey there, good-looking, glad to see you."

"Me too. Give me a hug," she said, walking toward him. They embraced and shared a light kiss, then Priscilla held him back at arm's length and looked into Tyler's brown eyes. "So how was it?"

"It was all very depressing. The city is crawling with FBI and ATF agents, not to mention the Kaufman police force. Then of course there's the media—they're everywhere."

"I know! I was watching it on the news. It's the biggest story right now. It's all that they're talking about. They're saying some prison gang, the Aryan Brotherhood, might be involved. Anyway, I was watching it on TV for a little while, but I turned it off about five minutes ago. I didn't think you would want to hear all that when you got home." She walked back into the kitchen.

"Yeah, well, I have had my fill of it for one day. I'll be back right back out there tomorrow. I have a meeting first thing in the morning with Russ, the FBI, District Attorney Mike McLelland, and the police chief. Also the sheriff and his merry band of dancing bears."

Priscilla laughed. She knew Tyler was cracking wise. "Here, have a drink." She handed him a large goblet of wine. "Go relax in the living room with Kano. We had our walk together. He did his business, and I cleaned up the garage corner where he goes on the newspapers, so you don't have to worry about that. Pizza will be ready in a few minutes, and I will come join you two."

No sooner had Tyler plopped down on the couch than his cell rang. It was his youngest son, Graham. "Hey, how's it going?" asked Tyler.

"It's all good with me, but what about you? I saw about the murder in Kaufman on the news. I know that's your region. Can you talk?" asked Graham.

"Actually I'm home. Just walked in the door a few minutes ago. Yeah, I was out there first thing this morning. If you've seen the news, you know it's a circus. It's a whopper for sure. They don't come any bigger than this."

"Yeah, it's all that's on right now," said Graham. "So how did it go today?"

"For the first day, about like I expected," said Tyler. "The suspects were slick, had things pretty well planned out. But at the same time they were very lucky. Picked a funny spot to commit a murder, but it takes all kinds."

"Yeah, I saw that. I was thinking the same thing. Right outside the courthouse. Damn, that took me by surprise," exclaimed Graham.

"You and a lot of other people. It doesn't really compute. Makes me think it was personal."

"You think? The news is all about the Aryan Brotherhood. They were saying that one of their members is in the Kaufman jail awaiting trial on a murder charge and that Hasse was going to prosecute the dude."

"That is the way many people are leaning, but it's way too early to circle the wagons, especially with a prosecutor. All they do is make people mad. Well, I should say half the people. There are those who like to see criminals go to jail."

"But you're right, they can piss a lot of people off, and those are the kinds of people that will shoot your ass down on the street."

"Well, I guess you have learned a thing or two hanging around your old man," laughed Tyler.

"That one was a no-brainer. Anyway, I just called to see how you were doing and wanted to tell you to be careful and keep your gun clean."

"Appreciate the call. It's all good here. How about on your end? Have you talked to Ian?"

"Yeah, I just got off the phone with him. Told him I would give you a call and give him a shout back. We know that you'll be busy until this gets solved," replied Graham. "Things are fine, just working. Is Priscilla over at the house?"

"Yeah, we're about to have pizza. I've got to be back in Kaufman first thing in the morning."

"Tell her I said hello. I'll let y'all get to your meal. Keep in touch and don't get yourself shot."

"Try not to. Thanks for calling, Graham."

"All right, Dad, love you."

"Love you too, son." The line went dead. Graham was in his early twenties. He managed a popular Mexican food restaurant in the Dallas area called Chuy's. It was incredible how popular it was. A couple of hippie dudes had opened the first one in Austin, Texas, back in the seventies. Now there were more than forty of them throughout the United States. The one Graham managed had a waiting line on Friday and Saturday nights of fifty or more people. It was all about the food and laid-back atmosphere; zany about covered it. The bar area had an open nacho car, meaning car as in hood and headlights, with the loaded nacho fixings where the engine should be. The place was the hot Mexican food destination for families, teens, and adults of all ages. Graham was a people person; the job fitted his personality to a tee.

Tyler picked up the remote and turned on the TV. He searched for a Dallas Maverick's game and found it. They were playing the Cleveland Cavaliers in Cleveland. Was Tyler going to be able to stop thinking about this case? Not no but hell no. If it wasn't such a high-profile case, Tyler could have put it out of his mind fairly easily; he had been doing this for quite a few years now. But this one, not so much. He didn't have that many cases that made national news. No, this one would be in the forefront of his mind for a good while. Maybe if it didn't get solved soon, the agencies such as ATF or Homeland Security would drop off the radar, but the Texas Department of Public Safety and the Federal Bureau of Investigations would still be working this case for the long haul. For them it wouldn't go cold for a long, long time.

This murder was in the Texas Rangers' jurisdiction, Field B, otherwise known as Company B. There would be no letup on their end until this case was solved. What was nagging Tyler was the thought that this was just the start of what lay ahead. Tyler was going to be wrapping his mind around this one for the foreseeable future. But if he could just enjoy this Mavs versus Cavs game, that would work for him, even for the short term.

Priscilla came into the living room with two salad plates and sat them on the coffee table. Tyler had one of those tables with a hinged top that could be raised to make food easier to reach. She went back into the kitchen and returned with plates of pizza and some napkins. To Tyler, the pizza smelled great; he was hungry. He took a couple of bites of his salad and then started in on the pizza. "So how was your day?" he asked Priscilla between chews.

"Well, when I left my classroom, I went straight home and turned on the news. There was so much coverage on about the murder. Must admit I watched all of it." She chuckled to herself. "And I saw you off in the distance. Some of the reporters were complaining that they weren't getting information as quickly as they would have liked. I saw a segment of you talking with Russell. It looked as though it was early in the morning."

Priscilla knew Major Wilson as Russell, as did Tyler. But when Tyler was out in the field around FBI or other agencies, he kept it more professional and referred to him as Major Wilson. Tyler and Russell Wilson socialized quite a bit together. They had worked in the field when Tyler came on with the Rangers. Wilson had been in the department for about ten years before Tyler hired on; he had learned from one of the best. Wilson was good and he had taught Tyler all he knew; the rest Tyler was figuring out on his own.

The two of them deer-hunted together and socialized at each other's homes. Russ wasn't a country music two-stepper and he didn't listen to rock, so he and his wife didn't hit the night spots with Tyler and Priscilla, but they were close friends. The two of them had had each other's backs in some pretty hairy spots a time or two over the years; few things made for better friends than someone getting your ass out of a dangerous jam. It's not like you forget that kind of thing.

Tyler and Priscilla finished off the pizza and salad and relaxed on the couch watching the fourth quarter of the basketball game. Tyler had another large goblet of wine after his meal; he was hoping it would help him sleep. The Mavs had put a whipping on the Cavs. Dirk went off on them for thirty-five points; that was one bad-ass German. After the game, the two of them went to bed; it was going to be an early day for both of them. The next day was Friday, a school day for the kiddies and Priscilla. Tyler just hoped he could relax his mind enough to sleep.

*****

When Priscilla came into the kitchen at 6:00 a.m., Tyler was already up and dressed. "Well, good morning, Ranger Tex Davis," she said, smiling.

"Well, good morning to you, Senorita Delgado."

"Did you sleep well?" she asked.

"Much better than I thought I would. What did you put in the wine?"

Priscilla laughed. "I'll never tell."

Tyler shared a smile with her. "Here's some coffee." He poured her a cup and set it on the counter.

"Muchas gracias, senor."

"I'm out of here, senorita. I've got to be in Kaufman by eight. I don't want to get caught up in the traffic. I'll call you this evening and let you know what's up." They hugged and kissed.

"Tyler, be safe. I'm worried for you. These killers are vicious."

"I'm with you on that one. I will be. Teach those kiddies their ABCs."

"That's my job," she laughed. "Bye, Tyler."

"Bye, Priscilla." Tyler walked out the back patio door and fired up his Chevy. *Here we go*, he thought to himself. *Day two of "Let's go find the Kaufman killers."*

CHAPTER 6

Tᴜ ʟᴇʀ ᴡᴀs ʟᴏᴏᴋɪɴɢ ꜰᴏʀᴡᴀʀᴅ ᴛᴏ this morning's meeting with Wilson and McLelland. It was promising to hear that McLelland had his suspicions about Eric Williams himself. Tyler arrived at the courthouse at 7:30 and went to Mark Hasse's and Mary's offices. When he walked into her office, Mary was seated at her desk. "Good morning, Mary, I'm Tyler Davis with the Texas Department of Public Safety. How are you?"

She looked up from her desk and seemed as though she didn't get much sleep the previous night; there were noticeable rings under her eyes. "Well, honestly, Mr. Davis, I'm a little frightened right now just coming to work. My husband wanted me to stay home this morning, but I thought I should come in so I could be of some help, especially after what happened yesterday. Oh, I remember you. Mark prosecuted one of your cases not long after he came to work here. Back in 2010, wasn't it?"

"Yes, that's correct. He also prosecuted a couple of my cases in Dallas before transferring to Kaufman. Mary, you're safe here at the courthouse. I don't think the clerical staff has anything to worry about."

"Well, I hope you're right, Mr. Davis. It's a shame what happened to Mark. He was such a fine man."

"I thought very highly of him myself."

"If you're here for Mark's case files and laptop from yesterday, I gave them to Mr. McLelland a few minutes ago. He said he was taking them to the conference room on this floor. It's down the hall at the far end of the building."

"Yes, I know. I'm to meet with him at eight. The reason I stopped by was to ask about Eric Williams's old secretary. Does she still work here?"

She probably didn't realize it, but her mouth had dropped open. She stared at Tyler a moment before she answered. "Well...yes...yes, she does. She works for another justice of the peace. Their office is just down the hall. Room 215."

"What is her name?"

"Theresa...Theresa Smith."

"Thank you, Mary. It was good seeing you again." Tyler walked out of Mary's office in search of Room 215. It was only three doors down. Seated inside the inner office at a desk was who Tyler thought to be Theresa Smith; after all, this was Room 215.

"Hello, Ms. Smith."

The woman, about in her early to midfifties, looked up from the desk. She was quite attractive, with a slender build, long straight brown hair, and a thin face. "Good morning. Yes, I'm Ms. Smith. How can I help you?"

"Good morning, I'm Tyler Davis with the Texas Department of Public Safety. I was wanting to ask you a few questions."

"What is this about?"

"This is dealing with official police business. I would like to speak with you in a more private setting. Could I take you to lunch later today?" This was the second time this morning and just seconds apart that a woman stared at Tyler. Theresa Smith had a quizzical expression on her face, trying to think how she should respond.

"Well, I'm quite busy. Could you tell me what this is about?"

"It's a matter I would rather not talk about here. You do take lunch breaks?"

"Of course I do, I have an hour. I take lunch at eleven."

"Perfect. Would you meet me out front of the courthouse at eleven? I'll drive, and you can pick the place."

"All right, fine…but I don't see how I can be of any help, especially if this has anything to do with what happened yesterday morning."

"No, nothing about that. I just have some routine questions about the day-to-day history of the courthouse. See you out front at eleven. Thank you."

"Fine, then, Mr. Davis, but I'm so very curious."

"I'm sure you are. See you then and thank you."

Tyler left Theresa's office and walked to the conference room at the opposite end of the building. As he entered the room, he saw Major Wilson, DA McLelland, SAC Collins, and FBI Agent Thompson seated at the table looking at the laptop. All four of the men were reading over the pending case of the Aryan Brotherhood member that was in the Kaufman jail. As Tyler walked up behind them and looked at the screen, Major Wilson turned to him and asked, "Did you read over this arrest, Tex? What did you think?"

"Yes, sir, I did. What caught my attention was that he has a brother already serving a lengthy sentence down in Huntsville. If the Brotherhood is involved with this murder, that, I believe, would be the link. Let me show you something." Tyler leaned forward and began to punch the computer keys. He brought up a previous case prosecuted by Mark Hasse. "See there? Mark Hasse put the brother in Huntsville three years ago on an attempted murder rap. Now the other brother is up for murder one for killing a biker over another heroin deal that went south. There is plenty of motive to go around, I know from experience. It's easy to piss those guys off. Hell, they stay pissed off."

Collins turned to Tyler and said, "What we've been hearing from our intel is that the 211 Crew out of Colorado, not the Aryan Brotherhood, is planning a hit. This information has been coming from our informants inside the Colorado penal system. Now these informants are not 211 Crew members, mind you, but from the general prison population. The 211 Crew are as tight as breeding snakes, so of course that makes what we've heard very sketchy, but it's been out there for a while now. It's led us to believe that something is brewing." Collins got up from his chair and sat on the tabletop. "What we did not expect was a hit coming here in Texas, so what we're asking ourselves here is this: was our intel wrong or was Hasse the mark? It's imperative that we look at all angles. There hasn't been shit about a Texas hit. That being said, Mark Hasse is dead, and someone quite vicious pulled this off. So with this being more like an assassination, it's making us consider everything. You know how we think in law enforcement, Davis. Coincidences are building blocks, and building blocks are what we build Texas prisons with."

He has a point, thought Tyler. If what he was saying was true, and Tyler was sure it was, then this intel was bare bones at best. The only way to know that prison gang intel was solid was if a member turned state's evidence, and this only happened when a member was ordered to do a mark and wanted out. It was blood in, blood out for these gangs, and some of them didn't want to go back to prison, especially for the rest of their lives. Without a 211 Crew member or Aryan Brotherhood member turning rat, all intel was hearsay. The Hasse murder could have been the mark all along, as far-fetched as it seemed; the two prison gangs could be working together. Maybe the 211 Crew did this hit for the Brotherhood, and the Brotherhood would reciprocate and do one for them. Anything was possible. It was still very early; they had to keep their minds open.

Major Wilson rolled his chair away from the table and looked at Tyler, who was still standing behind the chairs. "Tex, before you got here we talked about your thoughts on Eric Williams. Of course, what we're doing here is tossing out all possibilities. There is no way we can afford to get sidetracked here. Mike here does think Williams is a possibility. He just doesn't think he has the means to pull it off. There were two of them. Who would have driven for Williams? Again, two suspects makes us think gang members."

"Davis, when Agent Thompson told us this morning that you talked to him about Williams yesterday after going through Mark's case files, I was on board big-time," said McLelland. "He hated Mark Hasse and he hates me. If anyone has motive, he's at the top of my list. But that being said, I don't see how he pulls it off. I don't see who would have driven the car for him, and I also don't think he has that kind of nerve. I think of him as a little weasel. Major Wilson, on the other hand, wants you to follow your instincts. Eric Williams does need to be ruled out."

"Tex, you're assigned to investigate Williams," said Major Wilson. "As of right now, he's just as much a possibility as anyone. He has to be eliminated as a suspect. You're going to have the full cooperation of the Kaufman police force. Mike here has already talked with Chief Burns and Sheriff Allbright about their officers working with you. Trying to tie Williams to the Crown Vic has gotten us nowhere. There is no record of him or any family member ever owning such a car. Collins and his agents are going to pursue the connection between the 211 Crew and the Brotherhood. The other Rangers are going to look into the local drug gangs as well as try to locate the getaway car."

Collins spoke up. "We are bringing in a special agent who trained at Quantico to infiltrate the Kaufman jail and attempt to garner information from the Brotherhood suspect before his trial. As good as this man is, it still rarely works, especially with Brotherhood members, but we're going with it. There can't be another prosecutor murdered here in Texas, or elsewhere for that matter. We need to get to the bottom of this, and as of now we really don't have shit."

"Tex, do you know where you want to start?" asked Wilson.

"Yes, sir, I do. I want to have a canvass done on Eric Williams's neighborhood. I want this done by the Kaufman police. I want to find out if he was home yesterday morning. I want Williams to think this is just routine police work, that he's not being looked at very hard. If he is involved, he needs to make a mistake. I want him to make a mistake."

Tyler had it all planned out in his mind, like a chess master moving chess pieces. "Next, I want to talk to someone who knows Eric Williams intimately. As we know, many people spend more time with their coworkers than they do with their families. For this, I've already set up an interview with Williams's secretary from when he worked here. Theresa Smith. I'm taking her to lunch this afternoon. I want to talk to her away from the courthouse so as not to get rumors started—not that they haven't already. But right now, I want to go back to the crime scene to look around. I have some time to kill before I meet with Ms. Smith."

"All right, Tex. Does anyone have anything else for Davis?" asked Major Wilson.

"Seems to me, Davis, you've spent time thinking this through," said Collins. "No wonder Wilson talks so highly of you. That's all I've got. Let's be sure and keep the lines of communication open between us. This could go anywhere."

"Will do, sir," said Tyler. He turned and walked out of the conference room on his way to East Grove Street. He never did sit down.

CHAPTER 7

TYLER STOOD ON EAST GROVE Street at the very location where Hasse had been slain. The bloodstained pavement was no more. The City of Kaufman had it cleaned the night before. It was a stain that they had no intention of letting their residents see walking to and from the courthouse. Not this blight on their fine city, no. What they wanted to see were the persons responsible brought to justice.

Tyler looked at the spot that had been Mark Hasse's parking space; he then looked across the street where the Crown Vic had been parked. He turned and walked to the intersection where George Hamilton had witnessed the murder, mentally counting the steps as he did so. Fifty-one yards, he thought to himself; that is quite a distance to see much of anything. Tyler began to think about what he did have. There was the make, model, and color of the car. Also a motive, the race of the driver, a well-planned hit, and the street confrontation. Not bad for the second day, he thought. Plus it's still early. Tyler looked at his watch. *Now let's go have lunch with Ms. Theresa Smith and see what else turns up.*

*****

Theresa came out of the courthouse a few minutes before eleven. Either she was hungry, very curious, or both. Tyler was waiting outside on a bench. "Hello, Ms. Smith. I'm parked right here in the front." There was a police presence outside, but the officers recognized Tyler, so he was allowed to pull up front. He opened the passenger door, and she got in. When he was behind the wheel, he asked, "Which way and where to?"

"Turn left here," she said. "It's down a couple of blocks. You'll make another left. I'll tell you when."

"Well, now I'm curious. Where are we going?" asked Tyler.

"Jalisco's Mexican Grill. I hope you eat fajitas. We can share. You look like you eat fajitas."

"Oh, yes, ma'am, I eat me some fajitas."

Theresa Smith laughed. "I thought you might, Mr. Davis."

"Call me Tyler."

"All right, Tyler. Now you must call me Theresa."

"Now we're working together," Tyler said as he turned to smile at her.

They were seated at the table waiting for their meal. Both had ordered the iced tea, and Tyler was adding sugar, while Theresa was drinking hers with only lemon. The restaurant was busy. Tyler hoped that meant the food was good. "Well, Tyler, I got the skinny on what you wanted to talk to me about."

"Oh, how's that?"

"Mary, Mark's secretary. She came by my office soon after you left and told me you had asked about my working for Eric Williams. Actually, I was relieved. I thought you wanted to ask me about the murder. I don't have a clue about that. I have no problem talking to you about Eric. I like him quite a bit. I worked for him for several years. He was very pleasant to me. I think he got a raw deal on his theft case. When he was arrested, I thought they were joking. A lot of people at the courthouse feel the same way, though they might not say it."

The waiter brought a steaming skillet of beef fajitas to the table. The two of them began to pile the meat and veggies on a tortilla. Between bites, Tyler asked, "What was Eric like?"

"He was a little quirky. You know those little scooter things, those Segways? Well, he would ride one of those to work, carrying his briefcase. It was kind of funny to see, but like I said, he could be quirky."

Theresa was a talker. Tyler was loving this. "Anything else quirky or that stands out about Eric?"

"Well…" She paused to work on fajita number two. "He is really, really smart. He is a member of Mensa, you know, that organization that represents really intelligent people."

"Oh yeah."

"Yes, and he liked to tell people about it. He could rub some people the wrong way, but I don't let that stuff bother me. He always treated me okay."

"Did you ever see him lose his temper?"

"Mr. Davis…Tyler, I've seen everyone in that courthouse lose their temper. I think it just goes with enforcing the law."

"What about making threats or threatening someone? Did you ever see or hear him do that?" Tyler asked.

"I did hear something like that come up at his trial, but he never threatened me," Theresa explained. "He never raised his voice to me. No, I can't say that I personally heard him say that to someone. Now he might have been on the phone in his office and I would overhear him say he was going to get 'that SOB' or 'that asshole.' I figured he was talking about a criminal case, not just anyone."

"Refresh my memory about what Eric looks like. I met him once, but it has been several years now."

"He's close to six feet, taller if he's wearing his boots. Guess he weighs a little over two hundred pounds, medium to large build."

"And his wife, did you know her?"

"Of course, I worked for him for several years," replied Theresa. "She would sometimes come by the office, and they would go to lunch together. Her name is Kim. She's very nice. A real looker too. Well, she used to be. Some serious health problems have beset her in recent years. Then the stress of Eric losing his job—it's taken a toll, I think. I've seen her around town, and she looks twenty years older than she is, and those years haven't been kind to her. If you knew her, you wouldn't recognize her from, say, eight to ten years ago. She's changed that much."

"And how well did the two of them get along?" asked Tyler.

"Okay, I guess. They seemed happy enough. Eric was pretty demanding. He likes for things to be perfect. I just had to work for him. I didn't have to go home with him. Kim might have been a lit-tle…how should I put this…stifled."

"Why do you say that?"

"Think about it," she said, looking at him like he was an idiot. "If you're married to someone and only perfection will do, that's got to stifle anyone. Let the small stuff slide, I say. Eric sweated too much of the small stuff."

"So you think she was under his thumb, so to speak?"

"Yeah, I think so. I did get that feeling, in what little time I spent around them."

They had finished off the fajitas, and the waiter brought the check to their table. As they were leaving, Tyler thanked Theresa for taking the time to speak to him. As Tyler was paying at the register, she again expressed to him that, even though Eric came off a bit unusual, he was not the kind of person who could murder Mark Hasse. But a much different picture came out about him from the trial transcripts. *I really have my work cut out for me*, thought Tyler as he drove Theresa back to the courthouse. *Need to find a getaway car, need to find a driver, and, of course, need to find a killer,* he kept thinking. This was where the help came into play, the help being the Kaufman police.

Finding out that Williams was a Mensa member supported his intuition that the killer was smart; that was one more caveat. But smart or flat-out dumbass, whoever did this was a cocky, lucky fucker. Tyler wondered if the killer had the sense to realize just how lucky he had been. Some really smart people have zero common sense.

As soon as he dropped off Ms. Smith, Tyler planned to go straight to the police station and have Sheriff Allbright set up a canvass of Eric Williams's neighborhood. Tyler wanted to find out if someone saw him leave his house Thursday morning, but Tyler wanted to make it seem as though the canvass was just routine. No Department of Public Safety and no Federal Bureau of Investigation agents, not yet; just the Kaufman police. If he was a genius and he did seek control, then he would be like a cat playing with his food before killing it. So for now Tyler was going to stay in the background, play dead. Be patient, let Eric think that he's not being looked at closely. Maybe, just maybe, he'll slip up. Someone needs to. As of now, nobody had Jack, as in Jack Shit.

*****

The police station was just a few blocks from the courthouse. It was half past noon when Tyler arrived. He went to the front desk and told the attending deputy that he had an appointment with Sheriff Allbright. After phoning the sheriff, the deputy directed Tyler upstairs to Room 220. Tyler entered the office and found Sheriff Allbright sitting at his desk. "Hey there, Davis, have a seat," said the sheriff as he stood up to take Tyler's hand.

Shaking the sheriff's hand, Tyler greeted him, "Afternoon, Sheriff, good to see you again."

"So McLelland tells me that you're wanting me to have my men conduct a canvass of the Williams' neighborhood this afternoon, and you're wanting to be involved, is that right?" asked Allbright.

"Yes, sir, I'd like to meet with the men before they go and meet back up with them when they return, only I don't want to be part of the canvass. For now I would like only local police to question Eric Williams. I want to make it look as routine as possible, no DPS or FBI. That will come later, if necessary. I don't want Williams thinking that he's being looked at very hard," said Tyler.

"All my men are on call after what this town has gone through the last couple of days. I'll have one of my best sergeants get a group of officers together. Shouldn't take but a couple of hours. Be back here at my office a little before four. Sergeant Cox will have them ready by then."

"I appreciate it, Sheriff. I'll meet with you back here. Thanks again."

As Tyler was walking down the stairs, he took his phone from his jacket pocket and pushed for Russ.

"Yeah, Tex, what've you got?" asked Major Wilson.

"I'm leaving the Kaufman police station now," replied Tyler. "I just met with Sheriff Allbright. He's getting his men together for this afternoon's canvass. That should get rolling around four. Before

I came here, I had my interview with Eric Williams's secretary over lunch. That turned out to be quite interesting."

"Oh yeah, how so?" inquired Wilson.

"Did you know he was a Mensa member?" Tyler asked.

"No, I didn't know that. You think that's a big deal?"

"I get by on common sense, Russ. I took one of those Mensa tests in *Reader's Digest* a few years ago and felt like a dumbass. You've got to be a smart fucker to get in with that group," Tyler replied.

"Knowing you, you probably got 80 percent of the questions right and still thought you sucked. What else did she tell you?"

"She sang his praises, said he wouldn't hurt a fly, but she also said he liked perfection and that's just a nice way of saying control."

"So what was the gist of the interview?"

"He's still prime for me—control freak, genius-level IQ, has motive, knows firearms. Would like to find out if he was home or not Thursday morning. If a neighbor says they saw him out watering his grass that morning, it won't feel the same, but until I can rule him out he's got my interest, big-time."

"Works for me, Tex. Okay, let me know how the canvass goes. Preston's wanting to know about it too. Call me as soon as you know something. I especially want to know if he was seen leaving his house."

"You got it, Russ. I'll holler back at you this evening." The line went dead.

When Tyler walked out the front entrance of the Kaufman police station, he looked across the street at all the media vans and trucks. He looked at his watch; he had lots of time to kill before four o'clock. He had a thought. It might not pay off anytime soon, but it could be a game changer later. He walked to his truck and opened the hatbox he kept in the back seat; inside was his favorite smoke-gray cowboy hat. He put it on and looked at himself in the truck's side mirror. *Hell, son, you look like a true-blue Texas Ranger. Handsome fucker too*, he thought, laughing to himself. He turned and walked across the street into the waiting throng of media cameras and reporters.

CHAPTER 8

AT A QUARTER TO FOUR, Tyler made his way up the flight of stairs to Sheriff Allbright's office. Seated in front of the sheriff's desk was a rotund police sergeant. He sported a neatly trimmed moustache on a ruddy complexion, his eyes a piercing blue. "Davis, I would like you to meet Sergeant Cox. He will be in charge of the men conducting the canvass. They're assembling downstairs in the conference room," said Sheriff Allbright. "Eric Williams lives in a quiet neighborhood a few blocks from here. I want you two men to coordinate your plan and report back here to me."

Tyler shook hands with the sergeant. He had Scotch-Irish written all over him. Tyler took the seat next to him and said, "What I have in mind, Sergeant, is letting your men do what they are trained to do. I'm going to remain in the background. Eric Williams will know that he is a suspect due to his employment at the courthouse, especially being linked to Hasse through his trial. With Kaufman police conducting the canvass, he'll think it's just routine police procedure. If he is involved in this murder and thinks my department or the FBI is extremely interested in him, he'll be more careful. I don't want him careful. The two things that we need to know is if Williams was seen leaving his house Thursday morning and, secondly, if any of his neighbors had seen a white Crown Vic in the vicinity. The sighting of the Vic could be at any time, not just Thursday morning. Did someone see a white Crown Vic a month ago, or yesterday? From what little I've learned about him, I think he's too smart for that, but we'll never know unless we ask."

Tyler leaned forward in his chair, putting his elbows on his knees. "I'm going to follow your men to this neighborhood. Shortly after they begin their canvass, I'm going to drive down Williams's street to get a visual of the house. At a later time, I'm going to attempt to interview him. I want to see where he lives. After the canvass, I'll meet up with you and your men back here and we'll hear about their reports. How does that sound, Sergeant?"

"Works for me, Davis. My men are downstairs ready to go," said Cox. He might have looked like a Lowlander, but he sounded like a Texan. "Let's get 'er done. I'll introduce you and go over the questions with the men. We're burning daylight."

"Let's do it," said Tyler as he stood. Nodding to the sheriff, he turned, walking toward the doorway with Sergeant Cox on his heels.

As the two men reached the door, Sheriff Allbright boomed at Tyler, "Davis, before I forget, Mike McLelland is holding a press conference tomorrow at noon. It's being held at the town square, in case you want to be there."

Tyler stopped at the doorway. "Wouldn't miss it for the world, Sheriff. Thanks for letting me know."

Sergeant Cox and Tyler went downstairs to rendezvous with the waiting Kaufman police officers. The sergeant had eight men going to work in groups of two to handle the house-to-house canvass. The grid was to cover about twelve blocks out from Eric Williams's residence. His street, then north, south, east, and west. Tyler was going to park around the corner from Williams's block and wait for the canvass to start. At his discretion, he was going to drive down Williams's street to identify his home. After he got his visual, he would just have to wait for the results. Could these men get lucky?

What Tyler wanted to hear was that a neighbor had seen Eric Williams leave his home Thursday morning. At the very least, that would give Williams opportunity, especially if he didn't have an alibi for his whereabouts. Only problem was, people rarely paid much attention to their neighbors, especially in quiet residential settings. But hell, you never know. Canvassing was an essential part of law enforcement protocol. Many a time what seemed the most inconsequential observation by a witness had led to the solving of a case. Yes, it could be tedious, but it was a tool used in virtually every investigation. If Eric Williams was involved, Tyler needed to search his home. For that to happen, he would need a warrant. To get the warrant, he needed probable cause. It was like wanting a date with a pretty girl: if you don't ask, you'll never know.

The Kaufman police officers rolled out of the parking lot ahead of Sergeant Cox and Tyler. The plan was for Cox to park around the corner from Williams's street after his men had started the canvass and wait for Tyler to join him. Tyler could have easily found Williams's street with his cell phone's GPS, but he was working with these men, so that's what he planned to do, work right alongside them.

When Sergeant Cox was two blocks from Williams's street, he pulled his squad car over and parked, waiting for Tyler, who was following directly behind him. Tyler parked behind the sergeant and joined him in the front seat. "Two blocks up on the right is Williams's street," said Cox. "About halfway down on your left is his house. You have the number, right?"

"Yeah, I've got it here in my phone and on my laptop," replied Tyler.

Looking out from the cruiser, the two men could see the Kaufman police cars parked up ahead. They were empty; the officers had begun their canvass. Tyler was feeling hopeful anticipation that some helpful information would come from this. He said a short prayer to himself.

"Okay, Davis, I'll meet you back at the station. While my men do their canvass, I'm going to cruise the streets, especially after what happened yesterday morning. I want the public to know that we're looking out for them," said Cox. "After you drive down Williams's street, go get a bite to eat. My men will be here for a couple of hours, till dusk at least. Whoever they don't interview this evening, they will attempt to contact tomorrow. If we get to the station before you, I'll give you a call and let you know we're back. You good?"

"I'm good, Sergeant, thank you. See you at the station." Tyler left the cruiser and went back to his truck. As he watched Sergeant Cox pull away, he decided to wait about ten minutes before he drove to Williams's street. He looked at his watch; it was just half past four o'clock. Tyler knew that what Cox had told him was correct, that the officers would make note of who was and who wasn't home. This was imperative; all the neighbors needed to be interviewed. Yes, it was tedious, but this method often paid off. The police had to be diligent; solving crime was 90 percent boredom and 10 percent excitement. The old "no stone unturned" adage wasn't a cliché when it came to successful police work. Impossible crimes had been solved by the most dogged investigations, and easy ones had gone unsolved by a lack of effort.

Tyler checked his watch and put his truck in gear, going up the two blocks and taking a right onto Williams's street. When he was a quarter of the way down the street, he saw Eric Williams himself standing on his Segway, thumbing through the mail at his mailbox located at the end of his driveway, dressed in camo. *He is a quirky bastard*, thought Tyler. *He still drives that thing around.* Williams didn't look up as Tyler drove past. He made a mental note of Williams's house as he drove past. Sheriff Allbright was correct; it was a quiet suburban neighborhood, and Williams had a nicely groomed lawn with a modest-sized home. Tyler had met Williams several years earlier at the Kaufman courthouse. He looked heavier than Tyler remembered; he had put on twenty or more pounds. What a coincidence, that he was outside when Tyler drove past; what were the chances? And what's with the camo? Theresa said he was quirky. She had hit the nail on the head. Was he quirky enough to kill? That's what Tyler intended to find out.

*****

Tyler drove to a Burger King and went inside to order. He got the big fish combo meal and took a seat at one of the tables. Well, there he had been in the flesh, thought Tyler, on his little scooter. He did fit the description of the shooter as far as physical size and weight. Then again, he fit the size of the average American male, give or take an inch or two. Not exactly the kind of description that bites you on the ass.

Tyler was going to finish his meal and drive to the police station and bullshit with FBI or Homeland Security agents to kill time until Sergeant Cox and his men returned. Maybe there would be a fellow Ranger there. If he got really bored, he might watch the Hamilton video. What he really wanted to do was hear from the officers doing the canvass; each minute seemed like an hour. *Just chill, Tyler. Roll with it, man, roll with it*, he thought. In the back of his mind, he didn't have high expectations that the canvass would prove fruitful; he wasn't being negative, just realistic. He figured that if Williams was involved, he would be smart enough to not make this easy, but he wanted the skinny on the canvass anyway. You never know…

Tyler needed a mental distraction, so he pulled out his phone and pushed "girlfriend."

"Hey, what's up?" answered Priscilla.

"I'm still here in Kaufman. Won't be home until later tonight. I wanted to give you a heads-up so you can make some plans," replied Tyler.

"Okay, I'll follow through with what I talked to you about last night, meeting up with Jacquelyn and her boyfriend for dinner. I can swing by your house after and take Kano for a walk. Do you think you'll be home ten-ish? I'll wait for you," she said.

"Yeah, I should be home by then. That would be nice."

"How is it going?" asked Priscilla.

"Just doing the tedious stuff, trying to gather information that will help with the investigation. I'm killing some time right now. In an hour or so, I'm meeting with some officers who are on a canvass. Don't think as of yet anything much has turned up from the other agencies. If it had, I would have heard about it by now. So, you know, slow going," he replied.

"Well, Tyler, I'm sure something will turn up for you soon."

"All in good time. You know the mantra. 'Just roll with it.'"

"Yes, I've heard that a time or two, or three, or…"

"Okay, I got it," laughed Tyler. "Here's a big, sloppy thank-you in advance for taking Kano for his walk."

"No problem, sweetie. I love you. I'm going to call Jacquelyn. See you at your house, bye."

"Bye, babe."

That was some good news; Priscilla taking Kano for his walk later that evening. Now Tyler wouldn't have to call his next-door neighbor, Mrs. Knuester, and ask her. Not that she minded. Mrs. Knuester was a retired lady who had three dogs of her own. Her husband had died a couple of years back, and she had gone from one dog to three after his death. If Tyler called and asked, she would take Kano along with her dogs to the park just over the neighborhood creek bridge. He paid her for it; she tried not to take the money, but Tyler insisted. It's not that he felt she needed the money, not by seeing the car she drove and how she dressed. But the park had a "pick up after your dog" rule, and if she was willing to pick up his dog's crap, Tyler was sure as hell going to pay her for it. Not to mention her walking him. At first he gave her checks, but noticed she didn't cash them, so now he gave her cash. Tyler told her to spend the money on her grandkids, so she conceded.

When Tyler was gone for extended periods, he took Kano to the Rover Ranch, a kennel in McKinney. Tyler liked the kennel's owner, and it was a very nice place. It was only a twenty-minute drive from Tyler's house, and even closer to Priscilla's. She would sometimes pick up Kano for him when he was coming back into town from a late flight so Kano didn't have to stay over an extra night. It worked out all around.

*****

When Tyler got to the Kaufman police station, he was glad to see that Ranger Jamison was there, or Steve, as Tyler knew him. Steve said he had spent the day working with the Kaufman police trying to get a lead on the Crown Vic, going to local storage facilities in search of the vehicle. They hadn't had any luck. Everyone was working some angle.

Jamison and Tyler went to the downstairs conference room to shoot the shit. The video camera from the previous morning had been removed, and the table was now centered in the room with all the chairs around it. The two Rangers sat and had talked for about an hour when Tyler's phone rang. It was Sergeant Cox; he and his men were back. They were waiting for him upstairs in the conference room next to Sheriff Allbright's office. Tyler headed that way.

When he got upstairs, everyone was seated at the table. Tyler took the seat closest to the door. When Tyler was seated, Sheriff Allbright got right to the point. "Which of you men talked to Eric Williams?"

"I did, Sheriff," said Office Hoskinson. "Eric Williams and his wife both came to the door and took my questions. They both expressed shock at hearing about the murder, and each of them stated that they were home yesterday morning. I asked them if they or anyone they knew owned a white or cream-colored Crown Vic. They both said no. I asked them if they had security cameras on their home. They said they did not, and I observed no cameras. I concluded the interview by advising them that if they thought of anything that could be useful to the investigation, to please let the Kaufman police know. They assured me that they would. Officer Daniels was my backup."

This time it was Sergeant Cox who directed his question to the officer. "Hoskinson...when you questioned the neighbors on Williams's street, did any of them see the Williams leave their home in the early hours of January 31?"

"They all answered negative, Sergeant. I was told by several neighbors that the Williams park their cars in the garage and that, as far as they could remember, the door was down and they were not seen to have left," replied Officer Hoskinson. "Now there were a few homes where we got no response. We can follow up on those residences tomorrow."

Again it was Sheriff Allbright. "Did any of the homeowners on his block have security cameras on their homes?"

"No, sir. Everyone we asked said they had none, and Officer Daniels and myself observed no cameras. Both of us made a special effort to look for them as we had been instructed," replied Hoskinson.

"Did any of you get a lead on security cameras?" asked Sergeant Cox.

"I'm the only one who did, Sergeant, but it was a block over from the Williams's residence and the street behind his street. Plus, the home is located in the middle of the block. Wouldn't be of much use at that location," replied Officer Shaver.

"I can't believe this shit! One fucking person has a security camera on their home in a twelve-block grid? This is 2013! There are neighborhoods that have them at every other fucking house!" said Sheriff Allbright in exasperation.

"That's in the city, Sheriff. This is a quiet, small-town neighborhood," said Sergeant Cox.

"I know, I know, goddamn it! I just felt that was our best shot!" replied Allbright.

"Hoskinson," said Tyler. "What was their demeanor like, the Williams? I mean, when they talked about the murder of Mark Hasse?"

"They expressed shock. Each of them stated that they couldn't believe someone would do such a thing," replied Hoskinson. "The wife, Kim, stated that it was a terrible tragedy. She did seem sincere. Both Mr. and Mrs. Williams had the look and response of all the people we spoke with. They were somber."

"Hoskinson, how tall is Mrs. Williams?" asked Tyler.

"Well, sir, I would say she's about five feet five."

"Does anyone else have anything they think is pertinent to the investigation?" asked Sergeant Cox. No one spoke up. "For you officers that have duty tomorrow, get together with your notes on who needs to be interviewed inside the grid for the follow-up. I know it didn't seem to get us anywhere, but we are going to run the full grid. For those of you that are off, enjoy your Saturday. Dismissed."

"Hold on, men." It was Sheriff Allbright. "I know that there are many people on this police force who think this murder was carried out by a gang, be it the Aryan Brotherhood or whoever. And that might be so…but as of right now, it could be the fucking tooth fairy. No one, and I mean no one, as of now has a solid lead. So when you're in the locker room shooting the shit and someone says we're wasting our time doing this or that, just remind them that a case of this magnitude can't be solved looking in one direction. Remember that! Dismissed."

When the officers filed out, the only ones left in the conference room were Allbright, Cox, and Tyler. "That wasn't much help," said Tyler.

"It doesn't mean he didn't leave his house, just that none of his neighbors saw him," replied Cox.

"Oh, I'm with you on that, but it would have been really nice to hear that a neighbor saw him leave in the early morn. At least we would have had something to go on. As of now we don't have squat," said Tyler.

"We don't know that he's involved anyway," said Sheriff Allbright. "You heard what I said to my men. I'm not trying to sound like a hypocrite. I'm all for investigating him until he's eliminated or until the perp is caught. And I know Williams has motive. He has to hate Hasse after losing his law license, but I've known him a long time. It would surprise the hell out of me if it was him. I'm a betting man, and I believe that when the dust settles, he won't have any on him."

Tyler was expecting as much from lots of people, and the sheriff was no exception. Tyler appreciated his honesty. And he had just expressed to several of his men to keep an open mind—in a very stern manner, mind you. Plus, Tyler was getting the full coopera-tion he had been promised by the police chief; he really couldn't ask for more. As of now, Tyler didn't know who the hell had killed Mark Hasse. He just had a strong gut feeling. Had Tyler been wrong before? Does a bear shit in the woods?

"Well, Sheriff, everyone with ties to the victim is a suspect, and Major Wilson wants me to pursue this until he can be eliminated as a suspect. I do appreciate you gentlemen letting me work with your men and all their help," said Tyler.

"We're here to help any way we can," said Sheriff Allbright. "You out of here for the evening?"

"Yes, sir, I am. Guess I'll see you two at the press conference tomorrow," said Tyler.

The sheriff and sergeant acknowledged that, and the two bade him adios. As Tyler exited the police station, he walked past the media trucks and reporters out front; there had to be over a dozen parked across the street. When he got in his truck, he called Major Wilson to give him an update on the canvass. Wilson didn't answer; he returned the call just a few minutes after Tyler was on the highway headed home.

"Hello, boss," said Tyler.

"Tell me some good news, Tex," said Wilson.

"Wish I could, Russ. The canvass turned up nada," replied Tyler.

"Damn."

"I'm with you. No one saw shit, and what's even worse, no one in the neighborhood invests in security cameras. We don't have a fucking thing."

"All right. You hear about the press conference?"

"Yeah, Sheriff Allbright told me."

"I'm having everyone there. See you at noon, Tex."

"All right, Russ, see you there." Heading west on the Highway 175 toward Dallas, he turned up the radio. Yeah, Tyler was feeling more than a little disappointed. The evening didn't go anything like he had hoped. He tuned the radio to the local blues station, KNON 89.3. About thirty minutes into the ride, they played "Bad Luck Life." *That's about right*, thought Tyler. *That's about fucking right.*

CHAPTER 9

Priscilla and Tyler slept in on Saturday, if one could call getting up at nine o'clock sleeping in. The press conference from District Attorney Mike McLelland wasn't scheduled until noon, so even a few extra hours in the sack was welcome. Tyler didn't really sleep much; he mostly just laid there with his eyes closed trying to rest. Now, he did get some good loving last night, and that had a special way of putting a positive spin on any man's day, whether he slept soundly or not.

Priscilla had plans to go shopping with some girlfriends and do lunch. The two of them made breakfast together; Tyler scrambled the eggs, fried up the link sausage, and made toast. Priscilla handled the fruit, juice, and coffee. She also set the table. It was relaxing for both of them to have a casual breakfast together. During their meal, Priscilla's phone rang.

"I need to get this, it's Justin," she said. "Hi, Justin, what's up?" Her son Justin lived in El Paso with her brother while attending school at UTEP. He was majoring in criminal justice, following in the footsteps of his father, the DEA agent. Justin also played football for the Miners as a defensive tackle. He stood about six three and weighed two forty. "All right, let me call you back in half an hour. I'm having breakfast with Tyler. He's about to leave. I'll call you and we can discuss it some more. I will. Bye, Justin." She hung up. "He told me to say hello to you."

"What did he have to say?"

"What do you think? He wants money," she laughed.

"Yeah, what the hell was I thinking?" said Tyler, returning her laugh.

Tyler liked Justin. He was really laid-back and helped out with Kano quite a bit when he was home for the summer. The DEA agents in El Paso who worked with his father had given Justin a drug dog that they retired when the dog turned eight. It's all about youth, even with dogs. His name was Bunker. When Justin stayed with his mother during summer break and Tyler had to go out of town, Justin would look after Kano and let the two dogs chill together over at Priscilla's house in McKinney. It was a nice break for Kano not having to go to Rover Ranch. Tyler liked the ranch but knew that Kano enjoyed being with people he knew, and it also gave Justin some spending money, since Tyler paid Justin what the ranch would have cost him.

"When you call him back, tell him I said hello," said Tyler. "I'm going to jump in the shower."

Priscilla did call Justin back while Tyler showered. Her plan was to meet her girlfriends from his house since going home to McKinney would take her in the opposite direction of the shopping destination with her friends. They were to meet up at the Shops of Legacy, an upscale shopping area in west Plano. Priscilla kept a lot of clothes over at Tyler's for just such an occasion.

Tyler came into the living room dressed in a suit and wearing a new cowboy hat.

"Oh my, don't you look nice." She smiled. "And sporting the new hat too, I see."

"Yeah, well, we're there to show our support to the district attorney. All the media will be covering it. Russ will want us to show America how it's done in Texas," laughed Tyler.

"And all the womenfolk will want to move to Texas once they get a look at you, Mr. Tyler Davis," laughed Priscilla.

"Yeah, and when they get here they better behave, or I'll have to put their asses in jail," said Tyler, smiling.

"That better be the only place you put their asses," laughed Priscilla.

"I'm out of here. I don't want to be late. You have fun this afternoon. I'll give you a call later," said Tyler as the two of them embraced
and kissed.

*****

As Tyler pulled away from the house, he thought to himself that
this was day three since Mark Hasse had been slain. How many more
days would follow before those bastards were apprehended? He wondered. All in good time, he thought; all in good time. But that was
the problem: nothing was good about it. It was like a hunger pain
gnawing on his backbone. He couldn't sleep. It was right there all
the time, like it was pasted on his forehead. Every passing day meant
someone else could be murdered. This crime didn't have the ring of
one and done. Tyler just knew in his gut that whoever did this was
planning on number two…hell, maybe three and four if they weren't
caught. *Sons of bitches*, thought Tyler.

Then there was yesterday's canvass—nothing but blanks. He
didn't really expect that much, but as a Ranger one still hoped to be
wrong. *Give me a fucking bone, a little something to chew on, Jesus.* No
one had shit! Talking with Jamison the previous night at the Kaufman
police station, they had shot blanks too. Nothing but a lotta nada.

Tyler did know that every Texas State Trooper would be on the
lookout for the getaway car. He almost felt sorry for people driving
white or cream-colored Ford Crown Vics. He knew they would be
pulled over, scrutinized, questioned, and have their tags run. All this
with the utmost caution and not a very friendly demeanor, since the
trooper might be stopping someone who had murdered a deputy
district attorney of Texas. They would get the once-over…twice, and
the what-for.

And Tyler *almost* felt sorry for them. If the State Troopers
weren't out risking their lives doing their jobs, Mr. and Mrs. Joe
Public wouldn't be safe. They couldn't stop all crime—case in point:
Mark Hasse—but they were going to do their damnedest to stop the
next one. You couldn't fault them for trying. And Tyler knew at this
very moment, his fellow State Troopers were giving their all to find

that car if it was anywhere on the Texas state highways. They cared not one bit less than Tyler did.

*****

Tyler parked a couple of blocks away from the town square. Hell, he had to; there were media trucks and curious onlookers everywhere. Then there was the police and law enforcement presence; this press conference had drawn quite a crowd. As Tyler approached the square, he saw the microphone set up just above the steps. Off to the left, he spied his fellow Rangers and Major Wilson standing together. He headed that way.

The media with their camera crews, microphones, and reporters were gathered at the bottom of the steps. The FBI and Kaufman police were on the right side of the upper steps. It was an impressive show of unity. Tyler greeted his coworkers, and they waited patiently for the press conference to begin. It was 11:45; it wouldn't be long now. At straight-up twelve noon, District Attorney Mike McLelland walked up to the microphones and in a clear voice addressed the media, the citizens of Kaufman, the people of Texas, and the United States of America.

"First off, I want to say that Mark Hasse was a tiger in the courtroom. He had an absolute passion for putting away the bad guys and enjoyed nothing better. Mark Hasse was a great storyteller and just an all-around good guy. People just really liked him." Mike McLelland paused for just a brief moment as he scanned the crowd gathered below him. "I hope that the people who did this are watching, because we're very confident that we're going to find you. We're going to pull you out of whatever hole you're in. We're going to bring you back, and let the people of Kaufman County prosecute you to the fullest extent of the law."

Again he paused for just the briefest of moments as he gazed out toward the crowd. "My office can't wait to prosecute the 'scum' that did this. To the residents of Kaufman County...be rest assured...me and my prosecutors will park in the same lot Mark Hasse parked in. We'll still make the walk and still show up, and we'll still send the bad guys out of Kaufman County every chance we get. We're not stopping…we're not slowing down…we're still doing our job. Thank you."

After District Attorney McLelland spoke, there was a noticeable buzz coming from the crowd. As he stepped away from the microphones, Chief of Police Burns stepped forward to say a few words. He was followed soon after by Sheriff Allbright. But the man who got national airtime was Mike McLelland, standing at those microphones wearing his black Stetson, showing the world that good guys can wear black hats. He told the citizens of Kaufman, the State of Texas, and the country how they conducted business in Texas. If you couldn't feel it on TV, you could sure as hell feel the passion and emotion standing there in person. The irony was that none of the people gathered there knew that this had just started and that, before it was over, it was going to get much worse.

CHAPTER 10

AFTER DA MCLELLAND, CHIEF DAVIS, and Sheriff Allbright concluded speaking, the three men walked to the bottom of the steps to take questions from the media. Major Wilson and the Rangers walked to the tables located behind the media throng in the center of the town square. Here it was relatively quiet; most of the crowd was out front, gathered around the steps.

Major Wilson addressed his men once they were seated together at a nearby table. "I know I've had you men going in different directions on this case, so now that we have this chance to discuss the situation as a group, let's take this time to bring everyone up to speed on where you're at or what you're thinking."

Steve Jamison spoke up. "Major has had me working with the Kaufman police inspecting storage facilities looking for the Crown Vic. So far we've turned up nothing. That hasn't been exhausted as of yet. I'm meeting with the Kaufman police this afternoon to widen our search to the surrounding area to see if anything turns up."

Lieutenant Jose Vasquez was next to address the Rangers. "Major Wilson, myself and Richard spent yesterday going over intel concerning the prisoner in the Kaufman jail. As you know, he's associated with the Aryan Brotherhood. He has a brother, also a Brotherhood member, who is doing life in Huntsville for attempted murder. The FBI has a strong belief that the connection to Hasse's hit could be found there. Now, no Brotherhood members were seen in the area on the day of the murder. No intel coming from informants, and nothing coming out of the Texas prison system. As of now we have nothing solid in that regard."

Ranger Roger Miles was next to speak. "Clint and I have been working on this hit being carried out by a local biker gang. They do keep a fairly low-key presence here in the Kaufman area as of late. They get in a few bar fights now and again, but they seem to want to stay on the down low, so as to not draw unwanted attention to themselves. The group seems to be content to run their drug activity with as little police interference as possible. We have interviewed some local informants with minor ties to the gang, but so far that hasn't led to anything useful."

"Now they do have a clubhouse on the outskirts of Kaufman, located in the industrial area south of town," interjected Ranger Clint Jacobs. "What Roger and I intend to do next is have surveillance set up on the clubhouse in compliance with the Kaufman police. What we want to know is if there is someone hanging with this club who has been suspected of committing such a murder in Texas or another state. Maybe they put a contract in."

Clint looked around the table at the Rangers. "The thing with these dirtbags is that there are quite a few of them. Some of them are some low-life fuckers. I don't know how they ever got out of prison. Over the years, several of them have been sent up on drug charges, sexual assault, and pimping. And that's the minor shit. But two years ago, their leader got twenty-five to life for attempted murder. A new leader was voted in and has them keeping a low profile. He goes by Polar Bear. He's an albino, creepy-looking fucker, who's spent twenty years in the Texas penal system for an assortment of crimes. He's a scary dude. As Roger said, lately they seem content with their area drug trade and mainly just partying at their clubhouse. But one or more of them could want revenge for past busts. They have more than a few friends in the pen who were put there by Hasse or some other prosecutor here in Kaufman. Anyway, that's where we're at as of now."

Tyler was up next to tell what he had been doing on the investigation. "The Major had me look over Hasse's case files the day he was murdered, to see what might stand out as far as suspects. Don't know if y'all remember, but about two years ago there was a justice of the peace here in Kaufman who was convicted of theft. He was charged with stealing video monitors from the county storage facility. He was offered a deal to plead to a misdemeanor theft charge and lose his judgeship but keep his law license. He decided to take his case to court. He lost, so he was disbarred."

Tyler looked around the table at his coworkers and continued. "While reading the transcript of the trial, I came to find out that this ex-judge was a member of the Texas Guard and a small arms instructor. Also while reading the transcripts, I came across witness testimony that called his character into question. That being said, there were several testimonies that held him in very high regard. I mentioned this ex-judge, Eric Williams, to Major Wilson. Turns out the Major had previously been told about his suspicions of Williams by DA Mike McLelland." Tyler looked around the table, and every Ranger was staring at him and seeming to hang on to every word. So far, this was better than anyone else had come close to as far as even a half-assed strong lead.

"So...Major Wilson has instructed me to pursue this individual until he can be ruled out. Yesterday evening, I worked with the Kaufman police on a twelve-block canvass of his neighborhood. The canvass resulted in nada. No one saw him leave his house Thursday morning. There are no home video security cameras in the neighborhood, and no one has seen a white Crown Vic being driven by Mr. Williams. I will say this: until proven otherwise, I want to stay on his ass until I know for sure he's not our killer. I've got the gut feeling. I just can't shake it."

"Well, Tex, now that you've slept on it, where do you want to go from here?" asked Major Wilson.

"Don't know if I really slept on it at all, sir...mostly just laid there with my eyes closed," laughed Tyler. The other Rangers laughed and smiled along with him; they had all been there before. "What I do think is that his residence needs to be watched. *If*...as in if I had a three-foot dick, I'd be a porn star." All the Rangers burst out laughing. Tyler smiled along. "*If* someone had seen him leave his house the morning of the murder, we would have probable cause, especially if he couldn't verify an alibi. And if he is involved, his wife is covering for him right now. So what I want to attempt to do is put surveillance on his home. I want a search warrant."

"And how the hell do you plan to do that without his knowing it?" asked Major Wilson.

"Well, sir, as I said, I *want* to. Don't know for sure I can pull it off," replied Tyler. "But this is a small town. I grew up in a small town. Everyone knows everyone, or at least knows someone who knows someone. Okay, here's what I'm wanting to try. The cops I worked with yesterday, they worked the grid. I want to talk to them and see if they know someone who lives on Williams's street. It's a distinct possibility, especially in a small town. If so, I want to ask them if I can set up a camera in their house to video Williams' home. I know it's still a long shot, but look, where are we now? Everyone here is like me—we're all fishing, and no one's had a bite."

"Hell, I think it's worth a try," said Vasquez.

Thank you, Joe, Tyler thought to himself.

Major Wilson stood up, and his men could tell he was pondering his response. They all sat there quietly. "All right, Tex, I know you... You've slept on this, even if you did just lie there with your fucking eyes closed." The Rangers broke into a light laugh. "You've got to give it all to me, because this sounds dicey. I'll have to run this by Preston before I give you the okay. This could be dangerous for the homeowner. If Williams is our man, he's a deranged fucker. No telling what he might do if he knew a neighbor was spying on him."

"Oh, yes, sir, I've thought about that. I plan on doing this with the utmost discretion," replied Tyler. "Here's what I have in mind. There were eight Kaufman police officers who did the canvass yesterday evening. But two worked Williams's street. I want to start with them first. See if they know anyone that lives on his block. If not, I'll move to the next two. I will conduct my questioning as though I'm just trying to get a feel on the canvass. I know loose lips sink ships, so I don't want anyone knowing exactly why I want this information. Say I do hit pay dirt and find a close neighbor. I plan on going to them asking for their help and stressing that they keep silent on what they're helping us do. If I feel that they can't do that, or they refuse, I shut it down."

Major Wilson was still standing up as he listened to Tyler. He stood there for almost a minute before he responded. "All right, Tex, I like it. I'm not going to say shit to Preston about this until it's on solid ground. But you're not to put shit in anyone's house until I run this by Preston, comprende?"

"Comprende, boss," replied Tyler. The two longtime friends locked eyes. They both knew what the other was thinking—*let's do what we need to do to put the cocksuckers that killed Mark Hasse in prison.*

"Anyone have anything else?" asked Major Wilson. No one spoke up. "All right, back to what you've been assigned. Keep me informed should anything come up. Don't shoot yourselves in the foot."

Major Wilson was right; Tyler had lain in bed last night trying to think which way he should proceed. The idea had come to him because there had been no video surveillance around Williams's home. All that would have been needed was just one such camera. *So,* thought Tyler, *let's put a camera there.* Now they couldn't have a security company put one up in the neighborhood. With Eric Williams scooting around on his Segway, he would be wise to that in a second. No, the only way to pull this off was by subterfuge. Tyler was going to have to get lucky. He needed to find an accomplice, but at least he had a plan. When his head had hit the pillow the previous night, the only plan he had was getting pussy. Besides that, his mind was void. Finally, this idea came to him. He might have actually slept a bit afterward.

The Major couldn't be faulted for being concerned with a neighbor's well-being. If this worked out and Williams was involved, they would receive congratulatory backslaps that would knock them over. On the other hand, if Williams was involved and found out he was being spied on, he just might be crazy enough to retaliate against the neighbor. Then heads would roll, as in Wilson's and Tyler's. But they faced some form of risk every day; that's what Rangers did, try to put the sorry-ass kidnappers, child molesters, arsonists, rapists, and murderers in the state pen.

Wilson and Tyler had taken their fair share of risks already. In fact, Major Wilson had about a ten-year head start on Tyler. Each had consoled one another and their loved ones while standing next to a hospital bed. So whether it's lose your job or lose your head, it's never about losing. It's all about cleaning the shit off Texas streets. Rangers had been doing this for a long, long time…never mind the damn risk.

CHAPTER 11

Tyler got up from the table and began to make his way toward the steps where the press conference had been held. He intended to try and locate Sergeant Cox. He wanted to find out where Officers Hoskinson and Daniels could be found. He heard his name being called from behind him. It was Major Wilson. "Tex, hold on there a minute."

Tyler turned around and waited on Wilson to catch up with him. "Yeah, Russ, what you got?" he asked.

"Let's you and me go grab a bite," said the Major.

"Works for me, Russ, but give me a minute. I want to see if Sergeant Cox is still around. I want to have him hook me up with the two officers I told you about, the ones who canvassed Williams's block," said Tyler. "This shouldn't take long. If I don't see him around, I'll find him later at the station. Wait here at the steps. We'll take my truck."

"No problem, Tex, take your time," said Wilson.

The two Rangers walked together to where the press conference microphones were set up. At the bottom of the steps, the DA was still being interviewed by reporters. It had been a little less an hour since the press conference ended. The area was still packed with media and curious onlookers. Sure enough, there was Sergeant Cox, standing next to Sheriff Allbright, who was talking to some reporters.

Tyler turned to Major Wilson. "There he is, Russ. I'll just be a minute."

Wilson nodded and waved him on. Tyler bounded down the steps toward the Sergeant. When Tyler got to Sergeant Cox, he noticed that Sheriff Allbright was deep in the middle of a conversation with reporters and Cox was just standing there listening in. Tyler tapped him on the shoulder. "Oh, hey, Davis, how you doing?" Sergeant Cox extended his hand for Tyler to shake. *Damn*, thought Tyler, *all this man needs is a kilt and some woolen knee-high socks.* With his red hair, pocked nose, and blue eyes, he had Scottish warrior written all over him. The surname Cox did originate from several areas of Great Britain.

"Hello, Sergeant, could I have a minute of your time?" asked Tyler, taking the sergeant's hand in a firm grip.

"Sure, sure," said the sergeant, as the two of them stepped away from the reporters. "What do you need, Davis?"

"Just wanted to do the follow-up with Hoskinson and Daniels. Are they working today?" asked Tyler.

"Yes, they are," said Cox, looking around. "They were both here for the press conference, but I don't see them about right now. They might have returned to the station. You want me to have them follow up with you? Can you come by the station this afternoon?"

"Yeah, if you would," said Tyler. "I'm going to have lunch with Major Wilson. I can come by the station after that."

"Tell you what, take your time. I remember the two of them were going back to finish up some interviews with the canvass," said the sergeant. "How about I have them meet you at about six o'clock? They will be ending their shift around then. I'll have them wait for you."

"That works for me, Sergeant, I appreciate it," replied Tyler.

"All right, my boy, I won't forget. These kinds of things don't slip this mind," he said with a chuckle as he tapped the side of his head.

"Okay, Sergeant, I'll catch up with them at the station at six. Thanks again."

The sergeant waved his hand to acknowledge Tyler and turned to join Sheriff Allbright, who was still very much involved in conversation with reporters. Tyler turned and motioned for Major Wilson to descend the steps. They needed to walk through the crowd to get to Tyler's truck. As they began to walk into the crowd, some reporters came forward to ask for interviews. The two Rangers politely declined and soon made it to the street away from the throng. As they made their way toward Tyler's truck, they came up to Wilson's Caddy.

"Hell, Tex, I'm right here," said Wilson.

"Works for me, Russ."

"Where do you want to go?" asked Wilson.

"How about Jalisco's Mexican Grill? You do an enchilada plate?"

"Shit, yeah. I'll drive, you navigate."

"Let's do it."

*****

Seated at the table at Jalisco's Grill, Major Wilson said, "I don't envy Roger and Clint having to deal with the biker gang. They can get crazy, especially if they're wired on crack or, shit, crank…that's even worse."

"I'm with you. We've had our fair share of run-ins with those types, remember?" laughed Tyler.

Laughing, Wilson replied, "Shit, how could I forget? They put your ass in the hospital. I thought Priscilla was going to die of dehydration from crying."

"Yeah, that was a rough go. But Roger and Clint can handle themselves," said Tyler. "Clint got his black belt, what, two years ago? They don't want to fuck with either of them, especially Clint. He's already fucked up some well-deserving individuals. He's the kind of Ranger that makes you want to obey the law."

"You got that right, Tex," said Wilson. "Now, you probably know why I wanted us to do lunch. I want to pick your brain on this Williams, Eric Williams. I'm all for you eliminating him, but you're the best I got, and I spent the last two days with the FBI. All they talk about is the Brotherhood. I must admit, if this Williams isn't the shooter, I want you on the best suspects. I know this Williams has motive, but the skinny is he doesn't have it in him. He's just hot air." Wilson looked across the table at Tyler and then said, "Then there's the two of them. Who does the driving for Williams? I know you've thought this out. I need you to enlighten me, Tex."

The waiter approached the table to take their order. "We're going to have two beef enchilada plates with charro beans and rice. We both want the chili con carne on the enchiladas and two ice teas please," said Tyler. "Oh yeah, and flour and corn tortillas."

"Can I get you gentlemen any more chips and salsa?" asked the waiter. Each of the Rangers declined; they had no intention of filling up on chips. The waiter left to fill their order, and Tyler and Wilson returned to their conversation.

"Russ, I know exactly where you're coming from, and I know that you have to report back to Preston," replied Tyler. "So here's everything I've got." Tyler made a mental note to himself before he started. Yeah, he only had a gut feeling, but shit, no one had a solid lead, and this was day three. And Tyler didn't want to work the same angle that the whole fucking FBI was working. He was going to sell this, and if he was wrong, so be it; he had been wrong before. But he had been right many more times. "I think this was a very personal hit."

"I know you do, but why exactly?"

"The main reason is where the hit took place. Who would do that?" asked Tyler. "I'm thinking a gang or cartel would do a hit outside his residence, a drive-by. Or even at his front door. Shit, Russ, Mark lived alone. He wasn't married."

"Fine, good point. I'm listening."

"*Another thing, and this is really just as much a biggie as the location. No, it is bigger!* The confrontation on the street. The shooter waits to confront Mark. Not to ambush him but to confront him. Engages him in conversation. Calls him a 'cocksucker.'"

"Whoa...where did you hear that?" asked Wilson with an incredulous look on his face.

"From George Hamilton."

"I interviewed him for an hour at the scene. I asked him a dozen times if I asked him once: did you hear any discernable conversation? Each fucking time he said no! Stated he was too far away to hear shit! Now you're telling me he heard part of the goddamned conversation?" Wilson was getting pissed.

"Calm down, Russ. During my one-on-one with him at the station, I pressed him on that. He said he might have caught that just as the shooter was pulling his pistol. If that's all he left out, he's still batting a thousand in my book," said Tyler.

"Yeah…okay, go back to your points," grumbled Wilson. "Fuck, witnesses always tell you something they don't tell me."

"All right. Like I said, there's the location, the confrontation, then there's the driver. With the getaway car parked where it was, so that the shooter could approach Hasse as he walked down the sidewalk and not come up behind him, to me that shows personal commitment from the driver," said Tyler.

"Where are you with that, Tex? The driver. Who would have driven for Williams? That's been the big one for everyone that's considered Williams. What's your take?"

"Okay…ready for this one?"

"I'm all ears."

"Kim, Williams's wife."

"You got to be fucking with me. His ol' *lady?*"

"Yeah, Russ, it makes perfect sense. She probably hated what happened to her husband as much as he did. Together they lost everything. She didn't work. He was the sole provider. They lost their health insurance, and she's sickly. I got that from Williams's former secretary. The wife is probably on board with the trial being a political vendetta—the term echoed by the defense at trial was 'witch hunt.' I must admit I think there were some personal politics that came into play myself. Eric should have seen the writing on the wall and taken the plea. Anyway, there's the fact that Williams is a quirky little bastard. Well, it takes a quirky little bitch to marry a quirky little bastard. She's my driver."

The waiter came to the table with their food. This gave Major Wilson a moment to think about what he had just heard. The thought of the wife being involved never remotely crossed his mind. Wilson didn't think it crossed *anybody's* mind except Tex's. Damn, he could think outside the box like no one he had ever met. Wilson cut into an enchilada.

"Damn, Tex…that never crossed my mind. You just might be on to something here. Shit, you put a lot of thought into this, which I knew you'd do. So tell me about the surveillance. What are your plans there?"

"I'm thinking first and foremost about the safety of the home-owner. That is, if one can be found. Then strictly a need-to-know basis, again with the ultimate safety of the homeowner in mind. Next, the equipment installation. Everything will be inside the home. Jason has all the stuff I need in the lab. The camera will be disguised in a window, and I will go to the cooperating owner's home in the evening as though I'm just a visiting guest. You know the video equipment is idiotproof, easy as hell to install. I'll have it up and running in half an hour. The real challenge for me is finding the right person or persons and having them agree to help us."

"I like it, Tex, I really do. The wife as the driver…who would have thunk it? That one was stumping me. Couldn't see past Williams being good for it because of that. I mean, who's going to help an ex-judge knock off a district attorney in the early morning outside of a courthouse? Yeah, it could be the wife. She could hate just as much as the husband. You know what they say, two peas in a pod."

"Do me a favor, Russ," said Tyler.

"Sure, Tex, anything."

"When we leave here, let's find a place to shoot a few games of eight ball. I've got to kill about two hours before I meet up with those two police officers. I'll play you five dollars a game."

"You're on. Loser racks."

Tyler knew he'd accept at five dollars a pop. Tyler rarely beat Russ. Hell, Russ had a pool table at his house, and Tyler could rarely beat him before that. But thirty or forty dollars was worth it. Tyler didn't want to talk shop at the police station for the next two hours, and losing at pool beat feeding the pigeons at the park.

CHAPTER 12

Tyler was able to park at the police station parking lot that evening. With the press conference taking place that afternoon, and reporters trying to make deadline for Sunday's newspaper circulation, even media trucks and reporters were lighter outside the police station, since Sundays had the biggest paper sales of the week.

It was a few minutes before six o'clock when Tyler entered the station's lobby. It had cost him thirty-five dollars to kill the last two hours. He needed to brush up on his eight ball game. He saw Officer Hoskinson standing at the counter talking with the desk officer on duty; he was dressed in street clothes. Daniels was nowhere in sight. Tyler walked over and greeted Hoskinson and asked where Daniels was. Hoskinson told him he was still in the locker room getting changed and would be right out; it shouldn't be much longer.

"When he comes out, y'all meet me out front. I want to talk to you two about something," Tyler said. He only waited on them a couple of minutes before the two cops came out the front entrance. Tyler greeted Daniels and asked the two officers to follow him to his truck parked at the back of the police station. Tyler dropped the tailgate on his Chevy. "Make yourself at home, boys," he said. The two young Kaufman cops, dressed in their blue jeans and Western shirts, did what they had done thousands of times; they sat on the back of the tailgate and made themselves at home. All that was missing were ice-cold cans of beer.

"The canvass y'all finished up with this afternoon, did it go about like yesterday?" asked Tyler.

Tyler was about twenty years older than the two officers; some younger cops could feel like they needed to be on their best behavior around him, especially since he was affiliated with an elite branch of Texas law enforcement. Tyler was trying to keep this casual. There was a lot of tension in the area with the murder of Mark Hasse. Tyler wanted to break the ice with these young cops; he needed information while drawing as little attention as possible to the why. Kaufman wasn't tiny as far as Texas cities went, but with a population of just over six thousand, it was small enough that when people did talk, there was no telling how far it would go.

"Yes, sir, Mr. Davis." It was Officer Daniels who spoke up. "None of the people we talked to saw a white Crown Vic or saw the Williams leave their home on Thursday morning."

"You men knock off the Mr. Davis and the sirs. It's Tyler, and I'm serious. You're off work, it's Saturday evening, and I'm sure after we leave here, all three of us are going somewhere to chill out and knock back some cold ones. I'm just trying to put a plan together for later," said Tyler. He looked at Hoskinson. "It's Randall, right? Your friends call you Randy?"

"Yes, sir, they do," said Randy.

Tyler smiled. "Didn't you mean 'Yeah, Tyler, they do'?"

Randy let off a nervous laugh. "Yeah, Tyler, they do."

Tyler turned to Daniels. "What's your first name, Daniels?"

"David. My friends call me Double D."

"Okay, Randy, Double D, here's what we've got here." Tyler was standing in front of the tailgate as he was talking to the two officers. It was early evening, and the sun had set; it was starting to get cool. The parking lot was illuminated faintly by security lights on the police station perimeter. "DPS wants to get in good with a family on Williams's street. We just want to keep an eye on the neighborhood, you know what I mean?" The two young officers nodded their heads. "And y'all can see there's media everywhere, and people gossip, especially in small towns. I should know, I grew up in a small town, and everyone knew everyone else's business."

"That's for damn sure," said Randy.

"Exactly," replied Tyler. "So if DPS can find that special family to be our eyes and ears, it's not something we want everyone knowing. You can see that, huh?"

"Yeah, you want Williams to let his guard down, and if he knows he's being watched, he won't do that," said Double D.

"Right," said Tyler. "What the Texas Rangers need is for you two officers to keep this conversation between us. Now telling you that doesn't mean that you're keeping anything from your police department, because DPS and the Kaufman police are working together. But it's on a need-to-know basis only. This is for the safety of those that may help us. Understand?"

The two officers turned and looked at one another. Sounded good to them; normal police procedure.

"What I'm wanting to know is, do either of you or someone else on your force know someone who lives on Eric and Kim Williams's street?" Tyler asked this almost holding his breath while waiting for their response.

Double D turned to Randy and said, "Remember when Sergeant Cox had us muster together yesterday afternoon for the canvass, Mark said that his sister lived across the street from Eric Williams. You talked to the husband yesterday. He said he would talk to his wife when she got home, and if she had seen anything he would have her call the station. You should have their number with your notes."

"Yeah, I remember. I didn't think it was a big deal," said Randy. "He said he didn't see anything that would help us."

Tyler felt like he had been shot out of a cannon. A Kaufman cop's sister living across the street from the Williamses; he couldn't believe it. Tyler acted like they had just told him the earth was round. "Oh yeah, Mark's sister, huh? Which one was Mark? I know I met all of y'all yesterday, but I can't place him."

"Mark Cooper. He was the really tall guy, skinny, about six foot six. We went to high school together. He played center, I played guard on the basketball team," said Randy. "We both hired on with the Kaufman police force at about the same time. I know him pretty well but we're not close friends."

"So during the interview, you got their phone number, huh?" Tyler was downplaying this, but he was ecstatic. He just didn't want to make a big deal about it in front of the two cops; this needed to stay on the down low. But he was excited; this just might work out after all. No, he was going to think positive. This *was* going to work out.

"Yeah, Tyler, it's in my notepad. I was planning on calling the husband on Monday to follow up, check if he talked to his wife," said Randy. "My notes are in my locker. Want me to get you their number?"

"Yeah, get that for me, Randy. I'll give the husband a call and see if he'll keep an eye open in the neighborhood for us. Maybe something will turn up, you never know," said Tyler.

"Okay, be right back," said Randy as he hopped off the tailgate and walked toward the police station's rear entrance.

Tyler and Double D shot the shit about the Cowboys and the Mavericks and Sunday's Super Bowl while Randy was gone. Tyler learned that Double D wasn't a fan of Jerry Jones as general manager for the Cowboys any more than Tyler was. They both liked Dirk Nowitzki, didn't really care who won Sunday's big game, liked to deer hunt, and each shot the same make of bow: Matthew's solo cam, one of the best bows on the market. Soon Randy was back with the number.

"Here you are, Tyler." Randy handed a piece of paper to him. "I put their name on there with the number. I couldn't remember it at first. I talked with so many people, they all started to run together. Their last name is Ruby. So you're going to do the follow-up call and talk to the wife?"

"Oh, yeah. I'm going to talk with both of them. Thanks, Randy."

"No problem, Tyler. I know there's suspicion with the Williams dude, but most of the cops here think it was the Aryan Brotherhood that killed Hasse. But y'all have to look at everyone, don't you?" asked Randy.

"That's right…the ol' 'no stone goes unturned' theory," chuckled Tyler. "Thanks again for your help, men." After sliding off the truck's tailgate and shaking hands, they walked away. Tyler unfolded the piece of paper. *Kent and Martha Ruby*, read Tyler. He looked at his watch; it was only a few minutes past seven. Tyler took out his phone and punched in their number.

"Hello," came the answer.

"Mr. Ruby, I'm Tyler Davis with the Texas Department of Public Safety. How are you doing this evening?"

There was a brief pause on the other end of the line. "I'm fine, Mr. Davis...and you?"

"I'm good, Mr. Ruby. Was wondering if your wife is at home?" Again a brief pause, this one was just a little longer.

"Yes, she is. You caught us at a bad time. We're just on our way out for dinner," replied Kent Ruby.

"Is that right? Where are you going?"

"A pizza and pasta place here in town, the Pizza Paisan."

"Would you mind if I joined you for dinner? I have a couple of questions I would like to ask you."

"Mr. Davis, if this is concerning the investigation of Mr. Hasse, I'm happy to help in any way I can. In fact, my brother-in-law is with the Kaufman police force, but I answered some questions yesterday. Two police officers came by my door, and I answered their questions the best I could." Kent Ruby sounded a bit put off. "Now, if this is about my wife not being home at the time, I can assure you I asked her if she had seen anything out of the ordinary, and she said she hasn't. I don't see what else we could add."

"Mr. Ruby, the Kaufman police and my department appreciate all your help, but there is one matter that I wanted to go over with you and your wife. It would be a big help to our investigation." Tyler was trying to sound as calm and soothing as he could. "And dinner will be on me. I'll have DPS pick up the tab. Could you give me just a little more of your time? I can meet the two of you there."

"All right, Mr. Davis, we don't mind trying to help. It's just that there's so little we've seen or heard. Do you know the Pizza Paisan? It's on Oak Creek Drive."

"I'll GPS it on my phone. Are you bringing your children with you?"

"My wife and I haven't started a family yet. It will just be the two of us."

"Okay. I'll meet you out front. I'm wearing a light-gray suit. I was at the press conference this afternoon, had to look spiffy. Also, look for a gray cowboy hat with a very handsome man under it, six two, two thirty."

"All right, Mr. Davis," Kent Ruby laughed softly. "We'll see you out front."

Good news, they have no children, thought Tyler. That could have been a big problem, especially if they were older. They might not have been able to keep quiet, wanting to tell their friends. Then there was no telling where it would have gone. *But don't get ahead of yourself*, thought Tyler. *You haven't even met them yet.* But so far, so good; one positive checked on his list. Now he had to do a sell job, convince the couple to help him. He was going in cold as hell; he didn't know a damn thing about them. But now was not the time to dillydally; there was already one body in the morgue. Tyler needed to close this deal and get Major Wilson to sign off on it. Tyler put Pizza Paisan on his phone's Google map and pointed his Chevy toward Oak Creek Drive.

CHAPTER 13

Tyler arrived at the pizzeria before the Rubys. He knew who they were as they crossed the parking lot because they were sizing him up as they approached. The trio made introductions and were soon seated inside the restaurant. After ordering and putting the small talk aside, Kent asked what additional questions Tyler had for them. Tyler liked that—a man who got to the point.

"How well do you two know Eric and Kim Williams?"

Martha Ruby answered the question. "Not very well. My husband and I have only lived on the street for about a year. I believe the Williamses have lived there for about ten years or so. We found out from other neighbors that they were more sociable years ago, but when Eric lost his job they tended to keep to themselves, especially the wife, Kim. She is rarely seen outdoors, unless she's going somewhere in her car."

"So you don't visit with them at their house or have them over?" Tyler couldn't very well ask friends to spy on one another; that sure as hell wouldn't go over very well.

"I've never actually met Kim Williams," said Martha. "I do wave at her if she drives by in her car, and she returns my wave, but I have never actually spoken to her since we've lived across the street from them. Now, I have talked to Eric a time or two when I've been in the front yard."

Kent Ruby chimed in. "I've talked to him quite a bit when he's come by on his Segway. He's always driving that thing around. I think he thinks he's cool driving it around dressed in his camo.

Whatever floats his boat, but that's about as far as our socializing goes with them. Why are you asking, Tyler? I told the police yesterday that I didn't see them leave their house the morning Mr. Hasse was killed. When I left for work, their garage door was closed and that's all I remember. Martha leaves about half an hour after me, and she said she didn't see them leave either. And the Kaufman police didn't ask us how well we know them, so why are you asking?"

"The reason my questions are different than the Kaufman police is because I'm here for a much different reason. The Texas Rangers need someone on your block to help us in watching the Williamses' home." *Go on, Tyler, spit it out*, he said to himself. "I'm here to ask for your assistance in the surveillance of their home. I'm wanting y'all to let me and the Texas Department of Public Safety set up a camera and record the comings and goings of Eric and Kim Williams."

Tyler leaned back in the booth to watch their reaction. Kent and Martha turned and looked at each other, and then turned and stared back at Tyler. They both had the deer-in-the-headlights look. Each of them seemed to be waiting for the other to speak, and it didn't seem to Tyler that it was going to happen anytime soon.

"I know this is asking a lot of the two of you, and that this is catching you by surprise, but it would be helping the Texas Rangers tremendously in solving the murder of Mark Hasse."

"So you think he really did it? He's not just a suspect? But the one…the killer?" Martha had her voice back now. "I mean…I knew he got fired and all. I called my brother last night when Kent told me the police came by asking questions. My brother is a Kaufman cop, you know…but he said it was just routine police work. That some white supremacist group…the Aryan Boyhood or something like that…was responsible." Martha was on a roll. "He assured me we had nothing to worry about. Then, the very next day, we have a sure-as-shootin' Texas Ranger wanting us to spy on this neighbor! Now I'm more than a little scared. I'm really freaking out here!"

Tyler didn't expect a reaction any different from what he was getting; he knew if he could get someone to help him, it was going to be a hard sell. People weren't stupid; they would recognize the potential danger of what they were being asked to do. Tyler had his work cut out for him on this one. He leaned slowly forward over the table and clasped his hands together, thankful the food hadn't arrived yet.

Looking at Martha, he calmly said, "Martha, I don't know for sure that Eric Williams is the killer. If I knew that, I would have arrested him already. He is just a suspect I've been assigned to look at. The FBI have suspects that they are looking at. It's still an open investigation, and I'm trying to do what my boss tells me to do, and that is to investigate Eric Williams. And I'm trying to do that to the best of my ability. I know your brother is a Kaufman police officer. I met him yesterday, and what he told you is true. There are many people looking at potential suspects, one being the Aryan Brotherhood. But as of now, nobody knows for sure. We're pursuing leads. I'm sure, especially with your brother being a police officer, you understand that. So again, no, I don't know that Eric Williams is the killer, but that's why I'm here talking to you and your husband. I'm seeking help in trying to find out if he is involved. Yes, I know I'm asking a lot of both of you, and yes, there is potential risk involved, but if you'll hear me out I can explain how this can be accomplished with minimal risk."

Kent and Martha were still gazing at Tyler with incredulous looks on their faces. Just then, the waitress showed up with their order. Tyler had ordered a bottle of wine with their meal, and he was ready for a drink; he was sure that was ditto for the Rubys. After they were served, eating and drinking red wine, their demeanor seemed to relax a little.

Kent broke the silence. "Okay, Tyler, I'm willing to hear what you have in mind, but I will admit this sounds a little...too out there for us. But I did see the press conference on TV this evening when I got home from work and Mike McLelland did sound very inspirational. Especially when he said that he would park where Hasse parked and walk where Hasse walked and not be intimidated. To continue to bring justice to Kaufman. I'm with him. We can't let this scum—his word—scare us. So yeah...I'm willing to hear you out." He turned to his wife. "What do you think, Martha? Do you want to hear what he has in mind or not?"

After listening to her husband, Martha seemed to relax even more. She actually sat up a little straighter in the booth. To Tyler, she seemed proud of her husband for what he said; she certainly acted like it.

"Of course, Kent, let's at least hear him out." Looking at Tyler, she said, "Law has been a part of my family for generations, going back to my grandfather. He was a Kaufman police officer too, Mr. Davis, as well as my brother. My father probably would have followed in his father's footsteps as well if he hadn't died. A drunk driver killed him just before I turned two. He was only twenty-one years old. My brother Mark was just a baby. He was three months old. I sounded weenie a moment ago. Tell us, Mr. Davis, what would we need to do?"

Good for you, Kent, for stepping up to the plate, thought Tyler. Things seemed to be going south for a moment there; maybe the ship could be salvaged after all. Tyler certainly needed their help. "Martha, first of all, call me Tyler. This 'Mr. Davis' needs to be tossed out with the bathwater, especially if we start working together. What I have, equipment-wise, is a base station. All that is, is a self-contained recording device connected to a router that communicates with my computer. All equipment will be supplied by me. Besides your residence, all I need from you two is a receptacle to plug my base station into. The base is slightly larger than a briefcase. So router, ethernet cable, base station, and a small camera for video—that's it. All recordings will be through the router to my web address, so I can access the recordings remotely from my computer. Once it's installed, y'all will be done with me."

The two of them were listening intently, so Tyler charged on.

"Now the camera is small, about one and a half by two and a half inches. That is the only thing that will be exposed. But with it being so small, it's easy to disguise. In fact, at our lab we have all kinds of things to hide it in, from stuffed animals to trophies. It can be put on a windowsill. Even if someone is looking at it, they won't know it's there. What do you think? Sounds innocuous so far, huh?" asked Tyler.

"Yeah, it seems like someone would have to be inside the house to know it's there, and we don't do much entertaining," said Martha.

"Exactly, and I doubt I would have to keep it there too long. But if either of you want it removed, I'll come right over and take it out. Y'all are always in complete control," said Tyler. "As far as the installation time, it only takes about half an hour, max. As I said, a self-contained unit connected by some simple cables, plug it in, and done." The two of them were nodding their heads as if agreeing about the simplicity. "Then, for your safety, I'll come by in the evening to install it. Kent can pick me up out at the truck stop on the highway and drive me to your house. That way, my truck is never seen at your house. I'll look like a guest Kent is bringing over for a visit. Even if Eric Williams is out and about on his Segway, it would not be cause for suspicion. Do you know what room would be best to set up the camera in?"

The couple looked at each other. Kent said to Martha, "I'm thinking the front spare bedroom. The Williamses' house is just right there, across the street in perfect view."

Martha replied, "That's the only place that makes sense. It's perfect." She turned and looked at Tyler. "We only use that room when my mother visits."

"Let me butter you up a little bit here. Are you two fine Texas compatriots on board with this? Before you answer, let me tell you that I need to get approval from my Major, even if you agree. He is just as concerned with your welfare as I am. But before he can say yea or nay, you two need to say yes. Do you need to sleep on it?" asked Tyler. "Oh wait…I almost forgot. If you say yes, this is on a need-to-know basis, and no one needs to know. That includes your brother, Martha. There may be people who are sympathetic to Eric and Kim's plight. People in Kaufman might think they got a raw deal on their court case. This is a small town, and you never know how people think. None of your friends or family can know, as in not anybody, comprende?"

"Oh yeah, we understand. Screw Eric Williams and the horse he rode in on!" said Kent. "If he is the bastard that did this, we want to help catch him. Tyler, you seem to have a very well-thought-out scheme to watch him. Your plan doesn't sound risky at all by how you've planned it, so absolutely, we'll do it."

"And you, Martha, you good with this too?" asked Tyler.

"My husband was speaking for the both of us, Ranger Tyler. God bless John Wayne and God bless Texas. If it is him, let's get that outlaw son of a bitch," said Martha. Kent and Tyler burst out laughing.

CHAPTER 14

As Tyler pulled away from the Pizza Paisan parking lot. It felt like he was floating, and it wasn't from the wine; he only had two glasses. No, it was from the time he spent with the Rubys. With their cooperation, he at least had a direction to shoot for. As of that morning, he didn't have squat. Funny how in just a few hours, things could do a one-eighty. Now he needed the blessing of Russ. But with the Rubys not having children and Martha's brother being a Kaufman cop, Tyler was feeling like this was a lock. No time like real time, thought Tyler. He reached into his suit pocket, took out his phone, and called Major Wilson.

"Hey, Tex, how'd the meeting go?"

"Russ, you won't believe it. A Kaufman police officer's sister lives across the street from the Williamses. She's married, and they don't have children," gushed Tyler.

"Damn, Tex, you're the luckiest bastard I know. When are you going to try and meet up with them?"

"I just had dinner with both of them here in Kaufman. I left the restaurant parking lot ten minutes ago."

"You're shitting me!" Russ's voice was incredulous. "How in the hell did you pull that off tonight?"

"Okay, just the bull-rider version. I know it's late. One of the two young police officers I met with went to school with the brother, and both of them were on yesterday's canvass. While they were mustered together for the canvass, the brother mentioned to the group that his sister lived on Eric Williams's street. That's it! From there I got their number and invited myself to dinner." This was the part he really wanted Russ to hear. "Russ, they said yes to the surveillance."

This was about the fifth or sixth time Tyler had experienced silence after saying something to someone that evening. Finally Russ spoke. "Damn, Tex, you're not lucky…you're a certified miracle worker. Only you could pull off some shit like that. The fucking witnesses tell you shit that they don't tell FBI, me, or anyone else. Relatives live across the street from your suspect. The brother is part of your canvass. Shit, son, does your truck run on water? That's fantastic news. Good work, Tex. How the hell did you sell it to them?"

"Can't take credit for that, Russ. It was McLelland's speech at the press conference. The husband watched it this evening and didn't want to be a pussy. When the wife was freaking out, he stepped up big-time, shamed the wife. After that, she was following his lead. But it started with Mike McLelland."

"Well, he made quite an impression nationwide, from what I hear. It wasn't wordy but it didn't need to be."

"I'm with you, Russ. I'm glad we were there. I'll always remember that."

"Tex, try to get some rest tomorrow and be at headquarters Monday morning at eight. We've got a conference call with the Austin brass. We'll run your surveillance coup by Preston. Don't sweat it. From what you've told me, it's glue. You and Priscilla enjoy the Super Bowl tomorrow. Again, good job. You can pull off more shit than anybody I've ever seen. But that's enough, I don't want you to float off to heaven."

Tyler laughed out loud. "Monday in the a.m., Russ."

"Good night, Tex." The phone went dead.

Tyler had made plans with Kent Ruby to meet him at the truck stop up on the highway when he got off work on Monday. Since Tyler was going into headquarters on Monday, he would pick up the surveillance equipment then. Damn, he felt so much better. After nothing turned up with the canvass, he was feeling like he was adrift; at least now he had a plan. He picked up his phone lying next to him on the truck seat and pushed "girlfriend."

"Hi, Tyler, how's it going?"

"Things are looking up, I'm on 175 headed home. I thought the press conference was interesting as far as press conferences go. Mike McLelland's speech was inspirational, especially from the 'we ain't afeared' standpoint. Did you see it?"

"Of course, it's all over the news. He was really good. The 'pull you out of your hole' and the 'we're going to get you scum.' That was a big hit with the media. He sounded like he meant business."

"I was wondering how it sounded on TV. Being there, you could feel the emotion, like it was hanging in the air. I know it got people fired up—hell, I wanted to go down to the jailhouse and kick some ass."

Priscilla started laughing. "Tyler, you're so funny. But I know what you mean...it does piss you off. People do want that 'scum' caught, right."

"Not yeah but hell yeah!" agreed Tyler. "How was your get-together with your girlfriends?"

"It was good. Had lunch at the Shops of Legacy. I did some shopping, and the three of us went to the movies. Sally and Cindy had to get home, so Sam, Susan, and I went to see *Dallas Buyers Club* with Matthew McConaughey. It was really good, especially on the eyes. He's sooo...damn handsome. And he's from Texas. I just might drive down to Austin and try to find him."

Now it was Tyler that was laughing. "Well, you just do that, but don't call me if you get lost because I'll be pissed... Your ass can just stay down there." Now they were both laughing.

"No, really, the movie was good. We should see it together. I'd go again."

"I bet you will...I'm getting really pissed now," joked Tyler. "Did you buy anything special?"

"A couple of tops, just some things I can wear to school, nothing special. And you? How did it go after the press conference? Weren't you meeting up with Russ?"

"Yeah, we had lunch together, then shot some pool before I met up with two Kaufman police officers to follow up on yesterday's canvass. They did help me with a lead, so it was a good day."

"See, I told you something would break your way. Did you get my text about stopping by to take Kano for a walk?"

"Yes, I did. I appreciate that. You're a special girlfriend, thank you. Are you at home?"

"You're welcome, sweetie. Yes, I'm in my pj's watching the news. The McLelland speech is all over the place. It's all they're talking about, especially after today's press conference."

"Yeah, the media thrives on crime news. Nothing sells like blood in the street. But I understand. Not only is this a tragedy but it's a big whodunit. It's going to get major airtime. Who is the media speculating about? Is it still the Aryan Brotherhood?"

"Yes…them. I'm surprised Russ doesn't have you working on that. I know how much he likes you." Priscilla said this with a hint of disbelief in her voice.

"They're only possible suspects, no matter what the media thinks. The FBI is working that angle with Russ, Joe, and Richard. Not everyone can focus on the same suspects. As of now, no one really knows. I asked Russ to let me work my suspect. He and I talked about him over lunch. He's as good as any, actually better, in my book. I have a good feeling about this one."

"Well, I feel sorry for the guy you're looking at, because if it's him, I know you'll figure it out, poor bastard." She laughed.

Tyler laughed along with her. "Well, thank you, babe. Yeah, I feel good about him. He's definitely a possibility. And as I said, I got some good news this evening on a strong lead. I'm at a much better place this evening than I was this morning, so I'll take it."

"I know you and Russ know what you're doing."

"Want me to pick you up tomorrow and make the eleven o'clock Mass at the Cathedral? The Super Bowl party's not until later in the evening, and I'm off until Monday morning."

"Sure. Afterward, we can go to Aw Shucks and have a catfish basket with oysters. Then we can go to NorthPark and see Dallas Buyer's Club with Matthewww…" laughed Priscilla.

Tyler burst out laughing. "Yeah, okay, we can do that. Good night, babe. I love you. See you in the morning."

"Good night, Tyler. I love you too."

Things were looking up, thought Tyler. He turned up the radio, and Paul Thorn was singing "Don't Let Nobody Rob You of Your Joy." *Amen to that*, thought Tyler. He gunned the Chevy on down the highway. "Here I come, Kano. Here I come, boy," he said out loud. Home sweet home. Thirty more minutes; he could hardly wait.

CHAPTER 15

TYLER GOT UP SUNDAY MORNING and did his fifty crunches, then fixed himself a good breakfast of eggs, bacon, potatoes, and toast. Then he took Kano for a walk, stopping on the way at his neighbor's, Mrs. Knuester, to see if her dogs wanted to tag along. She let Tyler take Bruno, her boxer. Bruno and Kano seemed to get along very well. He showered when he returned home; he needed to be at Priscilla's by ten o'clock. The drive down Central Expressway to downtown Dallas would take about forty-five minutes from McKinney, and the Mass was at eleven o'clock.

Priscilla was raised Catholic. Tyler wasn't. When Tyler's father sold his gun store in Palestine, Texas, he moved the family to Dallas. Tyler's older brother, Mike, made a friend soon after they moved here who invited him to a church service in Highland Park. After a couple of months, Mike talked Tyler into coming to a youth choir practice. When Tyler got there, he looked around at all the pretty young girls and—Lordy, Lordy—he beheld what the Lord had created, so he learned to sing. Eventually, Tyler joined Highland Park Baptist Church, and at the age of sixteen accepted Jesus Christ as his Lord and Savior and was baptized. His first girlfriend was a choir member, Judy, a Miss Teenage Dallas runner-up. She was a stunner. Tyler lost more than his heart to Judy.

Over the following years, Tyler's beliefs had taken a path of ebbs and flows; today he considered himself a spiritual person more than, say, a religious one. And in the almost two and one-half decades since he had sworn an oath to uphold the laws of Texas, he had witnessed the good and bad of mankind, to put it mildly. To this day, Tyler still believed in Jesus Christ.

More times than he could count, he worked cases that took him out of town. On these trips, he shared motel rooms with members of law enforcement, be it FBI, fellow Rangers, or State Troopers. Sometimes late into the night when the conversation turned from the case at hand to sports or politics, invariably it would shift to personal beliefs (all helped along by the use of fermented beverages). Tyler would be asked, "How can you believe in God when you've seen all the shit we've seen?" or "How would a just God let this shit happen?"

Tyler would answer with "Yeah, there are horrible people doing terrible things to innocent people, but here you are…trying to do good and put an end to it."

So to Tyler, there was the rub. In the inner depths of his being, Tyler knew that in the universe there was the yin and yang, good and evil, love and hate, God and…the devil. The creative compilation for man's existence. On Tyler's life journey, he too had to cope with the dark side, so he chose a mantra of "just roll with it." To some, this might sound flippant. To Tyler, it wasn't; not in the least. It meant not being beaten down, swayed, or jaded by the evil he encountered doing his job. He was required to arrest those who chose to not even attempt to do their best. God gave them a choice; they chose. Everyone chooses. To Tyler, it was that simple: just make the right decisions. The quality of your life depends on it.

Tyler thought it amusing that a very popular movie that came out when he was a youth, *Star Wars*, also had a mantra. *May the Force be with you*. This was the mantra of the good guys, not Darth Vader and cohorts; they had turned their back on the Force. Tyler knew that long after dirt was thrown over his lifeless body, and when a thousand years had passed, there would still be Rangers like him, fighting the good fight. The good book states, "The wicked shall never inherit the earth." Why? Because there would always be enough good guys fighting to keep it from happening.

*****

Priscilla and Tyler didn't attend Mass regularly at the cathedral in downtown Dallas due to both of them living in the suburbs; it was quite a distance from their homes. It was special when they did attend, largely due to the church being so grand. It was the Cathedral Sanctuario de Guadalupe (Cathedral Shrine of the Virgin of Guadalupe), overseeing the second largest Catholic membership in the United States. It was located in what is known as the Arts District of Dallas. The church's cornerstone was laid in 1898 and was dedicated in 1902. The building's architectural style was Gothic Revival, with a single spire of 224 feet. Boasting some forty-nine bells and an average Sunday attendance of over eleven thousand patrons, it was a source of pride for the citizens of Dallas.

With Tyler having been introduced to the Southern Baptist church of his youth, he had trouble wrapping his head around Catholic priests not being allowed to marry. The pastor at his Baptist church not only had a wife but children. This didn't seem to be a problem with the congregation. Tyler felt that Catholics needed to lighten up, let the priests get some pussy, and have a family life, especially with the stigma of pedophile priests within the priesthood, not to mention the cover-ups linked back to Rome. Choices; it was back to choices. This is your flock; protect them at all cost. Have the priests that lead these flocks empowered in their lives, blessed with God's gift to man: love and unity of family.

Tyler wasn't throwing stones. He was well aware that Baptists, Protestants, Christian Fundamentalists, and their ilk also had their share of skeletons. This was the main reason Tyler had distanced himself from organized religion. He knew that when man got control of anything, that's what he wanted: control. Whether it be religion, politics, banking, or even law enforcement, things could get fucked up real quick. So Tyler did his best and "rolled with it." Maybe in a hundred years, the priesthood would change. Tyler did know it wasn't biblical: priests in the early centuries were married. If the Catholic Church could make changes to its doctrine centuries ago, it could certainly reverse itself today. The good people were going to have to make their voices be heard.

*****

After the service, Tyler and Priscilla went out for lunch at a popular Dallas seafood dive called Aw Shucks on lower Greenville Avenue. This area was old east Dallas, just blocks from the original Dr. Pepper bottling company. Also in the vicinity was Southern Methodist University, or SMU, where Major Wilson and his wife had gone to college. Aw Shucks was a small restaurant that only seated about sixty people. The patrons ordered at a counter and picked up their orders when called; no frills. But the food was great, and on weekends the waiting line was out the door and down the sidewalk; waiting times could reach an hour. Everyone from the Dallas well-heeled, as well as the nearby college kids and everyone in between, ate here.

Directly across the street was the Granada Theatre, an old movie theater that had long since been converted into a popular music venue. With the big movie complexes being built in the suburbs, the early movie theaters were perfect as music venues. They had something the new theaters didn't have: a stage. Priscilla and Tyler had seen the Fabulous Thunderbirds play there with Kim Wilson on lead vocals and Jimmy Vaughan on lead guitar a few years back. Jimmy Vaughan was the older brother of rock icon Stevie Ray Vaughan. Both of the brothers were Dallas natives, growing up in Oak Cliff, located just south of downtown Dallas.

Jimmy had moved to Austin and began playing with The Thunderbirds as a young man. All Stevie did was practice, practice, practice, inspired by his older brother, only to rocket to legendary rock god status with "Double Trouble" before his tragic death in a helicopter crash after a show in Colorado. While a student at UT, Tyler had a girlfriend give him a CD that the Vaughan brothers had recorded together just prior to Stevie's death. It was titled "Family Style" and was full of killer cuts. One of Tyler's favorites was "White

Boots." It made you proud to live in the city where Stevie and Jimmy Vaughan were born.

While having lunch, Priscilla asked, "Are you taking us to NorthPark to see *Dallas Buyers Club*?" NorthPark was the first climate-controlled, fully enclosed mall in the world, completed in 1965. "It's still early, and we have plenty of time to make it to Sam's Super Bowl party at least two hours before kickoff. You don't care about the pregame stuff, do you? Especially since the Cowboys aren't there."

"If the Cowboys were there, I'd be throwing my own Super Bowl party. They haven't sniffed the Super Bowl since Jerry fired Jimmy. I take that back—they got there with Switzer, but it was still Jimmy's team. Jerry's made some stupid decisions trying to play general manager. The main one was not drafting Steven Jackson when he fell in their lap. But don't get me started."

"So is that a yes or no for the movie?"

"Of course it's a yes," replied Tyler. "How could I deprive you of another chance to see Matthewwww?"

"No, really, it's a good movie. You'll like it," she replied, smiling at his inflection.

"I know, I'm just teasing you. Going to a movie sounds fine, and to me, that one's as good as any."

"Good. I do think you'll like it. Matthew McConaughey might get the Academy Award, he's that good in it. You'll see."

"Works for me. I'm ready anytime you are."

NorthPark was only a few minutes' drive from Aw Shucks, a short drive back up Central Expressway. The original mall had undergone several expansions over the years and was still very much *the* place to shop for Dallasites. Even after all these years, it had stood the test of time. It was a beautiful mall. There was so much money spent there that the upkeep was top-notch; the place looked like it had been built yesterday.

Tyler parked in the multilevel covered lot on the west end of the mall and went inside to the theater. Years ago, when the mall had first opened, the movie theater was separate from the mall; now it was located inside. It had been swallowed up and relocated completely with the expansions. Tyler did like the movie but thought it was a sad way for people to live and die. Thank goodness the stigma and care practices had changed for AIDS patients since those early days.

Next on their agenda was the Super Bowl party at Priscilla's friend Samantha's house. It was still early evening, only a little after five. Tyler was tired and had a busy day—hell, a busy week—coming up, but he was going to suck it up for Priscilla's sake. Her friend Sam was a coworker of Priscilla's, teaching at the same school. All the people there would be her school friends or friends of Sam and her husband. Tyler could socialize with the best of them, even if he wasn't excited about the Super Bowl teams. The Baltimore Ravens were playing the San Francisco 49ers in Super Bowl XLVII. Tyler would know quite a few people there, just not too well. Rangers have a way of hanging with other Rangers. What he didn't want to do was talk about the Hasse murder all night. He hoped the people there would focus on the game and not pepper him with questions. He knew it would come up, but not all night…please.

Sam lived in McKinney, a few miles from Priscilla. Her husband Jack was a high-level exec with Texas Instruments. They were loaded, living in a gated community on the west side of the suburb. Their home was huge, maybe six thousand square feet. It had a movie-viewing room, a pool, and separate guest quarters, and it sat on about four acres. Executives at Texas Instruments definitely made a lot more money than Texas Rangers.

When Tyler and Priscilla arrived, there was already a full house inside. The movie room wasn't being used for the game; everyone was in the den tuned to the big screen. There was lots and lots of food, as well as plenty to drink. Jack and Sam sure knew how to throw a party. There were at least forty people there, with a few wearing jerseys of the respective teams. Not many people in Texas really gave a shit who won this game. Tyler sure as hell didn't, but if he had his druthers it would be the Ravens. Hell, he had to root for someone.

Soon after arriving, Priscilla went to help in the kitchen and visit with her girlfriends. Tyler saw Jack talking with some other men. He grabbed a beer and joined them. "Hello, Jack, thanks for the invite."

"Well, look what the cat dragged in. How you doing, Tyler?" asked Jack, taking his hand. "What the hell is going on in Kaufman? Sam told me you were out there on the case. What a thing to happen. Is it who they think it is, the Aryan Brotherhood? That's what the media seems to believe."

"Jack, it's way too early to know. Lots of suspects are being looked at. Prosecutors make lots of enemies. Putting people in prison pisses people off, especially the ones put there. And sometimes they're still pissed when they get out."

"I bet they are. Here, let me introduce you to some of my friends."

Tyler was introduced to the men with Jack and joined in with the small talk, waiting for the game to start. He found a seat close to the TV soon after. He sat next to Sam and Jack's teenage son, Evan, and his girlfriend. That way, he didn't have to talk about Hasse's murder. Evan wanted to talk about the game. *Perfect*, thought Tyler. He stayed planted there. He knew he wouldn't see Priscilla during the game; she would be jawing with her friends. She came to socialize, not watch football. The Ravens handed the 49ers their first loss in a Super Bowl. It did turn out to be a good game, thought Tyler. But it was about time his Cowboys got back into the bowl game; it was pushing twenty years now.

Taking Priscilla home after the game, Tyler felt like he had left the party with minimal mental fatigue. He avoided talking about the Hasse murder most of the night, thanks mostly to Evan's interest in football. Evan had wanted the 49ers to win, so Tyler changed Super Bowl allegiance.

On his way home, he stopped to buy some groceries. When he got home, he took Kano for a short walk and then did a maintenance cleaning on his SIG .357 Mag pistol before hitting the sack. With the video conference early the next morning, getting the surveillance equipment together, and meeting up with the Rubys, he had a full day ahead of him. Now if he could only sleep.

CHAPTER 16

Tyler entered the security gate to the Company B headquarters at 7:05 Monday morning. There were several cars already parked in the gated employee lot. Wilson's Caddy was there as well as Jason and Rich's cars. This morning's video conference with the Austin brass would be mandatory for all the Rangers. It wasn't often that these took place; only the biggest cases got this much attention. A few years ago, these meetings were held as conference calls, on speakerphones. Now it was audio and video, everyone together on the big screen.

The building opened for the general public at 8:00 a.m. Linda Curry was the receptionist; she did the meet and greet and maintained the client appointments. Gale Walker was the office manager who oversaw the secretaries and clerical staff, who generally arrived by 7:45 a.m. These staff members were on the first floor. The second floor was where the Rangers had their offices. Only Major Wilson's office held an inner office for his personal secretary, Judy Poppa. The second floor also had a large conference room, where the video conference would take place.

The building had a basement that everyone referred to as the lab. Yes, it did have a forensic laboratory, but it held more than that. There was a small arms storage room, and a soundproof gun range that could accommodate three shooters. In addition, there was the weapons room, evidence room, and equipment room. This lower level was overseen by Jason Chime. He wasn't a DPS agent but rather a certified forensic laboratory analyst. He was also a graduate of the

University of Texas at Arlington, having received a degree in biology with a minor in computer science. He was a good kid (Tyler thought of him as a kid because he was the youngest employee at headquarters).

Jason had proved himself to be an indispensable asset, especially to the Rangers. He had only worked for DPS for two years, having been trained by Edwin Smoot to run the lab. The two of them had worked down there together until Smoot's retirement some six months before. Smoot had been the DPS lab tech here for thirty-five years, and he had been a damn good one, but the kid was ambitious and was holding his own in Edwin Smoot's absence.

When Tyler entered the security door to the building, he took the elevator down to the lab to get the surveillance camera from the equipment room. After retrieving the camera, he saw Jason coming out of his office.

"Good morning, Jason."

"Hey, good morning to you, Tyler. I see you're going to do a little spying," said Jason, nodding toward the base station Tyler was holding in his hand.

"Yeah, Jason…I might have a hot one."

"Going by the local news, y'all are involved in a real mess. Hard to believe someone would kill a prosecutor outside the courthouse, especially in broad daylight," said Jason. "The media is portraying it as an Aryan Brotherhood slaying, but you must have another suspect in mind since you have that spy cam. You mentioned hot—is he hot-hot, or is it too early to tell?"

"Good question. My brain says hot, my gut says hot…but there are people who know him, and they tell me he's not up to it. I've yet to interview him, but he has been questioned about his alibi. He lives in Kaufman, so we did a canvass of his neighborhood. That got us nowhere, hence the spy cam," replied Tyler. "As you saw on the news, the main focus is on the Aryan Brotherhood. The feds had intel coming out of Colorado that a hit was being planned. Nothing solid, mind you, but the mark was thought to be in-state, not a Texas hit. Seems the 211 Crew was marking it. So Hasse's murder doesn't fit. Then there is a local biker gang. They have a clubhouse in Kaufman, located on the outskirts of town in an industrial area. They're dope runners, all the shit from what I hear—smack, coke, meth. Maybe they're good for it. There are quite a few of them. Anyhoo, to answer your question, I feel good about my guy, but yeah, it's early."

"Well, if it's an alibi breaker you're needing, that spy cam will do the trick. It sees all and tells all. Never to be wrong or misled, until photoshopped," joked Jason.

"Shit, Jason, I hear you. If there had just been one of these," said Tyler, gesturing with the spy cam, "on my suspect's street, I'd have a solid idea about the guy right now! None of his neighbors had a security camera—zero. I know he knew that, Jason. He's a smart fucker. He's a Mensa member, so he'll cover his ass and then some. From what I've found out so far, he likes to boast. He thinks he's the smartest person in the room, and he probably is."

"I know that's right," blurted Jason. "You've got to be one high IQ'd mother to join in with the mental giants."

Tyler was nodding his head in agreement. "I hear you...and I want to talk to him so bad, but I feel like the time has to be just right. I don't think he'll give up much to just anybody. He'll want to play mind games. I did a short interview the other night out in front of the police station with some reporters. I hope they put me on TV. If they did, maybe my suspect saw it. That may be a catalyst for him to speak to me if I approach him. His ego would want to toy with me, like a cat playing with a mouse. I can feel it. But the time has to be right, so I'm waiting, staying in the background for now."

"Good idea, Tyler."

"Thanks. I've got to be on top of my game, Jason, to lure him out. Shame of it is, if it is him, I don't think he's done. If he was pissed enough to kill Hasse, he's just as pissed off at some other people. But there is no alternative—can't touch him without evidence or probable cause. No one has a solid lead on anyone. There's a funeral this week, and we're all just speculating." The last few days of frustration showed on his face. "So if he's the guy, this camera is my best shot. If there is another hit, and he says he's at home but I know different, I've got my search warrant. If I search his house, it's over, no matter how well he thinks he's covered his tracks, I'll nail his butt."

"Good luck, Tyler. I hope that works out for you. If there's anything I can do on my end, let me know. I'm here Monday through Friday, eight to five, except holidays. Hell, even then if they're paying double time," said Jason, kidding with Tyler. Jason wasn't being cynical; in law enforcement, you have to joke to lighten the mood, or everyone would go crazy. Same as doctors working in trauma; you see so much human tragedy that if you didn't crack wise now and again, your mind would blow like a 50-amp fuse (Rolling Stones nod). After two-plus decades, no one knew this better than Tyler.

"I'll keep you in mind if I think I can use you. Talk at you later. We have a meeting this morning with the Austin bigwigs."

"Again, Tyler, good luck. I hope you nail the bastard."

"So do I, Jason, so do I." Tyler walked to the elevator and pushed the up button. He had a conference to attend, and in this meeting no one would be cracking wise. No, sir, this meeting would be as serious as the proverbial heart attack.

*****

Tyler stepped off the elevator and went to his office to drop off the surveillance camera. He walked down the hallway and entered the conference room. Already seated at the table were Major Wilson, Lieutenant Roger Miles, Ranger Steve Jamison, and the rest of his coworkers. Tyler greeted the men, poured himself a cup of coffee, and grabbed a couple of pastries Judy had set out. He took a seat at the table. Mounted on the wall at the far end of the room was a large TV screen displaying the conference room in Austin. Seated at that table were the Texas Ranger Division top dogs, meaning Deputy Assistant Director Calvin Cook, Major Steven Reed, Captain Alex Ferguson, Captain Joe Williams, and an empty seat that would soon be occupied by the head honcho, Director Colin Preston.

The audio was on between the rooms, and the men were talking among themselves, just making light conversation, inquiring about each other's families and discussing last night's Super Bowl. Some of the men were looking over their notes while waiting for Preston to appear and start the meeting. It was 7:58; it wouldn't be long now, thought Tyler. He was finishing his second pastry when Director Preston entered Austin's conference room and took his seat. It was exactly 8:00 a.m.

"Good morning, gentlemen. Having to call this meeting under such tragic circumstances is a damn shame. The assassination of Mark Hasse in front of his courthouse—our courthouse—is a goddamned atrocity. I've been kept abreast of the investigation by Major Wilson, Special Agent in Charge Chris Collins, and District Attorney Mike McLelland, as well as Chief Burns and Sheriff Allbright. But it is you, gentlemen, my agents in the field, that I want to hear from this morning. You are the eyes and ears that I rely on. So all of us here in Austin want to hear from each of you. We are very interested in your thoughts concerning this investigation. Major Wilson, where do you want to start?" asked Director Preston.

Major Wilson had Jamison address the director and the Austin headquarters staff first. Since the getaway car was the best lead that anyone had, it was the logical place to start. Jamison explained how he was working in conjunction with the Kaufman detectives and police force to locate the Crown Vic. He told the officers they had searched registration records and poured over hours of closed-circuit footage in an attempt to get the license plates on the Crown Vic. The search also included storage facilities in and around Kaufman. Jamison told the director that the search had not yet been exhausted and that finding the car was very much a high priority.

Next to take the floor were Lieutenant Roger Miles and Clint Jacobs. The Rangers told the Austin headquarters staff about the local biker gang that was involved in the Kaufman County drug trade. Miles told them about the clubhouse the gang occupied on the outskirts of Kaufman, in an industrial area. He explained that the sheer number of members in itself posed a problem. With such a large group, pinpointing just two potentially involved in the hit was daunting. The Rangers also brought up that since the bikers were local, chopping the getaway car would have been simple if they were responsible. Drive it to a garage, strip it, torch it, and *poof*...no more Crown Vic. Lieutenant Miles told them about the junkyard that the biker gang ran in the same industrial area of Kaufman. The director and his staff were informed about prior arrests and convictions of club members and that some had been prosecuted by Mark Hasse. So there was plenty of motive for them to want to see Mark Hasse six feet under Texas soil. In fact, there were so many possible suspects it was difficult to keep up…almost.

Next up to the plate was Tyler; he had one more sales job to do. He wanted Preston to rubber-stamp his surveillance of Eric Williams's residence. He felt good about his chances and figured Russ had already discussed the matter with Preston, but still…you never know. It did involve the general public, so that in itself made it dicey. "Lord be with me," he muttered to himself. "Let it roll."

"Good morning, Director Preston, gentlemen. I'm sure you've been briefed on my interest in a onetime justice of the peace in Kaufman County, a Mr. Eric Williams. He was prosecuted and found guilty of the theft of county property, that being three video monitors taken from a storage locker belonging to the county. His defense claimed that the monitors were taken by Mr. Williams to be used for official business, video magistration from the county jail to his office at the courthouse. His attorney alleged that the charges were personal and political. The term she used was 'witch hunt,' a direct quote from the trial transcripts. The prosecution brought into question Mr. Williams's character and also the misappropriation of law library funds, for which he has a hearing pending. The theft case was prosecuted by both Mark Hasse and Mike McLelland."

"I'm familiar with Williams's case, Davis. Where exactly has this information taken you in regard to this investigation?" asked Director Preston.

"Well, sir, I felt Williams was a viable suspect due to his having motive, so I arranged a canvass of his neighborhood in conjunction with Kaufman police. I wanted to find out if he had been seen leaving his home on the morning of Mark Hasse's murder," replied Tyler.

"Yes, Davis, I know that the canvass turned up no eyewitness testimony on Williams's whereabouts that Thursday morning," said Preston.

"Yes, sir, that's correct, but I had a meeting with the two Kaufman police officers who did the door-to-door canvass on Williams's street.

I came to find out that one of Kaufman's police officers has a sister who lives on his block. I managed to obtain an interview with her as well as her husband, and they have agreed to allow DPS to conduct video surveillance on Williams's home from their residence. Eric Williams and his wife are each other's alibi. Both of them stated during the canvass that they were home the morning of Hasse's murder. As of now, I have no proof that this is the truth."

Here came the part that Tyler hated to say, but it had to be said. "If Williams is our perp and he has another murder in mind, it's imperative that we have proof of his leaving his residence. I feel that the two of them will continue to cover for each other, as they're doing now. I feel confident that the neighbors who have agreed to assist us will be discreet. I expressed the importance of their discretion for their own safety. The couple have no children and no close relationship with the Williams, not even a friendly relationship that can sometimes develop among close neighbors."

"That's a hell of a note, Ranger Davis. You're telling us that if he pulled off another hit, this surveillance would assist in his arrest." Preston had a dumbfounded look on his face as he continued. "In the meantime, someone else would have to die. I'm all for you wanting to watch the man. What I'm not for is someone else getting killed to get us to him." By his tone and look, the pressure of this case was raw, like a festering wound. Another death was not something Preston even wanted to consider, especially if it involved another high-profile member of law enforcement.

"Mr. Preston, I know that every man in this room feels exactly as you do. But as all of you have heard this morning, we're actively trying to find the assailants. From the getaway car to the biker gang, to the FBI working on the Aryan Brotherhood intel and my interest in Eric Williams, there are no solid leads. I would like nothing better than to search Williams's home, but my actions are dictated by law. We surely don't want them to strike again, but until there is evidence to move on, we have to continue to search for that break. Even if it's an ugly one."

"I know, Davis…I know. You're right, this is a very ugly business. No one knows that better than all of us here. You men, all of you men, I know are doing your best to solve this crime. Knowing all of you personally but not nearly as well as I would like, I'm proud to be associated with you as Texas Rangers. Keep up the good work. Together we'll find the sons of bitches who did this. And yes, as much as I hate to admit it, someone else could die. I know I sounded frustrated there, but I know we all are. How long has it been now? Five damn days! We have the whole goddamned state, FBI, ATF, and police departments statewide looking for these bastards, and no one is any closer than we were on Thursday. Well, gentlemen, it's certainly not from lack of trying. It's just the nasty nature of the beast. I—no, *we* here in Austin appreciate all your hard work and effort. No one knows more than we do how tough this job can be."

Director Colin Preston leaned back in his chair. "Davis, I like your initiative on the surveillance. Major Wilson, this is your call on how you want Davis to proceed. From my perspective, it certainly couldn't hurt. All stops are pulled. It's go fucking get 'em. You men know what's at stake here and where we're at. And as of right now it's not pretty. I'm not telling you anything you don't already know. That being said, we're here in Austin and you're in Dallas, and we're keeping you men from turning this around and putting these assholes in the penitentiary. Thank you again for the job you're doing. Should anything arise that you men need, let Major Wilson know, and I'll be sure you get it. As of now, there is no greater case on the books in Texas. This is it, men, good luck."

The Austin brass wished the Dallas Rangers good luck and said their goodbyes. Major Wilson and his Rangers did the same from their end. Captain Alex Ferguson stepped forward and turned off the video feed from Austin, and the screen went blank.

Major Wilson turned from facing the screen and looked at his Rangers seated at the table. "Well, as you men can see, there is plenty of pressure to go around. It's the same statewide, not just in Kaufman. I want to reiterate what you just heard. I'm also satisfied with the effort you've put forth so far. Solving this kind of murder is rarely easy. Y'all know what your assignments are, so get to them. Tex, you heard the man—carry on with your surveillance of Williams. If you men need anything, just let me know. If I can't get it, the Austin brass will. It's Katy-bar-the-door on this one, boys."

As this meeting adjourned, Tyler left the conference room with an optimistic feeling about the rest of his day. He had gotten the green light he wanted on watching Eric Williams, and he planned on watching him like a hawk. Yes, Tyler was feeling better about this positive turn going his way. What he didn't know was that trouble he couldn't imagine was just around the corner.

On the day of Mark Hasse's murder, he had thought to himself that this killing might just be the beginning of things to come. He had expressed that exact sentiment to himself time and again. And it was coming…at depths he couldn't fathom. The surprises coming his way were the kind delivered by the Brothers Grimm.

CHAPTER 17

Having several hours to kill before meeting up with the Rubys, Tyler decided to put the time to good use. He took the elevator back down to the lab and entered the shooting range. Inside was a foyer area that had a ledge to place ammunition, firearms, and targets. Hanging on hooks below the shelf were ear protectors, the kind that cupped the ears and are adjusted by sliding a small band of steel into a plastic holder above the head. Tyler pulled up his trouser leg to withdraw his SIG .380 from his ankle holster belted inside his cowboy boot. He kept his .380 loaded with Hornady Critical Defense cartridges. These bullets had six notches located on the bullet's frontal cavity. The cavity was encased with hard plastic to assist aerodynamics and bullet expansion. These FTX patented custom cartridges were designed for maximum mushroom effect. If Tyler did shoot someone, he wanted them to *know* that they had been shot.

In his shoulder holster, under his jacket, Tyler carried a SIG Sauer .357 Magnum, also loaded with high-expansion bullets. He used to carry a 9mm, but when the .357 came out in auto, he switched. The .357 had better "stopping power" over the 9mm. Again, if he was going to shoot someone, he wanted to stop them, especially since the people Tyler shot at would be shooting or about to shoot him. Tyler was baffled by the deaths of unarmed suspects across the country shot by police. Why were they shooting to kill? Shoot to wound, at the very least; wounding an unarmed suspect in the leg will stop him just fine. Outlaws shoot unarmed people in the back, even if they do carry a badge.

The SIG .357 was the most accurate semiauto on the market and ballistically the most consistent handgun cartridge Tyler had ever fired. He was an expert shot and shooting the most accurate auto helped to keep it that way. Of course, revolvers with extended barrels made for the most accurate handguns but carrying one under his jacket wasn't something Tyler was going to do. He was leaving that for Hollywood and Dirty Harry.

Tyler stepped through the opening door behind the bulletproof glass to the waist-high podium. He attached his silhouette target to the clips and pushed the forward button located on top of the podium. The target began to move to the far end on the gun range. This target had the outline of a human. When the target stopped, Tyler aimed for center mass and emptied his clip in a tight group with his .380. He reloaded his clip, put his pistol back in his ankle holster, and pushed the return button. When the hanger arrived, he attached a more detailed target on the clips. This target was of a criminal clutching a pistol extended out in front of his body, effectively blocking his chest area. This made for a more challenging target. Not only did it represent someone being fired upon, it also created a smaller target area: the head.

With Tyler being alone in the gun range, he was going to have some fun. He pushed the forward button, watching the target move downrange. As soon as it came to a stop, Tyler withdrew his pistol located under his jacket while simultaneously dropping to a crouching position behind the podium. Extending his right arm as he came out from behind the podium, keeping his body turned to prevent exposing his full-frontal mass, he fired off six shots in rapid succession. He did this is in less than five seconds.

He stood, putting his .357 back in his holster while pushing the return button with his left hand. When the target came to a stop, he looked at his point of aim on the pictured criminal target. Just above the bridge of the nose, right between the eyes, was a hole the size of a silver dollar. This hole was the result of five bullets grouped together. At the base of the neck, slightly below the Adam's apple, was a single hole, Tyler's last point of aim. "Teach you to point a gun at me, my man," Tyler said out loud, laughing to himself.

He unclipped the targets, wadded them up, and threw them in the trash can. He left the gun range, returning to his office to retrieve his surveillance equipment. He had a few more things to do in Big D before driving to Kaufman to meet up with the Rubys.

Tyler left Ranger headquarters, driving back to his house. When he got home, he went to his office, which used to be a spare bedroom. Very few homes in Texas had basements because of the warm climate; with no freeze line, it negated the benefit of a basement. In his office, he had built a gun storage and cleaning room in the walk-in closet. He had done all the work himself, enlarging the doorway and removing the door completely. Inside was his gun safe, and along the wall he had built a bench for cleaning and maintaining his deer rifles, pistols, and scopes. Above the bench were shelves where he kept gun lube, solvents, Tri-Hone knife sharpeners, and a full assortment of supplies to maintain his hunting and police weapons. He had also installed lights above the bench. It was quite a nice setup.

With Kano curled up under the bench, Tyler removed his .380 from his ankle holster and his .357 Magnum from his shoulder holster. He sat them on the cleaning pad he had unfurled on the bench and began to clean the pistols he had shot earlier at the gun range. After he finished, he cleaned up his mess and wiped down the gun mat, putting it away. He looked at his dog asleep under the bench. "Kano, want to go for a ride?" he asked in a loud voice. The dog bounded out from under the bench, doing circles in the gun room doorway. "Okay, let's go."

Kano took off for the back door. He didn't need to be asked twice. Tyler was pulling a small one over on his dog. Yeah, they were going in the truck, but just up the street to the park for a short walk. Tyler didn't have time to walk him there. Short drive or long drive, it didn't matter; Kano would love every second of it. If he was with Tyler, he was as happy as a pig in mud.

When Tyler returned home from taking Kano to the park, he went to his office to call his friend Stephanie, a criminal court judge in Dallas. Tyler first met her when she presided over one of his cases in Dallas. But how they became friends occurred a year after that case. Tyler had taken the DART train from his home in Plano to downtown Dallas to attend a seminar. He had not used the transit system before and thought he would give it a go, especially when he learned that it would drop him off three blocks from the hotel where the seminar was being held. On that morning's commute, he saw Judge Marshall. She told Tyler that she took the train daily to the courthouse and had been doing so for several years now. Over the course of that week, the two of them sat together each morning, and a friendship started between them on the DART train that lasted to this day.

Stephanie had invited Tyler and Priscilla to join her and her husband, Craig, at a Greek festival being held that weekend at their church. Stephanie's family was of Greek descent. From there, the couples had double-dated to movies, dinners, and trips to the Marshalls' lake house on Cedar Creek Lake, an easy hour's drive east of Dallas.

Craig Marshall had worked as an air traffic controller until his retirement a couple of years earlier. He was a very interesting person to talk to; he always had stories to tell. One story that Tyler thought was quite interesting was of Craig's first week on the job at the Dallas / Ft. Worth Air Traffic Control Center in 1985. He had witnessed singer Ricky Nelson's plane disappear from the control screen on New Year's Eve. Nelson and his band were on their way to perform at a New Year's Eve extravaganza in Dallas when the plane crashed in DeKalb, Texas. Everyone on board was killed, crashing just two miles from the nearest landing strip. Thus Craig had had a unique introduction to the life of an air traffic controller.

Craig now volunteered part-time as a chaplain for the Dallas Police Department, which he found very rewarding. What was unfortunate was that he had been diagnosed a little over a year earlier with malignant melanoma, the deadliest form of skin cancer. Tyler wanted to call Stephanie to check up on Craig's condition. Last he had heard, the prognosis was bleak. Tyler called Stephanie to see if she could do lunch that afternoon. He still had time to kill before he met up with the Rubys. The plan was to go to their house after dark. Tyler didn't want to take the chance of being seen by Eric Williams. Stephanie's secretary answered the phone at the courthouse.

"Judge Marshall's office, may I help you?" inquired Connie Winston.

"Hi, Connie, it's Tyler Davis. Is the judge busy?"

"Oh, hello, Tyler. No, she's not. Her case this morning was recessed until tomorrow morning. Let me put you through. She'll be glad you called. Hold on."

"Thanks, Connie."

"My pleasure, Tyler."

"Hi, Tex, I'm glad you called," answered Stephanie. She was one of the few people who called him Tex. When she learned that his college teammates and a few others called him that, she took it up. She thought it fit his personality. "What's up? I hope you called to invite me to lunch. I'm free all afternoon."

"Actually, I did. I'm headed to Kaufman later, but I don't have to be there until this evening, so I wanted to take a beautiful judge to lunch." Stephanie was quite attractive, with long, light-blond hair and beautiful gray eyes.

"Well, I fit the bill," she said, laughing. "Do you have someplace in mind?"

"How about somewhere casual? Do you know the Opening Bell? It's across the street from the police station on Lamar, by Bill's Records. Have you been there?"

"No, I haven't, but I know you know the best out-of-the-way spots. How about I meet you in front of Bill's? We can hoof it from there, say, in about an hour?"

"Works for me. See you in sixty."

Well, this will work, thought Tyler to himself. He could catch up with an old friend and pass some time before heading to Kaufman. Hopefully there would be some good news about Craig. It wasn't like his world was full of cheery news right now. If the news was grim, well, he wanted to be there for her. Tyler was sure she could use someone to confide in. The Marshalls had two children; their oldest, a son, was a Dallas police officer about to complete his second year on the force. Their daughter was in her final year of law school, following in the footsteps of her mother and grandfather. If Craig succumbed to the cancer, it would devastate the family. Soon Tyler would know the particulars; he was really hoping for some good news. Tyler put Kano in his garage kennel and headed for the truck. It would take an hour to get to Bill's.

Stephanie was already out in front of Bill's Record Store when Tyler arrived. Bill was a legend in the Dallas music business. His first store was in Richardson, Texas. He had converted an old super-market into a music institution, selling recordings that back then were only on vinyl. His Richardson store had a stage in the back where musicians would play on Saturday afternoons for free. These shows could include famous musicians who had come to Dallas for gigs at local clubs. Bill also sold T-shirts, posters, and zany patches. Bill's Records and Tapes was a very popular place to hang out in Richardson for years. But all good things come to an end, and Bill had to downsize. He moved to this new location on Lamar Street, just a mile from downtown Dallas. His new digs, though smaller, were in a great location. Down two blocks was Gilley's, the famous country music nightclub, and right next door to his store was Poor David's Pub, another live music venue in Dallas. Bill was well into his sixties now, still soft-spoken and puffing away on his cigarettes. Everyone liked Bill.

Tyler and Stephanie walked the quarter of a block to Belleview Street, taking a right for another quarter of a block to the Opening Bell, and went downstairs. The Bell was a quaint coffee bar with its own small stage where acoustic acts performed. It was part of the historic Sears building that was once the tallest building in Dallas. Most of the Sears building had been converted into loft apartments, a popular residence for the young Dallas professionals. It was now known as "the South Side of Lamar."

Tyler got lucky and stumbled on the Bell while buying music at Bill's. He'd asked Bill where he could get a bite to eat that was close by, and Bill directed him here. It served freshly brewed coffee, sandwiches, and delicious baked desserts from local bakeries. The atmosphere was very laid back, from the acoustic shows during the evenings to the daily patrons on their laptops or meeting up for cof-fee with their friends. Tyler could use some laid-back about now... big-time. He had been on many intense cases over the years, but that didn't make it any easier. So this short reprieve with Stephanie was as welcome as his Sunday with Priscilla. He would take all he could manage to squeeze in. He had no idea how long it might take to solve Hasse's murder.

The two of them ordered coffee, sandwiches, a blueberry muffin, and lemon crème pie. Tyler was going for the lemon pie; it was to die for.

"So you're on your way to Kaufman this afternoon? That's all that's on the news. It's such a shame about Mark. He was such a fine man. I got to know him quite well before he left for Kaufman. It's hard to believe what's happened. Does your department or the FBI have anything to work with? As far as solid suspects, I mean," said Stephanie.

"Not anything that anyone can hang their hat on. Sure, there is what you hear on the news—the getaway car and such. But as far as solid suspects, no one has anything. What's on the news is all speculation. The FBI seems to believe that the Aryan Brotherhood is good for it, but they don't really know who. It's embarrassing to say, but here we are five days later, and no one is any further along than we were on Thursday."

"Well, how about you, Tex? What iron do you have in the fire?"

"Russ has me working a different angle. You know I can't get specific, but I like my guy. People in Kaufman know him, and some say maybe, but most of them say he's not up to it. I'm to work him until he can be eliminated. I'm fine with that. He's as good or better than what the others are working on."

"Good for you. I know you don't like to feel you're spinning your wheels," said Stephanie, trying to sound encouraging.

"Well, let's not talk shop. Tell me how Craig is doing. Didn't he go in for some tests recently?"

At that question, Stephanie leaned back into the leather couch. She actually seemed to sink down into it. It was early afternoon and quiet in the café. They were sitting in the back. Only a couple of other people were inside, and they were closer to the front entrance, engrossed in their laptops. Tyler could see the pent-up emotion being released. Stephanie's whole body slumped at once. Her eyes glistened;

the color drained from her face. In a low voice, not much more than a whisper, she spoke.

"No, Tex, the results were not good. The cancer has spread to his brain. He only has weeks to a few months to live." With that, she leaned forward, cupped her hands over her face, and began to sob.

Tyler moved over on the couch and put his arm around her shoulders. She let it all out. It wasn't loud, but it was a complete release; her body shook. The strong facade was gone. Craig was losing the battle, and thus she was losing her Craig. Tyler held her as she leaned into him with her hands still cupping her face. In the dim quiet corner of the Bell, a heart was breaking.

*****

Well, so much for a laid-back afternoon, thought Tyler, as he pulled away from the parking lot. Stephanie's words were ringing in his ears as he drove on Interstate 30 from downtown Dallas headed east toward Kaufman. What bad news; the rounds of chemo had had little effect. Yeah, she was right; it had all happened so fast. Within a few months of seeing the melanoma and finally going to see a dermatologist—to this. What a damn shame.

The cruel monster was taking another victim. Here was another killer. So different from the one Tyler pursued, but so much the same. Tyler thought they were both equally heartless. Quite different, quite the same. People losing loved ones to tragedy. The world could use a lot more yang, thought Tyler. This was one Tyler just couldn't roll with. He pulled his truck over to the shoulder of the highway, and he too began to sob.

CHAPTER 18

Kᴇɴᴛ Rᴜʙʏ ᴇɴᴛᴇʀᴇᴅ ᴛʜᴇ ᴛʀᴜᴄᴋ stop restaurant, and seeing Tyler seated at the counter, took the stool next to him.

"Y'all ready for this?" asked Tyler.

"Hell, yeah," replied Kent. "In fact, we're pretty excited. We feel like we're doing espionage. It's not like we lead the most interesting lives here in Kaufman. You're spicing things up for us a bit, Tyler. In fact, Martha has been a bit frisky the last couple of days. I need to thank you for that, my man."

Tyler slapped the counter and let out a good laugh. Kent joined in and nudged Tyler with his elbow. "Glad to be of some help there, Kent," replied Tyler, smiling.

The waitress approached and asked Kent what he was having. "Just some coffee, miss."

"I can appreciate you two seeing the exciting aspect of this, Kent," said Tyler, "but it's a very serious matter. Now don't get me wrong. I prefer y'all having this attitude rather than being worried to death. At the same time, keep in mind that your neighbor could be a killer. But if you two keep this on the down low, y'all have little to worry about."

The waitress placed a fresh cup of coffee in front of Kent and topped off Tyler's cup.

"I'm not afraid," Kent said as the waitress walked away. "But I did put my twelve gauge under the couch and my nine-millimeter under our mattress." This got another laugh out of Tyler.

"Hell, man…I don't blame you. Don't blame you one damn bit," Tyler replied, slapping Kent on the back as he laughed. "I'd've done the same damn thing."

*****

It was dark when they pulled up to the Rubys' house an hour later. Tyler was dressed casually in jeans, long-sleeved shirt with the sleeves rolled up, and a baseball cap. The cap had a big T on the front; it was popular with Texas Ranger baseball fans. The Rubys' residence was directly across the street from the Williamses' home, but two doors down. It couldn't be any more perfect for the surveillance, thought Tyler.

Kent had drawn a picture of the neighborhood layout on a napkin at the truck stop. The spare bedroom was on the right side of the home, giving a perfect view of the Williamses' garage from the window. When Kent and Tyler entered the house, the three of them went into the bedroom. Martha had drawn the curtains, so Tyler began to set up his equipment. It was all very simple, really, as the unit was mostly self-contained.

Tyler set up his router on the dresser along a nearby wall. He placed the base station on the floor between the dresser and the window. After hooking up the cables, he had Martha turn off the lights, and he opened the drapes. There it was…the Williamses' house. It could be seen perfectly from this vantage point.

The Williams had their front porch light on, which would help that much more in the observation, but it wouldn't have mattered either way. The camera was designed to see in low light. Tyler had brought a vase that he could hide the camera in, but Marth had some plants on the windowsill. He decided to use what was there, so he set the camera in one of the existing planters. That way nothing would be altered in the window. After securing the camera, Tyler powered up the base station, router, and his laptop. There it was, pretty as a picture. Tyler adjusted the zoom to bring in just the Williamses' house.

"Damn, that's a clear picture," said Kent.

"I was thinking the same thing," added Martha. "It didn't take you very long."

"Yeah, this is top-of-the-line surveillance equipment," replied Tyler. "We've been fortunate to have great staff at our headquarters. They keep up with all the latest gadgets to help us do our jobs. We have a young lab tech who is the best. His name is Jason. The guy before him was really good too, but he retired not long ago. His name was Edwin Smoot. He was at DPS headquarters long before I hired on. Hated to see him go. He was a legend. You should see what we have in our equipment room. We can watch, listen, and follow with the best of them. I couldn't put GPS on Williams's car, though. Can't take the chance of something being thrown out of court. I don't have a warrant or probable case. I can't blow this one."

The Rubys couldn't see Tyler's expression very well in the dark bedroom, but he had a very satisfied look on his face. "I'm really excited to get this set up. I can't thank you two enough."

"Well, you're welcome! We're excited too," replied Martha. "This is actually kind of fun. We feel like we're smack-dab in the middle of one of Kaufman's most exciting murder cases."

"And you are, Martha, and that is what Kent was telling me earlier. And yes, I'm relieved that both of you are comfortable with what we're doing here. But as I told Kent, this is a very serious investigation. I can't stress enough that this surveillance be kept secret. No one is to know. Not family, not friends…no one." Tyler said this with his most earnest tone. "I'm more concerned with your safety than blowing the surveillance."

"We understand, Tyler. We've talked this over quite a bit since we agreed to do it over dinner together. Don't worry, we got this," replied Kent. "Come on, let's go to the living room and have a drink. I want to show you my shotgun. It's a Remington 1100 with a ventilated rib."

"Okay," said Tyler, smiling to himself as he followed the Rubys from the bedroom, closing the door behind him. "I'd like to see it. It's my favorite auto. I also have a soft spot for side-by-sides."

Joining the couple in their living room, Tyler and Kent talked guns and hunting while Martha made everyone drinks. The three of them sat and visited for some three hours. Martha turned on the radio, and Tyler introduced them to his favorite country music station, the Range. Neither of them was familiar with the station and seemed to be converts. Whether they were or not, they left it on the dial. No one brought up the surveillance the rest of the evening. It was just new friends visiting to get to know one another.

But the surveillance of the Williamses' home was at the forefront of Tyler's mind. He just couldn't help it. It was a big deal to him. He wanted to put these killers in prison; they needed to be off Texas streets. So if it was Eric Williams and his wife, he was glad the camera was in the next room. What he didn't know was that there was much more lurking just around the corner...so *much more*. In fact, he would soon doubt that the surveillance he had set up in the Rubys' front bedroom would amount to much more than a hill of beans.

CHAPTER 19

HAVING THE SURVEILLANCE ON THE Williamses' house didn't mean Tyler sat around watching their home all day on a computer monitor. It was just a tool to use if another crime was committed. As bad as that sounded, there was just no way to have Eric Williams watched 24-7. If he was the only suspect, that could have been accomplished, but the truth of the matter was, there was no main suspect. Not the FBI, or DPS, or Kaufman police had a prime suspect in Mark Hasse's murder. There were so many possible suspects, it was staggering. Hasse was a criminal prosecutor. Bottom line: they make a lot of enemies.

Over the following days and weeks, Tyler ran down dozens of possible leads to tie Eric Williams to the murder. He felt like Eric's wife, Kim, was good for the driver, but he wasn't sure. He worked with Kaufman police and the FBI to see if he could find a link to the Crown Vic through Kim Williams's parents. They both lived in Kaufman. Maybe the father-in-law helped Eric. Hell, Tyler didn't know, so he looked into it. Nothing.

Then there was Eric's brother. He lived in Fort Worth, and that was only about a two-and-a-half-hour drive from Kaufman. Did he own a Crown Vic? Nada. Where were these people when Mark Hasse was killed? All their whereabouts were confirmed. They sure as hell weren't on East Grove Street on Thursday morning the last day of January of this year.

But Tyler didn't stop there. He looked into close friends of Eric Williams, all the way from the Texas Guard to college friends, and even back to high school. This had been done as discreetly as possible, mostly by running background checks as well as Department of Motor Vehicle records. There had been a few moments of interest, like when an old college friend had owned a white Ford Crown Vic. But the friend had sold the car, and the new owner lived in Arizona. Tyler had verified it through the Arizona DMV.

Just as Tyler looked into every nook and cranny, so did his fellow Rangers. The biker gang's clubhouse was put under video surveillance by Rangers Roger Miles and Clint Jacobs with the help of the Kaufman police. An old house near the industrial site had been used to set up the camera. The house had been condemned by the city years ago but never torn down. The attic was used to place the camera, late at night under extreme stealth. The idea was to see if anyone from outside the core gang members showed up on a regular basis. The theory was that maybe the gang hired the hit men and were making payments on the contract. But it was a tough row to hoe.

The bikers did have many people coming and going from out of town to the clubhouse, but they knew what they were doing. To throw off detection of any criminal activity, they had decoys that came up clean. It was illegal to stop and search them without probable cause. It wasn't against the law to ride a motorcycle. If they did have members or cohorts moving drugs or drug money, the ones that carried it had no pending warrants. And the ones that did have outstanding warrants and were arrested and grilled extensively by Kaufman detectives for information about the Hasse murder. Nothing of significance turned up.

Then there was the FBI. They worked the Aryan Brotherhood angle hard. Major Wilson and Rangers Joe Vasquez and Richard Rossman worked many leads with them. They tried their best to put a couple of Aryan Brotherhood members in Kaufman on the morning of Mark's murder. Still nothing solid came up. Sure, there were potential suspects—hell, Tyler had a potential suspect. But that one really solid lead eluded everyone. Even the possible tie-in to the 211 Crew in Colorado had been investigated thoroughly. Still nothing.

And of course there was the ever-present media, questioning daily about what was being done. *Yeah, like we're sitting on our asses,* thought Tyler. The media wanted to know about the murder; the Texas Rangers wanted to solve it. It did go from days to weeks. The frustration did begin to mount. It was getting almost palpable. This was a murder that law enforcement didn't want to go unsolved. Not that they wanted any murder to go unsolved, but this was a member of the hierarchy.

Mark Hasse was there to complete our hard work, was Tyler's way of thinking. He oversaw the law being fulfilled. Without the prosecutors, the prisons were empty. And Tyler knew from almost two decades of doing this job that that's exactly where criminals needed to be. And a great many of them needed to be there forever, never again to walk among regular folks.

It had been about six weeks of the same ol', same ol'. It was late evening in mid-March when Tyler's cell rang; he was at home. "Yeah, Russ, what's up?"

"Tex, you're not going to believe what just happened!" exclaimed Major Wilson.

"Russ, I hope you're going to tell me that Hasse's killer just walked into the Kaufman police station and turned himself in."

"Fuck no! But it still might have to do with our investigation. Tom Clements, the head of the Colorado Department of Corrections, was assassinated at his house this evening. It took place less than two hours ago. Shot dead at his front door. His wife said a pizza delivery man killed him when he answered the door. The suspect got away clean. Shit, Tex, that makes two in less than two months. I just got off the phone with Preston. He thinks there has to be a link between this and Hasse. It's too much of a coincidence. I think he's right."

"Damn, Russ…I'm with you. Right off the bat it makes sense," said Tyler, as his mind was racing. "But then again, it's two different states, and the intel we had months ago was about a hit in Colorado, not Texas. So it could be a separate incident, not a serial assassination. Have you talked to Collins?"

"Yeah, he called me and then I called Preston. Where are you now, Tex, at home?"

"Yeah, I got home from Kaufman a few hours ago. I'm in the sack."

"Come to headquarters tomorrow morning. Call the other Rangers, and y'all be at the conference room at eight. Preston is going to call me back for a conference call with his staff. I'll see how they want us to proceed. After you make the calls, turn on CNN. The story should be breaking about now. Good night, Tex." The line went dead.

Just as Tyler thought, it was starting to get deep now. It had been six weeks since Hasse's murder, but if these murders were connected, it could be six days before the next one. Or then again, another six weeks or six months if no one was caught. *Good goddamn…just make the phone calls, Tyler*, he thought. *You have all night to lie here thinking about this shit.*

He made the calls to the Rangers; some of them had just heard about it from the news. Each one gave his opinion on whether they thought the murders were connected. It was split about fifty-fifty. This was something that they could mull overnight; opinions could change by tomorrow morning. After making the calls, Tyler turned on the news, and there it was.

Breaking news: Tom Clements, Colorado Department of Corrections Chief, assassinated at his home earlier this evening. His wife called 911 after finding her husband lying in the doorway after hearing a gunshot. Before opening the door, he asked her if she had ordered pizza. Clements's wife said she saw a lone gunman running from the scene. Neighbors of the couple stated that they had seen an older model "boxy" black car parked nearby the Clements residence just prior to the shooting, possibly a Lincoln or a Cadillac. The shooting had taken place just before 9:00 p.m. mountain time.

Tyler looked at the clock radio; it was a few minutes after eleven. Tom Clements had been killed over two hours ago. The information on the news was just the basics. Tyler knew that Russ would have a much more detailed account at tomorrow's meeting, especially after talking with Preston and the Austin headquarters. *Damn*…thought Tyler. Two prominent members of law enforcement murdered in less than two months. And not just murdered but assassinated. One gunned down in the street; the other shot in the doorway of his home. What the hell?

Shit like this just didn't happen very often; it was rarer than Bigfoot sightings. Was there a link? It was two different states, thought Tyler. That made him hesitate to lump them together. Then there was the intel that had been swirling around for months about the 211 Crew ordering a hit. Was it a package deal? Clements and Hasse? Were the Aryan Brotherhood and the 211 Crew in cahoots? That sure as hell didn't sound feasible to Tyler, but you never know.

Tyler had learned not to count out anything when it came to murder. Hell, your Sunday schoolteacher could be planning a murder because she liked the pastor and Betty Sue baked him cookies every Sunday. Look out, Betty Sue! Anything was possible when it came to murder, any fucking thing, and that was not rhetoric. Tyler knew of a case in New England not long ago where a pastor's new secretary had been murdered by a jealous parishioner. She saw the young woman as a rival for the pastor's affection and took her out with a .38.

He got out of bed and went to the kitchen to make some tea. He was going to need at least an hour to relax his mind before trying to get some sleep. After putting on the kettle, his phone rang.

"Hey, Priscilla."

"Hi, Tyler… Samantha called me and said I should turn on CNN. Did you hear about the Colorado corrections guy getting killed?" She had a tinge of excitement in her voice.

"Oh, yeah, I've heard about it."

"Well, I know things have slowed down on your investigation. Do you think this could be linked to your case?"

"Oh, babe, it's way too early to draw any conclusions, but yeah, it's possible. That's why I have a job."

"Well, I know it's late, but when she called, I was shocked! It sounded like what happened in Kaufman. A little like that, anyway."

"Oh, it's very unusual. I'm sure there are going to be a lot of questions about whether they're related. Shit…I'm asking them myself."

"I know…it's so weird."

"Russ called me about it just before eleven. He wants all of us at headquarters tomorrow morning. He's on the phone now with the Austin brass. I should have a clearer picture then. Right now, I just want to get some sleep. This is just more crap for me to think about."

"I know, Tyler… I know you don't sleep well when you're on a big case. I didn't mean to keep you up, but when Sam called, I just had to call you after what was on the news."

"It's all good. I'm fixing a cup of tea. I'm going to drink that and just lie in bed." Tyler said this with a light laugh.

"Oh, Tyler, I hope you can sleep. I'm going to let you go now. Call me tomorrow and let me know what's going on. At least we have some fun plans for this weekend. But I'm going to worry even more now that someone else has been murdered."

"Don't worry, Priscilla, this happened a thousand miles away. Probably has nothing to do with the *Hasse* case. But I will call you and let you know if this affects our plans. Good night, sweetie. I love you."

"I love you too, Tyler. Good night."

Yes, it was a thousand miles away, but Tyler was starting to get a feeling that this Clements murder just might get the ball rolling on the Hasse murder in some way. He didn't know why but it was there, in his head. He took his tea back to his bedroom with Kano on his heels and a healthy shot of Jamison in his cup.

CHAPTER 20

IT TOOK SOME DOING, BUT Tyler did his fifty crunches. He was dead tired. He doubted he had slept for two hours last night. When he got up, he checked his computer to see if Eric Williams had left his house for any extended amount of time. Nope… There he was yesterday, out and about on his scooter thing. Tyler figured as much. He didn't think Williams had made a trek to Colorado to knock off Tom Clements. That would have been way out there. But at least he knew for sure. Thank goodness for the Rubys.

The fact of the matter was Eric Williams had done nothing in the last few weeks to draw any attention to himself. He stayed around his neighborhood, occasionally puttering around on his Segway, dressed in his camo. He had done an interview with a reporter who had approached him a few weeks back. Again, he was standing on his scooter during the interview, out in front of his house. The newsfeed had been shown on one of the local news stations. He said he was shocked that he could ever have been suspected of the Hasse murder. Tyler had to admit he didn't look like a cold-blooded killer. Then again, Tyler had put many a person in jail that looked like the guy next door. That's what many of them were…the guy or girl next door.

Williams also said he understood why he was considered a suspect, and that, yes, he was disappointed about the outcome of his court case but had moved on. Eric stated that he and his wife were quite happy in their retirement and that they held no ill will toward anyone. He also said that the reason he was still free was because there was no evidence to tie him to the murder and that there never would be.

Tyler thought about that as he was getting ready to go to headquarters. If evidence turned up to tie the Clements and Hasse murders together, Williams would be right. There was little chance that he was involved in both murders. Oh, it was possible, but Tyler had been doing this for a long time. He had seen some far-out stuff. But Williams, Hasse, and Clements…plus a third party. That was just too convoluted. Tyler would eat his hat if that had any merit. And yeah, Eric Williams came off during his interview as a mild-mannered citizen, but Tyler had read the court transcripts. He wasn't quite the Boy Scout he made himself out to be on camera. Tyler knew he had a dark side. Hell, Tyler knew everyone had a dark side. The yin and yang were always present, but it wasn't a fifty-fifty split in anyone. Tyler knew it could run the gamut, from one to ninety-nine. And you didn't have to be a ninety-plus to kill someone. You just had to break fifty. Tyler felt Eric Williams would break fifty easily.

Tyler had to admit to himself while lying in bed last night that doubt about Eric Williams's guilt started to creep into his subconscious. He just felt this Clements murder was going to get things rolling. He just had a gut feeling, and he had learned to listen to his gut. His gut also told him that if—*if*—Williams was involved, he wasn't through killing. He was just biding his time, waiting patiently. This mental consternation was a constant for Tyler. This was why he couldn't sleep; all this shit was running through his head. And it had been almost two months now. He needed to get going. He had a conference to get to.

*****

When Tyler arrived at DPS headquarters, there were only two cars in the gated lot, Major Wilson's and Judy's, his secretary. She was a hell of a gal, dedicated to her job and a gem for Russ. She would have an assortment of snacks at this morning's meeting for the Rangers. She would also have any report typed up that Major Wilson wanted from the previous night's conference with the Austin brass.

Jason Chime pulled into the lot right behind Tyler, waiting for him so they could enter the building together.

"Morning, Jason."

"Morning, Tyler. Hell of a note. Someone's mowing them down, huh?"

"You got that right," said Tyler as the two men walked toward the back entrance. Tyler scanned his ID badge, holding the door open for Jason. "What brings you in so early?" asked Tyler as they walked to the elevator.

"The Major wants me to run some research on Clements and get some background on him. He wants to see if I can pull up something no one else has. I'm going to run some of Smoot's old files. I'm also going to call Smoot when I get to my office, pick his brain. He knows shit no one else does." Jason had a wry grin on his face.

"That's for damn sure," said Tyler, returning the knowing grin.

Tyler did know about the background information that Jason had on individuals, and yes, it had started with Edwin Smoot. Every law enforcement agency had information about criminals. They also had intel on employees, in the event of things like what had happened to Tom Clements. You couldn't afford to start from behind the eight ball. As far as personnel research, no one held a candle to Edwin Smoot. He had started with DPS in the prehistoric days, back when information was stored and collected on index cards. Then came computers. Smoot was in his element, like a duck to water. Not that he knew shit about them at first, but he learned big-time. Jason would tell stories about Edwin's computer skills. He claimed that even with his degree, Smoot had forgotten more than Jason ever learned. Edwin Smoot taught himself; he became an expert. Oh sure, he took the DPS computer classes, but Smoot also took evening classes on his own time. He never seemed to forget a damn thing, and he logged all of it.

He wanted the Dallas headquarters to have the most extensive criminal and employee information that existed. During his career, he had received numerous awards for helping to solve crimes with the research he provided. His degree was in chemistry, but his PhD should have been in computer science. The man was brilliant. He would have made J. Edgar Hoover proud.

Tyler rode the elevator down to the lab with Jason. Jason went to his office to do his research, and Tyler went to the ammo storage vault to get bullets for his .357 SIG. He had some time to kill and was going to blow off some steam in the firing range. After firing off a few rounds, he took the elevator up to his office to complete some reports. Not that there was much to report of late, but this was standard procedure: documentation. Soon it was almost eight, so he made his way to the conference room.

Tyler saw Jamison coming out of his office, and they entered the conference room together. The other Rangers were already seated at the table when they entered. All the men greeted one another as Jamison and Tyler poured coffee and helped themselves to some fruit and pastries. They joined the others at the table waiting for Major Wilson. It was almost eight.

When Wilson entered, Judy Poppa was right behind him. He took his seat at the head of the table while she began to hand out the reports.

"Good morning, gentlemen. That report that Judy is passing around has a lot more information than what you saw or heard on the news last night. It seems that the murder of Tom Clements was actually a serial murder." When the Major said this, you could have heard a pin drop in the room. "Mrs. Clements said her husband called out to her just before answering his front door asking if she ordered pizza. Well, gentlemen…two days before Tom Clements was murdered, a pizza delivery driver was slain and robbed of his uniform not but fifteen miles from the Clements' home. The suspect was not apprehended, and there were no clues to his identity."

"That's fucking sick," said Vasquez. "You mean the perp that killed Clements murdered an innocent pizza dude just to go to Clements's door with a pizza uniform on? The stupid fucker could've had a pizza box in his hand, and the man would have opened the door."

"That's exactly what the Colorado police now believe hap-pened," said Wilson, as he looked around the table. "The perp is believed to be deranged. As Joe so aptly stated, the killing of the delivery driver was unnecessary. The thinking is that, not only is he vicious, but he is of very low IQ. The delivery driver had a wife and three young daughters. He was only twenty-seven years old. Plus, the pizza gig was just part time for extra money. He had a career job."

"That is some sick bullshit," said Jamison.

"Well, let me assure you, Steve, that exact sentiment was expressed to me many a time last night and over the last several hours. It does seem that this bastard likes to kill. And he's not too picky." Wilson took a deep breath and slowly let it out. He then leaned forward on the table, resting on his elbows. He had the full attention of the Rangers. "So here's where we're at. I spent an hour on the phone last night with the Austin brass as well as another hour with the FBI in Colorado. Until there are ballistics run on the bullet that killed Clements and then compared to the ones that killed Hasse, we are not going to assume that this is a serial assassination. Now, that being said, all effort will be put forth to see if these murders are linked. We can't assume they are, but at the same time we can't assume they're not. Follow me?"

All the Rangers nodded. They understood that this was the only option for now. It just couldn't work any other way. The link had to be made or broken. No one could afford to stand idly by; critical evidence or suspects could go undetected.

"The bullet that killed Clements is on its way to Quantico. So are the bullets that killed Nathan Leon, the pizza delivery driver. It's in your report there. The bullets that killed Mr. Leon were at the Colorado Springs police station. The connection between the two murders wasn't made until last night. But at this time, the FBI in Colorado feel that the bullets will match. We'll know for sure no later than tomorrow." Wilson got up from his chair and walked to the coffeepot.

"What we do know is that the cars do not match. As you can see there, one is a black Lincoln or Cadillac DeVille, thought to be an early '90s model, and the Hasse car was a white Crown Vic." Wilson took his cup and sat back down at the table. "What does that mean? Not jack shit if this was a planned serial assassination. It just means that different cars were at the scene of these hits, that's all. They could be the same two that killed Hasse, just driving a different car now. See our problem? No one knows shit right now." Wilson's voice had an edge; he was frustrated.

Wilson continued. "What else do we know? That these murders were up close, brutal and personal. That says volumes about the killers. So where does that leave us? For the time being, about where we are now. Preston has instructed me to wait for the ballistics report from Quantico. If there is no match, we're going to take that into consideration on our end. Preston is assigning two Rangers from our Company D headquarters in Lubbock to go to Colorado to meet with FBI, the Colorado Bureau of Investigations, and Colorado police to investigate a possible link between the murders. At this time, he doesn't think any of you men need to be in Colorado. Now, that directive could change. But for now, we're at status quo until I hear otherwise. Keep in mind that Tom Clements was killed just a few hours ago. There's no telling what could turn up over the coming hours or days. Now do any of you have anything on your mind?"

All the Rangers sat quietly for a moment, giving whoever felt inclined to speak up a chance to do so. The Major had pretty well covered the subject. Learning that none of the Dallas agents were going to Colorado sat well with all of them. They were thinking that if these murders were linked, the Rangers from the Texas panhandle could figure it out with the help of the FBI. And having a high-profile murder in their jurisdiction that was still unsolved took precedent. So what was there to say?

"Shit…give me something," said Major Wilson. He was thinking that he needed to lighten the tension a bit. This pressure had been building up over the last few weeks, and this Clements murder was just another straw. "Open your trap, Tex. I know you've got something on your mind. You usually do," Wilson said with a light laugh. "If not, tell us a fucking hunting story or something."

The Rangers did laugh a little to themselves at the Major's quip. A little of the tension left the room. Even Tyler could feel it. Hell, he could always find something to say. "I feel like you covered it, boss. Speaking for myself, I don't want to go to Colorado. The panhandle

Rangers are a lot closer there than we are. And as far as how Preston views it, I'm in agreement. Let's wait on the ballistics, see if there's a match, then see how it shakes out with the agents in Colorado. If no definitive tie can be found between Clements and Hasse, then they have their case and we have ours. What's got everyone so worked up is just how rare these types of crimes are. Plus, they're similar and came so close together. Then with the Hasse murder unsolved, everyone is grasping for answers. I'm thinking that just maybe, until we know different, people are going off on a tangent."

"Major, I'm with Tyler," said Joe Vasquez. "Looking over this intel here, there are a lot of people who could have it in for Clements, especially the 211 Crew. To me it only makes sense to wait for things to shake out in Colorado. Especially with these murders taking place so far away from each other, and in two different states."

A couple of more Rangers spoke up and echoed those sentiments. All the men felt that a connection needed to be confirmed before jumping to conclusions. Keep it business as usual here in northeast Texas until evidence proved otherwise. Not much could be done on their end unless there was more to go on.

"All right, men, I'm going to leave y'all to it. If I learn any more over the next several hours, I'll be in touch. Preston is to call me with any new updates," said Wilson. "Now have Tex here tell you his story about shooting at a cougar during a bow-hunting trip last year. I've heard it, so I'm out of here." Major Wilson stood up to leave.

"Shit, I've heard that story before," said Vasquez.

"Me too," said Jamison.

"I haven't," said Miles. "I'd like to hear it."

"Damn, Tyler...you shot a cougar with a bow?" asked Jacobs.

"I said shot at, not shot," replied Wilson as he headed out the door. "Tell them the story, Tex." The Major was laughing as he walked through the door.

"Y'all want to hear it?" asked Tyler. "Hell, I'd be happy to. It's a good one." All the Rangers hung around for the story, even the ones who had heard it before.

"I was up in my elevated tree stand on a damp misty morning this last hunting season. I'd only been there for about two hours, having gotten settled thirty minutes before first light. Then I saw him walking toward me, but he was fifty yards away."

"So how big was it?" asked Miles.

"Oh, the sucker was huge…maybe one twenty pounds. He was all muscled up."

"Damn," replied Jacobs.

"Well, at that distance, it was too far to shoot. He walked to a tree that had fallen over and lay up under it. He was directly in front of me. So I stood up slowly on my stand to see if he would eventually come my way."

"How long did you wait?" asked Miles.

"Close to an hour. He never budged. And when he first got there, a squirrel barked at him for like…thirty minutes. Finally he shut up. I couldn't see the cougar, but I knew exactly where he was."

"Well, what did you do?" asked Jacobs.

"Like I said, it had rained early that morning, so I knew the leaves would be moist. There would be very little sound if I walked toward him."

"You were going to walk up on a sleeping cougar with just your bow?" asked Miles with an incredulous voice.

"No, I had my .357 revolver with me. I decided it was too much of a gamble to try and shoot through brush with my bow. Any little twig would have deflected the arrow, and he was under a fallen tree. So I quietly climbed down out of the tree and slowly began to walk toward him. Now I'm hunting river bottomland, so it's bushy as hell. I can't see but a little ways in front of me."

"Shit, man…this is getting good," said Miles.

"I covered the fifty or so yards making almost no sound, and there he was, lying beside the trunk. He was curled up sleeping, but there was a branch blocking his body. I could only see his legs and paws."

"Holy shit! How close were you?" asked Miles.

"No more than ten or twelve yards. Then I see him lift his head up and look at me over the branch. I could only see his eyes and the very top of his head. We made eye contact. I knew it was now or never. In a second, he would be gone. I took quick aim and pulled the trigger. He instantly did a complete backflip over the tree trunk and disappeared."

"Did you get him?" asked Miles.

"Well, this is where the story takes a turn. I know from experience that a wild animal can be mortally wounded and still run a good distance. So I cautiously walk around the tree with my pistol at the ready. I don't want a hundred-pound cougar jumping on my ass... especially a wounded one. When I get to the other side of the tree, I look around to see if he's out there dead. Now this is thick woods, so there's old logs and brush everywhere. There...off to my left, I see it. Some thirty-five yards away is brown and white fur. It's still, there's no motion. I liked the brown color, but not the white. Cougars aren't white. I walk over to the animal lying there, and it's a yearling deer with his head eaten off. It's what you call cougar breakfast. He was napping under the tree, soon to be back for lunch."

"So where was the cougar?" asked Miles.

"Your guess is as good as mine. I'm sure he's still out in the river bottoms snacking on deer. I rushed my shot. Flat-out missed him."

"That's still a pretty cool story," said Jacobs.

"Yeah, he would have made a nice trophy, but I was glad for the opportunity. It was exciting."

The Rangers continued to sit in the conference room for another hour or so and just bullshitted together. This was good for morale, especially after the last six weeks. None of them had any idea that they would be back in this same room very soon and the atmosphere would be far from light, before and after the meeting.

Tyler was correct about the Clements murder altering the Hasse investigation. He just didn't know it yet...but he soon would. It would cause him to question much of his previous thinking on the case. And it was just around the next bend.

CHAPTER 21

WHEN THE RANGERS LEFT THE conference room, Tyler walked into Judy Poppa's office. Her office wasn't particularly small unless compared to Major Wilson's, but it was beautifully decorated. She was seated behind her desk when Tyler entered the doorway. Looking up at him, she smiled. "Hi, Tyler. Would you like to speak to Russ?" The door to Wilson's office was closed; it was behind Judy and to the right. "Let me tell him you're here." She pressed a button on her desk phone. "Russell...Tyler is in my office. He would like to see you." She looked up. "Go on in, Tyler."

"Thank you, Judy," said Tyler as he walked past her desk to Wilson's door. When he entered the office, Wilson was on his landline phone. He motioned to the chairs in front of his massive desk. Tyler took a seat as the Major continued his conversation. After a couple of minutes, he hung up the receiver and then pressed a button on his desk phone. "Judy, hold all my calls with the exception of Preston." He then leaned back in his chair and smiled at Tyler. "Did they like your cougar story, Tex?"

"I believe they did, Russ, and I liked telling it," said Tyler with a laugh.

"I bet you did. It's a good one. Many a hunter has spent hundreds of hours in the woods never to see a cougar, much less get a shot at one. Especially with a pistol. Too bad you didn't bag him. Would have helped out the deer population where you hunt. No telling how many of them he's eating every year." Wilson clasped his hands behind his head. "What's on your mind, Tex?"

"Wanted to run something by you, Russ. You know I've wanted to interview Eric Williams, but I wanted to wait for the time to be right. I think the time is right."

Wilson studied Tyler's face for a moment. "Yeah? Why so?"

"We've both agreed that he's not going to open up to just anybody. Oh yeah, he's talked to reporters, but that's just giving his generic spiel. To really reveal something, he's going to want to talk with someone he feels is in his wheelhouse. Someone he can fuck with." Tyler reached into his jacket pocket and produced a can of snuff. He put a pinch in his mouth. "I'm thinking with Clements being murdered, the news media is going full tilt with speculation. Especially with people in Kaufman, the rumors will be flying. The interview I did outside of the Kaufman police station was on the news, and I believe Williams saw it and knows who I am. So if a Texas Ranger hot on this case comes calling, he'll be curious, maybe grant me a few minutes of his time. I'm also thinking that I can use this Clements murder to appear to grovel to him, make him think we believe these murders are linked, and that him being considered a suspect was a mistake. Thinking it may appeal to his ego."

"I'm listening...go on."

"All right. Now I go seeming to make amends. Tell him and the wife that I know their scrutiny brought them embarrassment and that DPS is looking for advice from a onetime justice of the peace. I just feel that the time is right to make a move. My plan is to go to his house playing it up to the hilt. I'll show up wearing a Stetson, expensive suit, high-dollar boots...make him think we need him. His ego will be in overdrive. He'll probably think people at the courthouse mentioned him and that's why I'm there. And if he doesn't buy that shit, he might still want to learn what I know. Either way it's win-win if he talks to me."

Major Wilson didn't respond right away. He sat there for a few minutes mulling over what Tyler had proposed. Yes, the subject of trying to question Williams in depth had come up between the two of them. Both men knew that you wouldn't get shit out of him at the police station. He would holler lawyer so loud it would be heard in Dallas. Not to mention he would feel disrespected with no evidence implicating him. He would clam up and not give anyone the time of day. Yeah, he was someone who had to be approached just right to garner information. Had to hand it to Tyler; son of a gun was always thinking. If Williams was the shooter, he had to slip up. Maybe, just maybe, he would reveal something in a one-on-one. As of late, things hadn't exactly broken their way on the case and the bottom line. Eric Williams had to be eliminated as a suspect.

"I like it, Tex. It just might work out. When did you want to do this?"

"Now. As in this afternoon. Leave here, go straight home, change into my best suit. I'm at his front door early this afternoon and that includes stopping for lunch. This Clements murder is big news right now. Strike while the iron is hot." Tyler was unable to conceal his excitement.

"I know you've wanted to talk with the man to get a feel for him. Yeah, Tex, it works for me. What are you waiting for? Get your ass on the road." Wilson did like it; he liked it a lot. This case was very much wide open. The Rangers couldn't very well let this Clements murder put a hold on their investigation. Wilson knew if they stood idly by, their wheels would be just spinning. It was all about grinding; it was up to them to make something happen.

"Thank you, Russ. I'll let you know this evening how it goes," said Tyler as he made a beeline for the office door. He didn't think he stopped smiling all the way home. This wasn't as good as slapping a search warrant in Williams's hot little hand, and of course he wasn't positive Williams was the killer, but it sure beat what he had been doing the last few weeks, behind the scenes, investigating. A one-on-one interview with a prime suspect was right up his alley. Tyler was good at reading people, especially someone he viewed as an adversary. He relished the opportunity.

The late-morning Dallas traffic was sparse, so it took very little time for him to get home and get changed. He put on his favorite light-gray suit along with his black alligator cowboy boots. He decided on the white Stetson instead of the gray one. Laughing to himself, he thought he'd go looking like the good guy. He chose the solid-gold Ranger mini badge and chain for his tie clasp, as well as the gold Ranger belt buckle. The belt was hand-tooled black leather with five-point sheriff badges emblazoned around it; at the tips of each star was a blue sapphire.

Standing back to look at himself in the full-length mirror, Tyler felt that he had that high-dollar official law enforcement look he needed to impress Williams. Tyler wanted him to think the top brass had come calling, just the kind of ego stroke Eric Williams would go for.

It was a few minutes past noon when he finished dressing. He took a minute to text the girlfriend and tell her things looked good for this weekend, saying he would call her that evening. He put Kano in the garage and then made tracks for his Chevy. Sitting in the cab, he hit rewind for the surveillance camera history on the truck's laptop, double-checking that Williams hadn't left home in the last couple of hours. So far, so good. He turned the ignition and hit the road to Kaufman.

In a little over an hour, he hoped to have a better feel for Williams than he presently did. Tyler had only met him briefly and that was years ago. He tuned to 95.3 on the radio dial and settled back for the drive. Jessie Dayton was singing one of Tyler's favorite tunes, "Mexican Blackbird," off his *South Austin Sessions* CD. Tyler owned it; he cranked up the volume.

*****

He pulled up to Williams's house just before two o'clock. He stopped on the way at Whataburger to quell his hunger pains. *Here goes*, he thought as he walked up the drive to the front door. He rang the doorbell and knocked on the door. Within a few seconds, Eric Williams opened the door with his wife standing behind him. Tyler spoke up as soon as the two of them made eye contact.

"Good afternoon, Mr. Williams. I'm Tyler Davis with the Texas Department of Public Safety. We met once years ago at the Kaufman courthouse. I doubt you remember, it being so long ago. I was wondering if I could have a minute of your time?"

Williams looked him up and down for a moment before answering. "Yeah, I remember…I remember everything. What's this about?"

"Well, sir, I'm sure you've heard about the murder of the Colorado Department of Corrections chief yesterday evening, Tom Clements?"

"Of course I have, it's all over the damn news. What does this have to do with me?" Williams's brow was furrowed. He had suspicion written all over his face. Tyler needed to break the ice and break it fast before the door closed in his face.

"Well, actually nothing. But with this turn of events, DPS now believes that the murders of Mark Hasse and Tom Clements was a serial assassination. I also know that you and your wife have been subjected to some embarrassment due to the investigation of Mr. Hasse's murder. My department is well aware of your years of service here in Kaufman as a judge. Being here gives me a chance to try and make amends from DPS for any mental anguish you and your wife might have suffered and at the same time have you share your expertise on who you think might be responsible for these two murders. We're convinced that they are connected. It's just too much of a coincidence for them not to be. It puts egg squarely on our face." Tyler noticed that Eric Williams's brow relaxed somewhat with his bullshit.

"No shit…this makes y'all look like dumbasses. I didn't have a fucking thing to do with Hasse's murder. I see now you're finally figuring that out." Now Williams looked pissed as he glared at Tyler. His wife was tugging on his shirtsleeve.

"Let me talk to you, Eric," said Kim Williams.

"Hold on a minute," said Williams as he shut the door and left Tyler standing there on the doorstep.

Oh shit! thought Tyler. He had wanted Williams to invite him in. What was his wife saying to him there? *Fuck!* What if he got shot down (not literally, he hoped) and not invited in? That sure would fuck up his day. All this for nothing. *Please open the door and invite me in*, thought Tyler.

Eric and Kim Williams left him standing there for almost five minutes. He thought about leaving. He sure as hell wasn't going to ring the doorbell again. He could imagine them laughing inside if they had no intention of talking to him. Then the door opened.

"All right, Mr. Davis, my wife and I will give you a few minutes of our time. Come in." Williams opened the door wide and shut it behind Tyler as he entered the living room. Kim Williams was standing at the dining room entranceway. "This is my wife, Kim. Have a seat."

Now Tyler could understand what Theresa Smith meant about Kim Williams's appearance. She did look much older than she was. Tyler had looked into both their backgrounds and he knew she was in her midforties. Having seen photos of her from a few years back, he knew she was once very attractive. Standing there, she looked closer to sixty, and it wasn't a pleasant sixty. Hell, Tyler had met women twenty years older who looked better. She had a sad, miserable aura about her. It made him want to know more about Kim Williams.

"It's a pleasure to meet you, Kim," said Tyler as he took a seat. Eric sat on the sofa across from Tyler.

"Can I get you a drink, Mr. Davis?" asked Kim. "Iced tea or coffee?"

"Yes, please. I'll have some tea, thank you."

"Sweet?"

"Please. And call me Tyler. No reason to be formal. We are in Texas, after all." Tyler smiled at her.

As she stepped into the kitchen, Eric said, "I saw you on the news a few weeks ago. You're the Ranger heading up the Hasse investigation here."

"Yes, I am."

"And how's that going for you? I haven't seen much of anything new until this murder in Colorado."

"No, you're right...things were getting a little slow. But this latest murder just might be the thing to get us to the bottom of this mess."

"So tell me, why exactly are you here? Please don't repeat what you said at the door. I heard all that. Did McLelland ask you to come see me?" Eric Williams was staring a hole through Tyler.

"Eric, I can assure you that Mike McLelland did not send me." This might be the only truthful thing he'd tell Williams this afternoon. "We had a conference this morning at our headquarters due to this Clements murder, and by its conclusion, my fellow Rangers, our Major, and I felt these murders were connected and that we'd been spinning our wheels looking too closely at Kaufman. We feel like it's gang-related and has to do with the 211 Crew out of Colorado. That's why I'm here."

Kim entered the living room with the drinks and took a seat next to Eric, handing him a highball glass. It looked to Tyler like whiskey on the rocks. Kim was having tea, same as Tyler.

Tyler continued. "I felt all along that you had nothing to do with the Hasse murder. I interviewed your secretary at the courthouse, Theresa Smith, and she told me you were not the kind of man to commit such a crime. Now of course, saying that, I wouldn't be much of an investigator if I went only by her endorsement of your character, but I didn't. I did investigate you quite thoroughly, and of course your name came up due to the court case, so there was a question of motive. But nothing came of it. And now I see why. Having an almost identical murder in Colorado is the reason. These murders were gang hits. Sure as I'm sitting here." Tyler hoped he wasn't laying it on too thick, but he thought Eric Williams just might have an ego big enough to swallow this shit.

"Of course my husband had nothing to do with Mark's murder. We both knew the man. And yes, we were angry about Eric losing his job. But murder…that's absurd," Kim said. She was looking directly at Tyler except for brief glances at her husband, as if to look for acknowledgement.

"Well, I'm glad to see DPS is now on the right track…finally. For someone to even think that I could shoot down a onetime coworker in the street like a dog, it defies logic. Then there were two assailants. Who would have driven the car for me? My wife? It's all so ridiculous. I'm a member of Mensa. I would never do something so stupid. As my wife stated, there is no way you would find me involved. We were both home in bed the morning Mark was murdered." Eric took a big swallow from his glass. He sat back smugly in his seat after his declaration, looking at Tyler. "Back to your being here. How can I help you?"

"As you can imagine, when Mark's murder first went down, any and all possibilities were on the table. Of course, I know you've seen the news and I'm sure read all about the possible suspects. Especially with your background in law and judicial prosecution, Eric, you know that much better than the average person anyway. So what came up in our meeting this morning was…could it be possible for the Aryan Brotherhood and the 211 Crew to be working together on these murders? My department has never heard of such a thing. I learned how intelligent you are when I investigated you. So who better to ask this to than someone who served this country for years and has a feel for what could or could not go down in this county?"

Tyler tried to look as sincere as he could. He leaned forward, placing his elbows on his knees, as to show keen interest in what Williams had to say. Was Eric buying this? He felt like he'd know with Eric's response.

Before answering, Eric looked over at his wife, and then turned back to Tyler. "Of course I've given that a lot of thought. I knew from what I saw on the news that the Aryan Brotherhood was of prime interest to the investigation here in Kaufman. Knowing that, I felt like the police were focusing too much on that one gang. There have been several members of the 211 Crew prosecuted in our courts here in Kaufman over the years. So with their incarceration in our prisons, naturally there will be collusion between the gangs. That's what I think you're seeing here with the murder of Hasse and now with this murder in Colorado—collusion."

Damn…he bought into this. He thinks he's the man, thought Tyler. "I see. What about later…I mean in the future? Do you think the suspects will kill again?"

"Oh, hell yes. I'm convinced more than ever my theory is correct. Something unprecedented is taking place inside and outside of our penal system. Mark my words, Ranger Davis, the Aryan Brotherhood and the notorious 211 Crew in Colorado are just getting started. Together they are working to eliminate high-profile members of law enforcement. Why? For no other reason than because they can. To spread fear. We both know it's blood in, blood out. You get released from prison, you're still at their bidding. Many of the members will never see the light of day. Even on the inside they call the shots. The consequences are well known—if you get the mark, do the job. If not, you'll pay. And if not you, a family member. Maybe a child or parent."

Eric said this like he was a fucking expert. You can't bullshit a bullshitter, thought Tyler. Eric Williams had been a justice of the peace here in Kaufman. He didn't prosecute high-profile cases. Never had, never would, especially now. His law license went up in smoke. He was talking like he'd put Osama bin Laden in a Texas prison. Well, at least he got him talking. Let's find out where this goes.

"Well, with you saying that, what do you think happened to the getaway car from the Hasse murder?"

"Oh, it's history. I'm sure it's been chopped. At best, it's in pieces. At worst, it's crushed."

Tyler felt like he had a good feel for the man now. His ego was bigger than he thought it was, and that's saying something. Before he left, he decided to direct a few questions to Kim. She hadn't said much. He wanted to see what she might give up. Hey, when you're given a gift horse, ride it. "Well, I'm not going to take up any more of you fine people's time. Kim, I want to thank you again for the tea. I hope what you've been through these last few weeks hasn't been too hard on you."

"It has been hard…on both of us," she replied. "What we went through with the court case living in this small town. Then for my husband to have been a suspect in Mark's murder. My goodness, it's been dreadful! You don't want to show your face around here. I can't begin to tell you how it's affected my health…just something awful. Mr. Davis, you can't begin to imagine the sleepless nights I've spent in this house."

"Yeah, and as far as my court case went, I was railroaded," Eric chimed in. "The cocksuckers had it in for me from the start. I was using those monitors for county business. Jealous sons of bitches. They were just too stupid to think of it. I can't lie to you, Davis, I'm not one bit sorry to see Mark Hasse gone, but I'm not stupid enough to shoot the man down in broad daylight. If it had been me, I'd come up with something much better, I can assure you. Thank God you're on this case. McLelland and the Kaufman police are far too stupid to solve it."

"Well, if it's not me, I hope someone figures it out. I'm going to leave you to it. Thanks for inviting me in and for all the good tips, Eric. I'm going to pass them on to my Major." Tyler stood up and started for the door. Both Eric and Kim also stood and began to walk just behind him. "Oh, I almost forgot. I do have one more question for you, Eric." Tyler turned to face them at the open front door. "On the Hasse murder, we have a witness who overheard the killer converse with Hasse just before shooting him. If it was an ordered hit given by a prison gang, why would the killer insult him on the street just before doing the deed?"

"Oh, that." Eric looked at the floor and then back up at Tyler with a wry grin on his lips. "Well, you never know about these things. Maybe the gang member had a prior case with Hasse. Maybe he just wanted to say hello before he blew the son of a bitch away."

CHAPTER 22

Holy shit! What a creepy couple, Tyler thought as he pulled away from the Williamses' house. Eric had done his damnedest to sell him on the Hasse and Clements murders being connected. Then when he posed that final question to Eric about Mark Hasse being confronted on the street by the assailant and cursed, what he said and how he phrased it, plus the look on his face, gave Tyler the chills. He only felt that way when his intuition was warning him.

That was one creepy dude; hell, they both were. He felt more suspicious than ever about those two. Mirror images came to mind. Tyler could feel the anger. Oh yeah, they tried to downplay it as best they could. But this wasn't Tyler's first rodeo. He had learned how to read people doing this job for almost twenty years.

Sure, he had made mistakes. More than a time or two, he had a feel for someone being good for a crime, only for them to be found not even remotely involved. And when that happened, he couldn't be happier. The worst injustice is putting someone behind bars who doesn't deserve to be there. And as much as Tyler loved his job, he was well aware that this had been done far too many times by lawmen. Tyler wondered how you could sleep at night putting people in jail that didn't deserve to be incarcerated by hiding or fabricating evidence. That's why he was okay with judgment day. May you reap what you sow. And knowing what he knew about the injustices that police had perpetrated on the innocent, it made him proud to be a member of the Texas Rangers.

DPS was such a small elite branch of law enforcement that they policed themselves like no other agency. It was the only branch Tyler wanted to join as a young man. As boastful as it sounds, they were the best of the best. Tyler would put Major Wilson in prison if he deserved to be there, and he knew Russ would do the same to him. They both wouldn't have it any other way. That was why they were such good friends. It was about doing what was right, not what was wrong. And it's not about ego; it's about public safety. Rangers are part of the public too, not above it.

What so influenced Tyler was his study of Texas Ranger history in his youth. He read about John S. "Rip" Ford, one of the most famous Rangers of his era who was once a mayor of two cities, a lawyer, a newspaper editor, and a medical doctor. In 1859, the Texas government sent his company of Rangers to Brownsville, Texas, to dispatch outlaw bandit Juan Cortina from the border town. He and his men did so in a brutal gun battle. Many of Cortina's men were killed, and Ford lost some of his Rangers. Ford stated that "his company of brave men knew their duty and they did it. They did right because it was right."

Preston had sent Texas Rangers to Colorado to investigate any links between the Hasse and Clements murders; if this proved to be true then Tyler was where he had been more than a time or two: dead wrong. But after interviewing the Williamses, he was almost convinced that wouldn't happen. But he knew *almost* wasn't shit. People didn't get convicted of *almost*. Hell, *almost* wasn't shit in anything that mattered. But until Eric Williams was cleared as a suspect, he was still on the top of Tyler's "could be" list.

He felt like he had just left the lion's den. There was the underlying feeling that Eric and Kim saw themselves as victims. Blameless victims. Eric, in his denial of involvement, had asked who would have driven the car for him. His wife? Yeah…Tyler could see that. Hell, he could see her coming up with the idea. Eric didn't know it, but Tyler felt like she was involved all along. It made sense to him. Maybe not to anyone else, but to him it did. And Tyler was thinking that Williams was counting on that. That's probably why he did it with his wife. No one would see it for what it was. Mensa smart.

And Kim, she had an aura of desolation about her. It was like she was beyond caring. She actually stated it, not wanting to leave the house. Once a beautiful woman who no longer wore makeup and had a slumping posture and a broken spirit. Creepy. Depressing. And Tyler felt that there was something about her that he was missing. He didn't know just what, but if things went like he was thinking, he would find out, putting an end to some nagging questions that plagued him. For now he was glad it was over. He was able to accomplish what he wanted, talking to the two of them in person. He did feel like if they met face-to-face again, it would be under different circumstances.

Hold on… Tyler thought to himself. *Back up, man. Stop for just a minute. What do you have on them? Not jack shit! This same thing came up in the conference this morning, not going off on a tangent. Are you grasping for answers because you have nothing and no one else does either? Because what you do have as far as evidence is "almost," "maybe," "could be," "gut feeling," "I think," "convinced"—exactly* nothing! *You're where you were six weeks ago, with fucking* nada. *Just that: they both started with N. That's it. Maybe they are just a pathetic couple.* Bottom line: after six weeks, Tyler was frustrated. *Pick up the phone, man, and call Russ,* he began thinking. *Take your mind off the interview. Do it right fucking now…*

"Yeah, Tex, did you meet with the Williamses?" asked Russ.

"Yep, he was home, so was his old lady. They left me at the doorstep for a few minutes before inviting me in. The wife wanted to speak to him in private. Had me worried for a second there. Thought they were going to leave me standing there with my dick in my hand. But I guess curiosity got the better of them. Talked to them for almost an hour."

"That's great news, Tex, but if they didn't admit to shooting Hasse, I'll have to hear about it later. I'm covered up here talking to everyone above my pay grade about this Clements murder. Some important information has come forth since our conference this morning. There is a suspect that Colorado has on their radar. He has family here in Fort Worth. I'm wanting to see you in the morning. Everyone is coming in again. Be here at eight. Do your report on the Williams interview and we'll discuss it tomorrow at the meeting along with what else has come up today. See you then, Tex." The phone went dead.

Damn, Russ sounded like he was frazzled. Tyler could only imagine what he was going through. He probably felt like a monkey fucking a football. Tyler was sure that everyone who had the slightest inkling of who was responsible for the Clements murder was wanting a piece of his time. The reason? The Hasse murder. People wanted to know if there was a connection to both crimes. Russ would be talking to the Austin brass, FBI, CBI, Colorado police, Colorado Corrections brass, as well as their Rangers who were sent to Colorado. Those were just the people that Tyler could think of off the top of his head. But hey, that's why Russ got paid the big bucks. He got things done.

Russ would do his damnedest to put together a comprehensive strategy to find out if the Clements murder had ties to Hasse's murder. What he also knew was that Russ wouldn't jump to conclusions; he would think his next move through. With the high-profile case in Kaufman, Tyler knew Russ would stay focused. He wanted the killing here solved. Getting pulled in the wrong direction was not his style. He would only follow evidence, not conjecture.

Tyler had been trained by Russ for many years, so he needed to remember what he had been taught. Keep an open mind. Think outside the box. Don't find yourself doing what you were almost doing on Williams's doorstep, holding your dick in your hand. Be patient…wait for something to break. Until then, look for the smoke and follow the waft. It'll take you to the fire.

*****

Tyler headed back west on the highway toward Dallas. He was going home to his office to start the report on the day's interview. He knew there would be more developments on the Clements murder by the end of the day. Less than twenty-four hours had passed from when he was killed the evening before. Russ had even mentioned that there was already a suspect who had ties to Fort Worth, which was in Company B's jurisdiction. Fort Worth covered four counties, the sixteenth largest city in America. For all Tyler knew, he could be going there the next day to search for the suspect. With this job, he had to stay flexible. His assignments could change day to day.

With Dallas, Fort Worth, as well as the forty counties in their northeast Texas jurisdiction, the Rangers sometimes got spread pretty thin. There was nothing easy about it. Tyler hoped that if Russ sent him on a jaunt to Fort Worth, that meant there was a strong lead linking the two murders together. His focus was on solving the Hasse murder. If there was no solid link, Tyler wanted another Ranger or two to go there. He knew Russ wouldn't pull him off the Hasse murder this soon unless he was told to do so by Preston.

Stop worrying, Tyler thought to himself. *You've got too much on your mind. Just chill. Go home, do your fucking report. Take the dog for a walk. See if your girlfriend will come over and fuck you. Watch some TV and when you get to the conference tomorrow you, Russ, and your coworkers will figure it out.*

The interview with Eric and Kim Williams was messing with his head. Hot damn, he was ready. Ready as he could be for something to break his way. Frustrated wasn't close to how he felt—*motherfucking* frustrated came somewhat close. Tyler punched the accelerator a little harder, turned up the volume on the radio, and continued west toward Dallas.

CHAPTER 23

For the Rangers to have conferences on consecutive days was rare. Major Wilson would usually meet with them in his office to discuss cases they were on by ones or twos. The meetings with all of them together were mostly held once a week, on Friday mornings. At those meetings, the Rangers would discuss each other's cases and brainstorm ideas to assist one another. It took too much time away from their jobs to meet together very often. It just wasn't feasible, especially with their jurisdiction covering so much of Texas. There just flat out weren't enough of them. But having two high-profile cases that were possibly connected made this necessary.

Tyler was up early. Again he hadn't slept all that well. Girlfriend didn't come over; she had a prior commitment with her daughter Jacqueline. He had finished his report on the Williams interview the evening before, soon after arriving home. To relax, he took Kano for a walk and then watched a movie on TV. Before leaving for that morning's meeting, he made himself breakfast, two egg-and-cheese tortillas with hot sauce. For the mental wake-up, he brewed very strong coffee. After showering and getting dressed, he rolled for the meeting. As he pulled away from the house, he hoped something really positive would come out of this conference; Lord knows the Dallas DPS headquarters could use a break.

Tyler ran into traffic on his way to work. He had left early enough to allow for this, but he was going to be cutting it close to making the meeting on time. He pulled in to the gated lot with ten minutes to spare. Scanning in at the security door, he took the elevator to the second floor and went straight to the conference room. He was the last Ranger to arrive, but he was on time, barely. Russ had yet to enter; all was good. He greeted his coworkers, poured a cup of coffee, filled a plastic bowl with fruit, and took a seat. He opened his briefcase and took out the report he wrote the night before on the Williams interview. Placing his briefcase under the table, he waited for Russ to enter and start the show. He didn't have to wait long; Major Wilson was never late. Tyler looked at his watch; eight o'clock. The side door to the conference room opened, and in came the Major.

"Good morning, gentlemen. Since our meeting yesterday morning, there have been some interesting developments with the Clements murder. A person of interest has surfaced. He has family ties to our state and to our jurisdiction. Fort Worth to be exact." As Wilson was talking, the side door opened, and Judy Poppa walked in with paperwork in her hands. She began to pass out the reports to the Rangers. The Major continued, never breaking stride in his presentation. "As you will see in the report that Judy is handing out, this suspect is considered extremely dangerous. He has been convicted of felony assault in Colorado and served time in prison there. In fact, he was just recently released. And it turns out he was released too soon for his crime. Brace yourselves, gentlemen. He got released early… on a clerical error."

"You've got to be shitting us," said Joe Vasquez.

"I wish I was, Joe, but that's the shameful truth," replied Wilson, with the same look of disbelief as they had.

"So there is interest in him by Colorado. How solid is it?" asked Richard Rossman.

"I'm going to answer that question and then tell you about him. After that, you men can draw your own conclusions." Wilson looked around the table, making eye contact with each Ranger before he continued. "He is a person of interest. There are no—and I repeat—no solid suspects at this time. There are several suspects that Colorado Corrections and CBI are interested in looking at for the murder of Tom Clements. That being said, none of them are solid at this time. The suspect with ties to Texas is named Evan Ebel, a known member of the 211 Crew. He has a brother and sister living in Fort Worth. They have no criminal background. He was paroled in January of this year and has since broken parole. His whereabouts are unknown. His nickname is Evil Ebel. He is a twenty-seven-year-old white male. He is tatted up. He has a swastika on his stomach, 'White Pride' and lightning bolts on his arms. Look at the photos at the back of the report. He also has some more colorful ones like 'Hate' and so forth. He's a real walking piece of art."

"He looks like a walking piece of shit to me," said Miles.

"Excellent observation, Roger," said Wilson with a wry smile. The Rangers lightly laughed at Miles's comment. "Now as I said, he is just a person of interest at this time. But he needs to be found if he's in Texas so he can be questioned and brought back to Colorado for breaking parole. Now, gentlemen, if he is the person who killed Clements, then he is probably also responsible for killing Nathan Leon. If that's so, he's a sorry, cold-blooded cocksucker. Please excuse me for speaking so highly of him." This time the laughter was louder.

"I want to volunteer to go to Fort Worth to look for him, Major," said Vasquez.

"So do I," added Miles.

"All right, I'll get to that, thank you," said Wilson, glancing at the two Rangers to acknowledge them. "Now we know from the meeting yesterday that the car seen at the scene of the Clements murder is a black Lincoln or Cadillac DeVille. We have a BOLO out in Texas for cars matching those descriptions. The thinking is that the car will have Colorado plates. But that is not a given. Plates can easily be changed, as you are all well aware of. There was no plate number reported from the scene, so we just can't be sure."

Major Wilson looked around the table at the Rangers seated there. His jaw was locked, and his countenance was intense. If Evan Ebel was in Texas, Major Wilson wanted him found and found now. "Before I give out assignments on who's doing what, we have more business to discuss. Oh…one more thing before I forget. As of yet, there has been no evidence found connecting the Clements murder to the Hasse murder. Does anyone have any questions?"

Looking over the reports in front of them and with Wilson spelling it out, no one had anything for him. It seemed pretty cut and dried. The Rangers needed to find this Ebel dude if he was in Texas, it was as simple as that. Jamison said, "I got it, Chief," and Vasquez stated, "It looks like it's all right here."

"Okay, fine," said Wilson. "As you men know, Tex has Eric Williams's residence under video surveillance. He has wanted to conduct a one-on-one interview with him for some time. The belief was that to approach this suspect the timing had to be just right. He was a lawyer as well as a justice of the peace in Kaufman before recently being disbarred. He knows to keep his mouth shut and why. Tex came to my office after the conference yesterday, and we decided that with the Clements murder hot news, the time to approach him was now. Tex informed me yesterday that he was successful in getting the interview soon after leaving my office. With my phone blowing up about this Ebel character yesterday, I haven't had a chance to hear his report. Tex is going to share that with all of us now. Tex."

Tyler looked around the table at his coworkers as they turned to give him their attention. "All right, y'all, I'm going to give you the eight-second bull-rider version. Seems at least some of us have a dirtbag to look for today. Yes, I was able to conduct a sit-down interview with Eric Williams and his wife, Kim, in their home yesterday afternoon. Eric recognized me from an interview I'd done a few weeks back that ran on a local news channel. He knew that I have a major role in the DPS case on Hasse's murder. I do believe that's why he agreed to talk with me—he was curious. As you're all aware of, I feel he could be good for the murder. There's motive, his knowledge of firearms, and so on...as you are all aware of. But I don't have shit either as far as one single bit of evidence. Saying that, meeting with him was eye-opening.

"He's angry. He attempts to hide how angry he is, but he's pissed. Then there was the wife. She's a dreadful mess. I do think she is someone who could be easily manipulated. The main thing I want to tell you is the comment he made just prior to my leaving, and yes, I do want us to discuss this in more detail, but today's not the day. Anyway, I asked him why the killer would converse with Hasse before shooting him and why he would insult him by cursing in his face. He said, and I quote, 'Maybe he just wanted to say hello before he blew the son of a bitch away.'"

"Whoa…that's some cold-blooded shit," said Miles.

"No shit," agreed Jamison.

"What did the wife have to say, Tex?" asked Wilson.

"She just sang her husband's praises. Said he couldn't do such a thing as kill anyone. In a nutshell, it was creepy. They're still at the top of my list. It would take some doing to knock them off of it. One last thing, and I'll let the Major get this manhunt rolling. Williams did his best to convince me that the murder of Hasse and Clements are connected. He tried to convince me that the 211 Crew and the Aryan Brotherhood are in cahoots to spread fear among law enforcement. Why? Because they can. His ego is bigger than Texas, y'all. I do know he's smart, but his common sense is out there…so is his opinion of himself. Just the kind of thing we encounter with sociopaths."

"Fuck, yeah, that's creepy as hell. Excuse me for sounding so professional," quipped Rossman.

"Tex, make copies of your report, and I'll make sure everyone gets one," said Wilson. "Joe, you and Roger get your wish. I'm sending you two to Fort Worth with Rich and Clint. Two of you go to Ebel's sister's house, and the other two go to the brother's house. As I stated earlier, the siblings have no criminal history. No known affiliation with the 211 Crew. Just find out what you can. Split up how you please, I don't give a shit. Decide amongst yourselves. You're big boys. Just let me know if they've seen him lately…as in any time since he's been out of prison. Also let me know…" He stopped in midsentence when Judy walked into the room and addressed him.

"Major, Preston's on the phone and he said it was urgent," she said, standing in the doorway.

Wilson looked up at her and then turned back to his men. "Y'all hold tight. I've got a couple of more things I need to go over." He left the room with Judy holding the door open. She closed it behind them as they left.

"This Evil Ebel dude sounds like a nutter, huh?" said Clint.

"No shit, Sherlock. Look how fucked up his tats look in these pictures," said Miles.

"How'd you like your daughter bringing that home?" joked Rossman.

The banter went back and forth between the Rangers for a few more minutes while they waited for Major Wilson to return to the conference room. He was gone for almost five minutes. Then their world changed in an instant. The side door to the room swung open with Wilson's face expressing great consternation. All the Rangers stopped and stared at him... *What the fuck?*

"Big fucking change of plans, men... Evan Ebel was in a gun battle with our State Troopers! It took place in Wise County less than an hour ago. Let's go—all of you! Rich, go get Jason and have him bring his camera equipment. Meet us in the parking lot. And hurry your ass up!" Rossman saw Wilson's face; he didn't have to be told twice. "We're taking the SUVs. Tex, you come with me. You too, Joe." Wilson was actually pointing at the men as he gave them the order. "We're taking three vehicles. Preston is flying in. Jacobs, you go with Jamison and Miles." Wilson spun on his heel and bolted out the door, hollering behind him, "Come on, let's get fucking moving!"

As Tyler exited the conference room, he was dumbfounded by what he had just heard. A shootout in Wise County involving Texas State Troopers and Evan Ebel. Whoa, Nelly! What a mental clusterfuck! Russ was as wound up as Tyler had ever seen him. He was like the rest of them: little sleep, long hours, and maximum stress. What a difference a day made. Yesterday, the Rangers left the meeting telling stories and doing some morale building. Twenty-four hours later... *fubar*! From one extreme to the other. This meeting had turned grim in a hurry.

CHAPTER 24

THE RANGERS WERE RIGHT ON Major Wilson's heels as they came out the security entrance leading to the gated employee parking lot. Rich was right behind them, explaining that Jason Chime was coming, bringing the camera equipment. The men piled into the black DPS State SUVs. The Department owned four specially designed Cadillac Escalades. Each came with bulletproof glass and bulletproof door panels. The headlights and taillights pulsed during daylight hours if switched on. Also located in the grille were red and blue flashers. These vehicles were only used for special tasks such as protection of dignitaries or politicians. They were also used by DPS Directors when they flew into Dallas. The Escalades were always kept fueled and completely maintained.

Tyler was driving the lead SUV with Major Wilson riding shotgun. Joe Vasquez was in the back. Steve Jamison, Miles, and Jacobs were right behind them, with Rich Rossman bringing up the rear. The three cars lined up at the security gate. Just as Tyler pressed the button to open the gate, here came Jason with his camera equipment strapped over his shoulder. He was running as he exited the security door. He jumped in with Rossman, and the trio of Escalades were off.

Major Wilson was on his phone from the moment he got into the vehicle. "Tex, engage the speaker system. Y'all need to hear this. Engage it for all three cars," said Wilson. Each Escalade could communicate together through the Bose radio speaker system. Everyone was talking at once in the three cars, including FBI Special Agent in

Charge Chris Collins, who was on the phone with Wilson. "Y'all shut up out there!" shouted Major Wilson. "You need to hear this!" It got quiet except for Collins's voice on the speakers.

"We should be pulling up to the crash scene in about twenty minutes, Russ," said Collins. "I've given you all I've got for now. Bring your men up to speed and I'll see you when you get here."

"Okay, Chris. We should arrive about forty-five minutes behind you," said Wilson.

"All right. See you then," replied Collins, and the line went dead. No one spoke in the cars; they were waiting on Major Wilson.

"Everyone can hear me, right?" asked Wilson.

"Yes, sir," came the chorus from the trailing Escalades. Then silence. They didn't want to piss him off.

"All right, then—listen up!" Tyler had the grille flashers on, and the pulse engaged for the head and taillights; the traffic was moving over. They were making good time. Tyler was pressing the accelerator, and the speedometer was on eighty-five. Wilson continued. "About an hour ago, a Montague County Deputy Sheriff pulled over a car matching the description of our BOLO. It was a 1991 Cadillac DeVille with Colorado plates. He was shot in the head by the driver."

"Oh fuck," said Miles.

"I know this is fucked up, but just listen," said Major Wilson. "After shooting the deputy, the DeVille took off. Passing motorists saw the shooting and called it in to the local police. Two of our own, Troopers Billy Smith and David Whitlock, heard the dispatch and went toward the scene. Smith ID'd the Caddy and gave chase. He was joined in the pursuit by Whitlock. This resulted in a high-speed chase, with speeds reaching in excess of a hundred miles an hour. The chase lasted some ten minutes until the Caddy crashed at an intersection, colliding with a tractor trailer. Our troopers approached the wreck, and the suspect came out firing. The suspect was shot at the scene by Smith, I believe. The suspect is believed dead but there is an ambulance at the scene and that is not verified at this time. Neither Smith nor Whitlock were injured during the shoot-out."

"Thank God," said Rossman.

"I hear that," said Wilson. "That's all I have now. If you have questions, now's the time."

"So it was this Ebel guy from this morning?" asked Joe.

"Yes, it was. Can't believe I left that out," replied Wilson. "He had a Colorado driver's license on his person."

"Is the deputy dead?" asked Jacobs.

"He was alive at the scene. That's all I know right now," said Wilson.

"You had him pegged, Major. Cold-blooded cocksucker," said Tyler.

"Unfortunately, I did. Too bad this went down before we caught him. At least Whitlock and Smith didn't catch a bullet," replied Wilson.

"That's the God's truth," said Miles.

"We should be at the crash site pretty soon. Let's shut this down and reflect. We'll have plenty to talk about in just a few more minutes. Tex, turn off the intercom," said Wilson as he turned and stared out the passenger window, slowly reclining his seat. Tyler did as he was told. Neither he nor Joe said a word as they drove the last half hour to the scene.

*****

Wise County was about an hour or so north west of Dallas. It was part of the city of Fort Worth, which encompassed four counties: Tarrant, Denton, Parker, and Wise. *What brought this Evan Ebel to Texas?* wondered Tyler as he drove to the scene. *Did he come here to visit his siblings? Did he murder Nathan Leon and Tom Clements as suspected?* With this shoot-out, it sure looked that way to Tyler. Was he also responsible for killing Hasse? Wise County wasn't that far from Kaufman. Was Tyler completely wrong about Eric Williams? It wasn't a far stretch at all to think he could be. This Evan Ebel dude was a cold-blooded SOB after what he pulled today. He had shot a deputy in the head and tried to kill two Texas State Troopers. It didn't get any more cold-blooded that that, whether or not he killed Clements.

Tyler knew both troopers personally. Hell, everyone in these cars did with the exception of Jason Chime. William "Billy" Smith and David Whitlock were part of the DPS family. State Troopers were Texas Department of Public Safety highway patrolmen. They did exactly what their title implied—patrol Texas highways. They were known in the state for their distinctive cruisers as well as their uniforms, which consisted of cowboy boots, hats, and dark-tan pants and shirts. The uniform color is referred to as Texas tan in this great state.

The State Trooper was an offshoot of the Texas Rangers. While the Rangers handled major violent crime, the Troopers enforced the law against highway crime: speeding, long-haul trucking violations, illegal immigration, drug smuggling, interstate sex trafficking, etc. The Troopers had jurisdiction in any county in the state, as opposed to local police, who were confined to the county they represented. While the Troopers wore uniforms, the Rangers didn't. They dressed business casual. Though many Rangers wore cowboy hats, it was optional, hence Tyler sometimes did and sometimes didn't wear his cowboy hats. All Rangers wore cowboy boots by choice, not requirement.

The Rangers recognized when they were getting close to the crash scene; traffic was backing up. Tyler drove on the shoulder to bypass the cars backed up on the highway. Following close behind him were the other Rangers. Orange cones had been set up to funnel the oncoming traffic to a single lane. Tyler drove between the cones, driving on the cordoned-off lane to within fifty yards of the intersection where they could see the crash. Even from a distance, one could see that the DeVille was badly mangled. *How in the hell did Ebel survive that?* wondered Tyler.

The Caddy was fucked up, and not just a little bit. The entire front end was crushed all the way back to the driver's door and then some. Ebel must have moved to the passenger side prior to the impact, thought Tyler. That appeared to be the only way he could have come out blasting. He sure as hell didn't exit the driver's door; it was crushed.

Exiting the Escalades, the Rangers walked as a group toward the contingent of police and emergency personnel at the scene. Special Agent in Charge Collins was talking to a group of police officers. There was no ambulance on site. If Ebel was killed, Tyler didn't think it was likely that his body would have been removed so soon. What's the story there? he wondered. Collins was talking to a man who looked to be the sheriff of Decatur. Also standing alongside them were Troopers Billy Smith and David Whitlock and FBI agents.

"Morning Chris, Trooper Smith, Trooper Whitlock," said Major Wilson, extending his hand to the men.

"Hello, Major. Didn't take you long to get here," said Collins, taking the Major's hand.

"Morning, Major, good to see you again," said Trooper Smith. He and Whitlock shook hands with Wilson.

"I hear you're the men of the hour, Smith," said Wilson, smiling at them both. "You did the department proud today."

"Well, sir, thank you," replied Trooper Smith.

"Where is the bastard? Is he dead?" asked Wilson, looking around expecting to see him lying under a blanket close to the car.

"No, he was carted off in an ambulance to a hospital in Fort Worth," replied Collins. "Paramedics found a pulse upon arrival. He was transported from the scene before I got here. From what I hear, it's just a matter of time. Don't think he's expected to survive his injuries. Between the crash and Smith here putting one in his head, it looks bleak for the man."

"Well, that's too fucking bad," said Wilson. "He seemed like such a nice guy." All the men exchanged glances, smiling. Not much love lost on cop killers among this group. "Let's take a look at what's left of the Caddy."

Collins, Wilson, Smith, and the other FBI agents began to walk closer to inspect the 1991 DeVille, or what was left of it. Jason Chime was already circling it, snapping photos. Tyler held back, and so did David Whitlock. "Hey, David. Not your typical day, huh?" asked Tyler, extending his hand out to Whitlock.

"Hell no, Tyler. Not typical by a long shot," replied Whitlock, taking his hand in a firm grip. "Had enough excitement to last me all year. Could say it was fun. Exciting, you know? Except for what happened to Deputy Boyd. His getting wounded takes the joy out of the experience, no matter how many deserving assholes bite the dust. Know what I mean?"

"I certainly do, David. I know exactly how you feel. But y'all did a good job today. I want to know exactly how it went down. Let's you and me take a walk down by our cars. I really want to hear this. I can tell by looking at this mess that it's a hell of a story."

The two of them walked a short distance from the crash scene to speak in private. When they reached the Escalade, they stopped and leaned up alongside the grille, which was still flashing.

"Go ahead, David, tell me the tale," said Tyler.

"Okay. I was on the highway here going west when a call came over my radio that an officer was shot farther up on 287, close to the Montague, Wise County line. The dispatcher said that the shooter was driving a black Cadillac with Colorado plates. Deputy Boyd had called it in before approaching the car. As I'm driving west, I'm praying that the perp didn't turn off on a farm road and disappear into the countryside. Last thing dispatch knew was that he was going south on 287, but I thought he might turn left on 380 and come my way. So shit, Tyler, I'm hauling ass that way trying to spot the Caddy. All of a sudden, Billy comes over the radio. He says he has a visual on the Caddy turning east on 380 and that he's in a high-speed pursuit. Fuck, Tyler, the perp is coming right to me, maybe fifteen miles west of my location."

Tyler shook his head slightly, as if trying to imagine what it was like to be in David's shoes at that moment. Having an active shooter who just minutes earlier shot a deputy now coming his way in a high-speed chase. "Damn, David, your adrenaline had to be off the charts," replied Tyler.

"Fucking A… I know you've been there, man. I wanted to spot that Caddy so bad. And knowing that he was coming right at me— whoa! Shit! My mind was going crazy." He stopped and looked at Tyler. "I'm giving you the cop-to-cop version, not the cop-to-brass version."

"Hell, David, that goes without saying. It's why I wanted to walk down here. Go on, it's starting to get good. I want everything—how you felt, all that good shit, before we get interrupted."

"So I radio Billy and tell him they're coming right to me and should be here in like six to eight minutes. He tells me to cross the median and wait on them, that they're hitting like a hundred. He tells me the perp is shooting at him from the car window."

"Holy shit…"

"I know, right? So I cross the median and wait on the shoulder with my flashers on. There is a small knoll behind me so I can't see but maybe two hundred yards down the highway. At a hundred miles per hour, they'll be on me like shit through a goose. I'm wanting to see this fucker something bad. I knew he shot Boyd. I'm aching for a shot at his ass." David turned to look at Tyler with a look of determination.

"I bet you did," replied Tyler. "Damn, David, you had to be geared up about now."

"No shit. Game is on, and it's coming right at me. This is career day. The radio is squawking, dispatch is yapping all this shit, Billy is telling me they're still coming east on 380. My mind is going a million miles an hour. I'm checking my gun strap—and bingo! There's the Caddy flying over the knoll like a bat out of hell!" David stepped away from the Escalade and turned to face Tyler. "This part is only for you. I don't think what I did was too smart in hindsight, but I was fired up."

"Been there, man. It's just you and me," said Tyler, reassuring him.

"Well, I turned on my siren and pulled to the middle of the highway, trying to get him to swerve and crash. I was only going about twenty. Well, he was on me in no time. I thought for a second there he was going to plow right up my ass. He just misses me, driving partly on the shoulder, partly on the road, blasting away on his horn. As I begin to pick up speed to give chase, here comes Billy. I drive to the shoulder to let him pass. He's doing about a hundred, lights flashing, siren howling."

"Damn, David, I would have loved to have been a part of this one," said Tyler, smiling at the thought. "But yeah…you might want to leave out the part where you tried to block the highway. You could have been engulfed in a fireball if Ebel rammed you. It could have been ugly. Yeah, he would have been dead, but so would you."

"Oh, I know! I caught a break on that one. Wasn't one of my brightest moments. I know I'm lucky to see my wife and kids again today. Anyway, I pick up the chase after Billy passes me, but he's got a big head start because of his speed. By the time I hit a hundred, they're a quarter of a mile ahead of me. After maybe a minute of hitting top speed, I see this intersection coming up, and Billy's car turned, blocking the road. Well, the few cars we passed had pulled to the shoulder to let us pass. They could see we were in a high-speed chase, so as I pulled up next to Billy's car, I could now see the wreck up ahead. It was about sixty yards away. I didn't see it happen. I was too far behind. Billy was waiting for me beside his cruiser. We began to run toward the crash with our guns drawn. We're closing fast, and he tells me to go right, to separate if we engage in a gun battle."

"That's some scary shit, ain't it?" asked Tyler.

"Fuck yeah… First time I've drawn my gun on duty, Tyler. I'm scared shitless. I'm just glad Billy is there with me. I know he can shoot his ass off. Some people say he's as good as you."

"Oh, he's good…damn good," agreed Tyler. "And it's normal to be scared. Cops who say they're not are lying their asses off."

"Well, within seconds, the both of us are just twenty-five or thirty yards from the wreck. I'm thinking the bastard has to be dead, the car is that fucked up. Smoke and steam are rising from the engine. Cars are stopping on either side of the crash, and people are running from the scene. And just as I think we're going to get to the crash and find him dead, he exits the passenger door and comes out blasting away—and he's shooting at me! So I drop to the ground and return fire. Then he sees Billy coming right at him and turns to fire at Billy. Don't think he had any bullets left in his gun. I didn't see a report, but he was aiming at Billy and he started firing. Billy dropped him in his tracks. Shot him in the forehead. He crumpled like a sack of

170

potatoes. I got up and started running that way. Billy stepped on his hand and removed the gun just as I ran up."

"Shit, David, what a story. Y'all kicked ass today. Way to fucking go!" said Tyler, smiling at Trooper David Whitlock. "You're fortunate not to have taken a bullet. I'm sure both of you will receive meritorious citations for your bravery."

"Thanks, Tyler. But as I said, I was scared silly. Never forget this day as long as I live. I'm sure of it," said David, returning the smile. "I was only trying to do my job and be there for Billy. I almost think he sent me to the right so he could close ground and get to him first. He was trying to protect me. I don't think he would admit it, but he got much closer to Ebel than I did. He made a beeline to the crash, and I went right. He's a bad dude…he's got balls of steel."

"He's been at this a little longer than you have, David. I know for a fact that this isn't the first time Billy has had to shoot his gun at a perp. But it was the two of you that nailed the bastard. It doesn't matter who shot him. Y'all had each other's back. That's what matters. You don't leave a brother hanging…and you didn't," said Tyler with total conviction. "This Ebel character might have killed three that we know of and he tried to kill both of you. I can't begin to tell you what a good thing you accomplished today. Go home this evening to your wife and kids and hug them. You're damn lucky to be standing here."

"Thanks again, Tyler. That means a lot coming from you. Hell, that means more to me than having it come from Preston. And I mean no disrespect, but you're the man."

"Bullshit! You're the man. I couldn't have done one thing better than you did today. You just might make Texas Ranger after today if you're interested. Let's walk back down by this crash. Major Wilson may want me to pick up Preston at the Decatur airport." The two of them walked back to the wreckage. An even larger contingent of law enforcement had shown up in the last thirty minutes. Tyler saw that the FBI forensic van had arrived and they were combing through the Caddy for items of interest.

Tyler walked over to Major Wilson standing at the back of the wrecked Cadillac DeVille. Vasquez, Jamison, and Miles were next to him. They were looking at some pieces of evidence displayed on a folding table that the FBI forensic team had set up. "There you are, Tex. Look what was found in Ebel's trunk," said Wilson, as he picked up a pizza warmer box with his latex gloves.

"Is that what I think it is?" asked Tyler.

"Sure as shit looks that way," replied Wilson. "And look here." Wilson held up a Domino's pizza hat in a sealed plastic bag. "There's also a hit list. I think it's in the forensic van now. Ebel had a list of Colorado corrections officers and judges on it. Tom Clements was crossed off the list. Mark Hasse's name wasn't on there, though. And then his pistol, nine-millimeter, same caliber that killed Leon and Clements."

"No shit...damn near seals the deal," said Tyler. "Ballistics, DNA of Nathan Leon, which will very likely be on the hat. He's the shooter. Who would have thunk it. Just two days later, he comes to Wise County and gets in a gun battle with two of our Troopers and bites the dust. Almost hard to fathom. Are you thinking what I'm thinking?"

"You mean about Hasse?" asked Wilson.

"Yes, sir," replied Tyler. "Even without Hasse's name on that list, it doesn't mean squat. The asshole probably couldn't spell Hasse."

"I'm sure that's going to be scrutinized to the hilt over the next few days or more," replied Wilson. "Don't even want to go there now. What I do want is for you and Vasquez to go pick up Preston and Cook at the Decatur airport. They should be landing about the time you get there."

"Yes, sir," said Tyler, turning to Joe Vasquez, waving for him to follow. As the two Rangers walked to the Escalade, Tyler was thinking about what the odds were of it being someone besides Evan "Evil" Ebel who had killed Hasse. He had to admit to himself that they weren't good about now. This was all very coincidental. Ebel was in Texas, gunned down not but a two-hour drive from Kaufman. He had a hit list; he killed a high-profile member of law enforcement in Colorado...just like Hasse. The murders were somewhat similar; not the exact MO, but close.

Then again, thought Tyler, there were differences too. Take the gun, for instance. The caliber used to kill Hasse was a .357 Magnum, not a 9mm. The hits were in two different states, and Ebel had family here. Maybe he was hiding out in Texas. With the Hasse murder just weeks old, it had law enforcement on edge, especially in northeast Texas. Ebel might not have realized Texas was so hot for him, especially if he didn't do the Hasse murder. He would have thought leaving Colorado and coming here was a safe bet.

Then there were the cars. They were different too. The odds... hell, Tyler was starting to think it could be, say, fifty-fifty. Yeah, this little episode here definitely threw a wrench in the works. He knew that with Preston and Cook coming into town, it would be balls to the walls. His weekend plans with Priscilla were out the window, that was for damn sure. What the hell, maybe the missing piece would be found to tie Ebel to the Hasse murder. Tyler was just saying to himself yesterday that he might be barking up the wrong tree with Eric Williams. Wasn't like he had something solid on him. Well, shit... Time would tell.

He and Vasquez reached the Escalades. He asked Joe to drive; he couldn't be bothered. Tyler got in the SUV and lowered the seat all the way back. When a Ranger did that, it was an unwritten rule among them: no conversation. They got so little sleep that it was a given. Tyler was going to take a catnap to the airport. Short and sweet. A precious few minutes to roll with it...

CHAPTER 25

TYLER WOKE UP SATURDAY MORNING on Easter weekend feeling like he had lived a year over the last week and a half. That's how long it had been since Evan Ebel had met his maker. He was brain-dead from Trooper Billy Smith's shot to the head. The plug was pulled on his sorry ass the next day. Tyler was pretty sure Saint Peter drop-kicked his ass to Hades as soon as he showed up knocking at the pearly gates. The bastard had created a disruptive upheaval that would make the Tasmanian devil look like a toddler.

Tyler lay in bed thinking back on all the turmoil the sum'bitch had left in his wake. It started with the murder of Nathan Leon, the innocent pizza driver whom Ebel bushwhacked for his uniform. This hardworking family man had lost his life to this sick fuck for the sole purpose of a disguise to murder another victim, Tom Clements. And what Tyler had learned over the last week was that Evil Ebel didn't just shoot Leon in cold blood; he mentally tortured him first. This sick fuck kidnapped Mr. Leon and forced him to recite some rambling bullshit about how inhumanely Ebel had been treated while incarcerated in a Colorado prison. Ebel recorded it…then shot Nathan Leon. It didn't get much more fucked up than that.

Poor, mistreated Evan Ebel. He felt he had a rough time in prison. So somewhere along the line, he decided to improve his life by tatting a swastika on his stomach to go along with his tats of "Hate," "White Power," and other such nonsense. In Tyler's opinion, if a person looked up to Adolf the "Cocksucker" Hitler, he was not on the path to earthly bliss. To top it off for poor Ebel, he was in prison for felony assault in the first place.

As Tyler leaned back in his bed with his body wracked with fatigue from overwork and lack of sleep, his mind wasn't near finished going over the last week. He thought about Mrs. Tom Clements going to the doorway of her home, only to find her husband lying in a pool of blood, gunshots echoing in her ears and the smell of gunpowder filling her nostrils. Only to look out and see the coward Evan Ebel retreating from the scene. Was Ebel through? Not no, but hell no. He took a jaunt to Texas, where, bless his little black heart, he fucked up some more lives. Several, in fact. Some mentally, some physically.

The one who took the physical brunt of his demented escapade to Texas was Montague County Deputy Sheriff James Boyd. All of DPS, FBI, and police had watched the dash-cam video from Boyd's cruiser. He had approached Ebel's Cadillac during the traffic stop from the passenger side. Deputy Boyd had his gun holstered, but his hand was at the ready. As he cautiously walked to the car looking inside, he was seen to collapse to the ground, with glass fragments exploding all around him. He was shot in the head as well as twice in his torso, then the Cadillac sped away.

It was disturbing to watch as passing motorists stopped to render aid. Fortunately for Deputy Boyd, he survived, but it wasn't for Ebel's lack of trying. The injuries he sustained would permanently affect Boyd for the rest of his life. Then there was his family going through the anguish of a husband, father, and son being severely wounded in the line of duty. Forever.

Tyler then thought back to picking up Director Colin Preston and Deputy Assistant Director Calvin Cook at the Decatur airport and driving them to the crash site. My God, they were pissed. Tyler felt like they were disappointed Ebel was brain-dead because they wanted the opportunity to shoot him themselves.

From that moment on, for the last week and a half, DPS had brainstormed almost around the clock to put together a comprehensive picture of just who, whom, why, and how these murders came about. Every form of research was attempted to find a link between

Evan Ebel and Mark Hasse's murder. Ebel's siblings in Fort Worth had been brought in an interviewed. Those who were believed to have associated with him since his release from prison were tracked down and questioned. His whereabouts were investigated and tracked. Searches for communication between the 211 Crew or the Aryan Brotherhood and Ebel had been conducted.

The Texas Department of Public Safety had been busy. Finding a connection between Ebel, Clements, and Hasse had been for naught. In spite of this, there were still many people who thought the crimes were linked. Just a matter of time before the evidence would be found was the common theory. Many lawmen felt it was too much of a coincidence.

So here we are a week later, thought Tyler as he threw back the covers and got out of bed. Easter weekend. He had today and Easter Sunday off. Yeah, baby. He was ready. Every muscle in his body ached. He had a wonderful weekend planned with Priscilla. They were having lunch with their friends Stephanie and Craig, then they were going to a party over at Russ's in the evening. Preston was still in Dallas, staying with the Major. He was flying out early the next morning from Love Field to Austin to spend Easter with his family. So he would be at Russ's party but not Cook, who had flown back to Austin the previous day. And as for Easter Sunday, Tyler and Priscilla were going to the Cathedral for Mass.

Tyler walked into his kitchen; he could smell all the food cooking. "Good morning, babe."

Priscilla turned and gave Tyler a kiss. "Good morning to you, my hunk of burning love," she said, laughing. "Go back and get in bed. I'm serving us on trays."

"Oh yeah, that works." Tyler went back to his bedroom and switched on the TV. No news channel this morning, he thought; this time it was ESPN sports center.

A few minutes later, Priscilla entered the bedroom, placing a tray full of food before Tyler. She was soon back with her own tray and joined him in bed. "It's going to be a little sad seeing Craig this afternoon, don't you think?"

Between bites, Tyler answered. "Yes, I do. But Stephanie said he was looking forward to our visit. Their kids are going to be there, so we should have a nice visit with everyone." He paused to take another bite. "Then this evening you'll meet Preston. I would have liked for you to meet Cook. He's got a great sense of humor. He kept all of us loose this last week, even under all the stress. I really like him. His wife insisted he come home as soon as he could for Easter. He took a commercial flight home. Preston's flying out tomorrow morning on the DPS plane. You'd like Cook. I like Preston too but Cook has the sense of humor that rocks."

"Well, maybe next time he's in town under better circumstances. The last two months have been unreal. I don't think I've ever seen you look so stressed, Tyler...ever. Thank God you're not working again this weekend. Especially with it being Easter. And after last weekend, you're having to work straight through all week. You need a break," she said with concern in her voice. "I'm also glad we're visiting with the Marshalls before going to Russ's. It gives you some time away from your colleagues. Just gives you a break from work-related stuff."

"Oh, I'm with you. Then again, seeing Craig will be a little stressful, especially under the circumstances. Sometimes seems you just can't get away from the crap." He looked over at Priscilla. "Hell, I'm sounding negative, huh?"

"No, there's some truth in what you're saying. There's the ebb and flow to life. Lately you've experienced a lot of ebb. Say next week you arrest the suspect on the *Hasse* case. Well, then, there's the flow! You would feel so much different. Remember your mantra, Tyler. Just roll with it."

Tyler smiled to himself at her encouragement. She was doing what all good mates did; that's why he loved her so.

Priscilla continued. "Speaking of suspects, how are things looking on your guy in Kaufman?"

"Well, it's funny you would use the term 'ebb and flow.' That is how I feel about him. There have been times I was positive it was him. Then comes this Ebel dude into Wise County. Blows the whole thing up for me. He seemed a million miles away after that. What keeps him at the forefront of my mind is that no one's been charged with Hasse's murder. So my guy is still very much viable. I just need that one break. But I don't feel nearly as sure about him as I did."

"Tyler, you never know, maybe that break is just around the corner. Then it will flow, flow, flow…and with tomorrow being Easter Sunday, I'm going to have the priest pray for you after Mass. I've planned it all week. I can't wait." She turned to gaze into his eyes. "You wait and see! Now, let's get up and take Kano for a walk. Then we need to get ready. We have a big day ahead of us." With that, Priscilla gathered up the trays and dishes.

*****

The drive to the Marshalls' didn't take long. They lived in Richardson, a suburb close to Tyler's home. It joined Plano to the south with both cities due north of Dallas. Stephanie and Craig no longer owned their lake house, having sold it soon after Craig became ill. It was where they had done most of their entertaining. This was another blow that cancer dealt to families, robbing them of the things they once did together like travel and hobbies.

A sad example was when Stephanie's father took the entire extended family to Greece for a holiday, and she and Craig could not go due to him being too weak. Stephanie could have gone without him, the trip was only for two weeks, but she told Tyler there was no way she would have gone, leaving him behind. A cure for cancer couldn't be found fast enough for Tyler. He had lost his father to the dreaded disease. His father had been a master gunsmith who sold his business when he was diagnosed with lung cancer. That was when the family had moved to Dallas to be closer to his mother's family. Tyler's father didn't want his wife and children to be so far away from loved ones when he died. His father actually lived longer than the doctors had first predicted. He was able to see his son play one year of football for the University of Texas. Yes, Tyler knew firsthand what families went through.

*****

"Hi, y'all come on in," said Lauren as she hugged Priscilla and Tyler in the foyer. "Mom, it's Tyler and Priscilla." She ushered them inside. "Come in, come in." Lauren took the bottle of wine Tyler brought and led them into the living room.

Lauren was the Marshalls' daughter. Her brother Josh and his wife, Dawn, were the next to greet them as Stephanie came out of the kitchen. "Hi, Tex, Priscilla. So good to see you both," she said as she wiped her apron before giving them both a hug. "Y'all come in here to the den and say hello to Craig." She lead them down the short hallway, and there was Craig sitting up on the couch with an intravenous tube inserted in his left arm. The fluid bag hung beside the couch. He didn't attempt to stand. He did look very frail, but his eyes were bright blue, and he had a big smile for them both.

"Hi, Tyler, Priscilla," said Craig in a soft voice. He held out his frail hand, which was shaking slightly. Priscilla bypassed his hand and gave him a hug while kissing him on the cheek. Tyler took his hand and gave it a light squeeze. In Texas, even a frail man would be insulted if you gave him a wet fish and called it a handshake.

"Good to see you, Craig. It's nice of y'all to have us over," said Tyler as he took a seat on a chair near the couch. There were blankets and pillows on the couch for Craig to use when he lay back down. Tyler was sure he had forced himself to sit up for their entrance.

"Craig sure was looking forward to your visit. Weren't you, Craig?" said Stephanie.

"That I was," said Craig, very softly. "That I was."

"Well, we're glad to see you, Craig, and we're hungry too," said Priscilla as she laughed with the others. "What is that I smell in the kitchen? Cookies?"

"Of course. I'm baking," said Stephanie. She was known for her baked chocolate goods. "Come in here to the kitchen and have a look-see." She glanced at the girls, and they followed her into the kitchen. She wanted to give Craig some time alone with Tyler and Josh. The girls could visit in the kitchen at the breakfast nook.

Josh helped his father lie back down on the couch with his pillows and put the blanket over his legs. He then pulled up a chair and sat next to Tyler. The two men were just a few short feet from the couch. With Craig being a Dallas Police chaplain before he became ill, and Josh a Dallas police officer, they wanted to hear all about Tyler's case. Tyler didn't mind talking to them in the slightest. It was just story time to him. These were close friends.

The three of them talked shop while the girls visited in the kitchen before lunch was served. Stephanie was happy for her husband to have this opportunity to visit with his son and Tex. She knew the curtain was closing quickly on Craig, very quickly. She could peer into the den from a service window in the kitchen. Her eyes misted as she glanced into the den to see them talking and laughing together, so thankful for this peaceful Easter weekend.

CHAPTER 26

THE MARSHALLS WERE STANDING ON the front porch waving good-bye to Tyler and Priscilla as they pulled out of the driveway. "Did you have a good time?" Tyler asked as he drove up the street.

"I really did. I know Craig didn't look very well, but it was so nice to see him again. He seemed really glad to see us too." There was so much emotion in her voice that Tyler knew she was holding back tears. She reached into her purse and took out a tissue to wipe her eyes. "It was a great visit but very sad. Poor Craig…he's so young. And the children. So sad."

Tyler reached over, took her free hand, and gave it a gentle squeeze. "I feel the same, but I'm glad we went over. I'm not so sure we'll see him again alive. He looked that frail."

"Stephanie told me he wanted to come to the den for our visit. She said he had been in bed for the last two weeks, so they moved him to the couch this morning. I'm glad we ate in the den so Craig could join us, even though he didn't eat anything." Priscilla put the tissue away and retrieved some makeup from her purse. She needed to compose herself; the next stop was Russ's and Katie's party.

"Yes, it was very nice… Do you want to stop someplace for a drink before going over to Russ's? It's still early," said Tyler, thinking Priscilla might need more time.

"No…that's fine. Just don't take the freeway. Drive the side streets. It'll take longer. I'm fine." She was still visibly upset. "I'll put on a CD." She picked the melancholy Randy Travis recording. It was perfect for their mood as they sat quietly together in their own thoughts on the way to their next visit.

*****

Russell and Katie Wilson lived in north Dallas in one of the nicest areas of the city. The residences had oversized lots with beautiful homes and large old trees. Tyler took the side streets, eventually turning on Royal Lane heading west through the Dallas neighborhoods. Priscilla was right; this route would take much longer, but it would get them there a little after six. It would work out perfectly.

Neither of them had seen Katie for several months now. Katie was a hoot. She and Russ got along like a house on fire. Tyler couldn't think of a couple he knew that was better suited. He had known Katie since he and Russ had started working together, so Tyler was glad that she and Priscilla had become friends when they started dating. With his knowing Katie and Russ for twenty years now, they were close friends. But Tyler needn't have worried; everyone liked Katie.

She was from a small town just north of Amarillo, Texas. Dumas, to be exact, fifty miles away from the big A. Russ had met her at a wrestling tournament for the Texas Amateur Wrestling Association (known to those in the sport as TAWA) when he was in junior high school. The tournament was held in Amarillo, and Russ pinned her brother in the championship match. Katie came up to him and told him he got lucky, then turned away in a huff. He had thought, *Who is this cute, spunky girl?*

Soon after, Russ spotted her at the concession stand and asked her for her number. It took more than a little persistence on Russ's part (as Russ tells it, and he likes to tell it); she was still hot that he had beaten her brother. After all, he hadn't lost that season, much less lost by getting pinned. But she finally relented and, as they say, all's well that ends well. And this one was not close to ending. Tyler was not exactly sure, but it was over thirty years of marriage and counting. They laugh about it today. And Russ and Katie's brother? They're thick as thieves now.

It's a poignant story, to say the least. The two of them kept in touch for years, rarely seeing one another because she lived in Dumas, and Russ lived in Dallas. And their being so young…well, it was hard to visit one another. What they did was make plans to attend SMU together. She enrolled when Russ was a sophomore and they married when he was a senior. Tyler was looking forward to seeing Katie. This was turning out to be a nice weekend. Tyler could use a stress-free weekend.

Yes, indeed, the last week and a half had been rough. Shit, week and a half…how about almost two months now? Nothing of significance had broken his way on the Hasse murder. And not just his way, no one's way. Well, there was one thing, thought Tyler—the Rubys, Kent and Martha. They had fallen perfectly into his lap. And they were so patient; he called them once a week to tell them that nothing had come of the surveillance, and each time they assured him it was no bother; the camera could stay for as long as he needed.

Now he was beginning to wonder if anything would ever come of it. So many people believed that the Clements and Hasse murders would eventually be connected, and if they were correct, then the Rubys camera was for naught. But what if it was Eric Williams and he gets away with it? That thought made Tyler ill. He pushed that thought to the farthest depths of his mind anytime it exposed its ugly head.

Back to the common theory of law enforcement: the 211 Crew and Aryan Brotherhood in cahoots. That's exactly what Eric Williams had tried to sell Tyler. At the time, he thought he was full of shit. Until Evan Ebel came to Texas. And not to just anywhere in Texas, oh no, but to Wise County. Less than a two-hour drive from Kaufman. Even several FBI agents felt that Ebel was involved in Hasse's murder to some degree. No, fuck that…most FBI agents thought so. Maybe they didn't think he was necessarily the shooter, only that he knew who was. Again, if that was true, it left out Eric Williams. Tyler didn't think for a minute he had a fucking thing to do with either gang. Just way too far of a reach for him. Possible, yes; improbable…much more likely.

Not that Tyler was shutting that door, he knew better than to do that, but very faintly cracked would about sum it up for him. He would have to see it to believe it. And Tyler understood perfectly where FBI and Kaufman police were coming from. He had wrapped his mind around that very thought many a time. On the surface, it made perfect sense. But the bottom line—and that was what came up time and again in Tyler's line of work—the bottom line was that no one really knows Jack Shit as of yet.

So back to Tyler's common theory: Eric Williams. He had thought about him so much he could recite his suspicions easier than he could spell his name. There was motive, street confrontation, a shooter, a driver, location, shooter's appearance, verbal insult, Eric's knowledge of weapons, and on and on. It was all right there. And then it wasn't. Circumstantial! Weak-ass fucking circumstances. Texas prisons were full of guilty people convicted with circumstantial evidence. But it was solid shit like fingerprints, DNA, closed-circuit cameras, license plates, blood, fibers, and on and on. Tyler had nothing even close to that. Not even close. And it was burning his ass up like shitting a fiery jalapeno pepper.

Calm your ass down, he thought as they pulled up to Russ's house. *Try to forget about it for an evening. Go inside to party and enjoy yourself with friends. Soon enough you'll be back at the grind. Monday will be here before you know it. Look at Priscilla and smile. Turn on the charm. Have some fun, relax.*

"Okay, we're here, let's do this," he said, smiling at Priscilla.

"Oh, good," she replied. "My mind was a million miles away. I'm so looking forward to seeing Katie and meeting Preston. But I'm still full from lunch with the Marshalls. I hope Katie doesn't notice if I don't eat."

"No worries, they'll be glad to see you. Come on." Exiting the car, they walked along the stone path leading to the backyard.

Russ and Katie had a big backyard. For Easter weekend, it was decorated with a festive theme. There was a five-foot-tall Easter bunny cutout holding a basket full of brightly colored eggs, her large ears poking out from her bonnet. Following behind her were cutouts of six baby bunnies, each one with its own basket of colored eggs.

The Wilsons had grandchildren, so Tyler figured there would be an Easter egg hunt here tomorrow. He sure didn't think this décor was for tonight's guests. It had the cheerful kiddie look.

Guests were milling around the back lawn by the firepit as well as the back deck. Tyler recognized some of the neighbors and saw some coworkers sitting at a table on the deck. As he and Priscilla walked up the deck steps, Tyler could see into the kitchen through the bay windows. It was full of people snacking off of food trays, drinking wine and cocktails. Sitting with the Rangers was Colin Preston. He took Priscilla over to introduce her. Preston had expressed wanting to meet her earlier in the week. He was good like that; he did his best to get to know a little something about each of the Rangers even though he was stationed in Austin. That in itself was no easy chore. Texas wasn't exactly a small state, and there were a lot of Texas Rangers. He had an uncanny memory for faces, but he also put out the effort, which the men appreciated. Preston was a good people person.

Standing up from his seat at the table, Preston stepped forward to greet Tyler and Priscilla. "Well, hello, Tyler," he said, taking Tyler's hand. "And this must be Priscilla. So nice to finally meet you." He embraced her and gave a warm smile.

"It's nice meeting you too, Mr. Preston," said Priscilla, returning his smile.

"None of that, Priscilla, call me Colin. My, aren't you lovely," said Preston, as he turned to wink at Tyler.

"Thank you. It's a shame you're not here with your wife, but I know it was business that brought you to town," she replied.

"Yes, and it's what has kept Tyler away from home most of the last week or so. We're trying to catch the bad guys," he answered with a light laugh. "Actually, it's kept the department busy here for some two months now. I'm constantly reminded by the media. They do a great job of that."

"Again, nice meeting you, Colin. I'm going to leave you men alone. I see Katie over there and I want to say hello."

"The pleasure was mine. Tyler is a very lucky fellow."

As she left to talk to Katie, Tyler and Preston went to the bar on the deck to get Tyler a drink. The music was playing over the outdoor speaker system. Russ had a variety of sounds playing, every-thing from rock to country. Tyler figured that Russ and Katie's son Doug had put together the tracks. He was a music major at Texas Tech. He had been accepted into the prestigious music program at the University of North Texas but opted for Tech in order to spend some time close to his relatives on his mother's side. The smell of barbecue was everywhere. Their next stop was the grill, where one of Russ's friends from the neighborhood was at work on the ribs. His name was Mike, and he was a great cook. His grill was the kind pulled behind a truck. It sat on its own trailer, and the front had a bull's head with long horns protruding from the head. Mike had backed it up the drive and parked it in the backyard. The grill was quite a sight, very large, able to hold over a hundred pounds of meat.

"Hello, Mike," said Tyler, as he greeted him with a handshake. "Damn, man, smells good as hell over here. Have you met Colin Preston?"

"Yes, I have," replied Mike as he nodded to Preston with a smile. "He's been over here more than once getting a plateful."

"I'm sure he has. Now you need to hook me up."

Mike put a slab of ribs on a plate for Tyler, explaining to him that he had started smoking the ribs the night before, assuring him that the meat would fall off the bone. Mike took his bull grill around the state, entering cook-off competitions. He had won first prize more than a time or two and had placed third or better multiple times. He could cook him some Texas barbecue, that's for damn sure. Russ and Katie had it going on: ribs, booze, good friends, and good music—what could be better? *This night is going to be fun*, thought Tyler.

The two of them walked back to the deck where Preston had been sitting to join the other Rangers still seated at the table. Russ was there now, so Tyler greeted him and his coworkers. Soon after, Katie and Priscilla came over to join them, squeezing in together at the table. They sat around talking, eating, and laughing for nearly an hour when one of the guests came to tell Katie that the house phone was ringing. She left and was soon back, whispering in her husband's ear. Russ got up abruptly, going into the house with Katie following close behind him. Soon she was back without Russ.

"Russ wants all of you men to go to his office. He said it's very important," she said, with a worried expression on her face. All the Rangers got up at once and walked across the deck to the back entrance of the house, with Katie following them. When the Rangers entered his office, Russ was still on the phone. His face was ashen, like he had aged ten years in the last five minutes. *What the hell...* thought Tyler. This didn't look good.

"Yes, he just walked in," Russ said into the receiver. "Davis, Jamison, and Miles are here too. Hold on." Russ held out the phone to Preston. "Colin, it's Chief Burns." Preston took the phone.

"Yes, Chief, this is Colin Preston." It was obvious by the sudden change of his expression that what he was hearing wasn't good news. "Oh my god...when did it happen? All right, we're leaving now...in about an hour...all right, Chief...good...we're on our way." Preston hung up the phone and took a moment before he spoke, looking at each man in the office. "Mike McLelland and his wife are dead. They were murdered in their home sometime this morning. Each of them was shot multiple times. They were found this evening by a neighbor and her son who had not seen or heard from them all day. We need to get going."

"Colin, I'll meet you out front. I have to get my gun from my bedroom," said Wilson, his voice stiff with shock. It didn't even sound like him. He turned to Tyler. "You men ride together, no sense taking more cars than we need. I'll be right out." He turned to Katie, still standing in the doorway. "Katie, don't let on to our guests. I don't want this to spoil their Easter. Tell Priscilla and Miles's and Jamison's dates that something minor came up and they had to leave. I know you'll see that they get home later. No sense in having everyone's night spoiled. I'll be back as soon as I can."

"Russ, you be careful," said Katie as the two of them embraced before he went upstairs to get his gun and cell phone.

Preston was in the DPS Escalade he had been driving while in town. He told Tyler to lead the way to the McLellands' house in Forney; he and Russ would follow. The men had left out the front door so that no one at the party would see them leaving. Tyler was in the street with his truck running with Preston behind him in the Escalade. They were waiting on Russ, but he wasn't but a minute or two behind them, coming out the front door and joining Preston in his car. Tyler hit the gas, and the two vehicles took off for Kaufman County.

*****

"Can you fucking believe this shit?" asked Miles, sitting in the back seat of Tyler's extended-cab Chevy pickup.

"And not just Mike but his wife too," said Jamison. "What a cold-blooded motherfucker… Has to be the same perps that did Hasse. Has to be. What do you think, Tyler?"

"That's exactly what I'm thinking… Jamison, open up my laptop there and turn it on," said Tyler, sounding excited. "Here, turn it toward me." Tyler began to punch some keys after turning on the overhead spotlight while still managing to drive. "Okay, keep pushing that arrow and tell me what you see. Tell me when a car comes out of the garage."

Jamison kept pressing the video surveillance recording of Eric Williams's house. It was running in reverse. Miles leaned forward from the back seat to watch the monitor with them. Jamison had it turned in his lap so Tyler could see the monitor, but with him driving it was mostly Miles and Jamison watching the recording.

"I'm back to six this evening and a car is pulling into the driveway," said Jamison.

"All right…" said Tyler, sounding more animated. "Keep scrolling back and tell me when the car left."

They all watched the monitor for quite a while. Tyler did have it speeded up to fifteen times normal speed, but for the longest time they saw no one leaving the house. "It's all the way back to early this morning and still nothing," exclaimed Jamison.

"Keep going…they had to leave sometime," said Tyler, sounding somewhat exasperated. The recording kept going in reverse. The timer showed 6:00 a.m.…then 5:00…then 4:00…then 3:00…

"What the fuck," cried Tyler. "When did those fuckers leave?" The timer kept reversing. Soon it was past midnight going into yesterday evening...11 p.m....10:00...9:00...8:00...7:00...6:00... Then there is was, backing out of the garage, Eric Williams's car.

"There, Tyler...you see it?" asked Jamison.

"Oh yeah, I see it all right. Damn, they were gone for twenty-four hours. Where the fuck were they?"

"Doesn't the wife have parents living in Kaufman? Maybe they spent the night over at their place. It is Easter weekend," said Miles.

"Yeah, that's possible," said Tyler. "Very good possibility. And they could have left early enough from there to do the deed and use the parents as an alibi. He's thinking this through. The fucker knows that his neighbors have been questioned by the Kaufman police. So what does he do? He leaves the night before, hours before the murder. No one at the parents' neighborhood is wary, especially like his own neighbors might be. Damn, Miles, you might have nailed it," said Tyler, believing that made perfect sense. "That does fuck up my surveillance somewhat. Not completely...but not exactly what I had hoped for. At least I know he wasn't home when the murders occurred. Now I just need to know where he was...or better still, where he wasn't. He'll need an alibi."

The men remained quiet in the truck for the remainder of the trip. The McLelland's home was just outside the city limits of Kaufman in the nearby town of Forney. Tyler knew exactly where the town was, but he had to GPS the address of the house. *Holy shit!* thought Tyler as he drove to what he knew to be a gruesome crime scene. *Holy fucking shit...*

CHAPTER 27

PULLING UP TO THE MCLELLANDS' home, the Rangers saw a large contingent of people. There were lots of police, both Forney and Kaufman officers. What was noticeably absent to Tyler was the lack of media. Not too many reporters working the Easter weekend, thought Tyler. He did see a couple, but they looked to be local and were kept well back from the house. Also standing around the crime tape were what looked to be the neighbors. Tyler let Preston pass him in the Escalade since he had his grille flashers on; Tyler followed him as close to the house as they could get, which was several doors down due to all the police cars and emergency personnel and their ambulances. When the men exited the cars, Preston had them muster together. He wanted to speak to the Rangers before they walked to the house.

"I was on the phone with Collins on the way here. He won't arrive for another thirty minutes or so. He was in Arlington visiting family when he got word. The bodies are still in the house. Collins has his forensic team coming to the scene. They will be even later than he is since they have to mobilize and it's Easter weekend." He looked toward the house and then back at the men before he continued. "The police have been instructed to stay out of the house until the FBI forensic team arrives. We are going to enter, but only in two small groups. First, Russ and I will go in, then the three of you will go in when we come out. Let's go."

Preston turned and walked across the neighbor's lawn as he went to the McLellands' home. He lifted the crime tape and held it up while the Rangers stepped under it. Chief Burns approached him when he was at the driveway. Another police officer was with him.

"Hello, Preston," said Burns, as he turned to the officer next to him. "This is Sheriff Klein. He's the sheriff here in Forney. Let me tell you, it's not a pretty sight. We've done our best to stay out of there as much as possible. Just confirmed that they both were dead and checked the home for an intruder."

"Hello, sheriff," said Preston as he shook hands with Klein. "Okay…I and my men are going inside in two small groups. Collins and his team should be here soon. Have your men clear the street as much as possible for the forensic team. I want them to park in the driveway. Then block off the street and don't let anyone enter. If they live on the street, they'll just have to walk to their home. We'll open it back up when the team leaves." He turned and looked at Russ and the Rangers. "Let's do this." He walked up the sidewalk to the front porch with the Rangers following.

The front door was open, and Cynthia McLelland could be seen from the porch laying facedown just inside the foyer. She was maybe eight feet from the entranceway. Shell casings littered the floor. Blood was pooled under her body. It had dried. As Russ and Preston approached her body, the Rangers were peering into the house from the front entrance. They looked across the living area to what looked to be the hallway leading to the bedrooms. Lying at the hallway entrance was the body of Mike McLelland. He had a substantial amount of blood pooled around him, maybe twice as much as his wife.

Russ and Preston walked from Cynthia's corpse to Mike's body, being careful not to step in the blood. As the two men stood over Mike's body, they talked quietly. The Rangers could not make out what they were saying. Soon they were back. "All right, you men go have a look," said Preston when he stepped out on the porch.

Tyler slowly entered the foyer and stooped down beside Cynthia's body. It looked to him that she had been shot as soon as she answered the door and fell back onto the floor. She had blood all over her back where the bullets had passed through. She probably took no more than two steps before collapsing. Jamison and Miles were standing just behind Tyler. "Looks to me like she took the shots just as she answered the door."

"Yeah…looks like that to me," said Miles. "Caught completely by surprise, I'd say."

"But look at the shot to her head, it came after she hit the floor. It's in the back of her skull," said Tyler, pointing to the entrance wound. "Looks like the shooter shoots her as she opened the door. She falls back turning, and lands facedown. Then after she's down he puts one in the back of her head. He was making sure she didn't live to tell the tale."

"Yeah, the ones on her back are definitely exit wounds," said Jamison. "That head shot was the coup de grâce. He took aim for that one."

"Exactly. He never stepped in the blood," said Miles. "He must have shot her again before he left. Look how much blood is under her. I think her heart was still beating."

"Looks that way to me," replied Tyler. "He puts her down when she answers the door. She's falling as the shooter sees Mike standing in the hallway. He turns his attention to him and blasts away. After shooting Mike several times, he's confident he's dead. So he turns his attention back to Cynthia and puts one in her head. Poof, he's out the door. Long gone. Over in seconds."

The three of them walked around the sofa that made a path from the foyer area to the hallway entrance. Mike McLelland was lying there with his feet just shy of the hallway carpet. He was also on the tile floor. The tile ran from the foyer to the hallway before the carpet started. Only the living room had carpet on this side of the house.

"What do y'all think?" asked Tyler. "To me he was standing here when the door opened, and he didn't have time to react. They're both in their pajamas. I think the shooter got them out of bed. Cynthia answered the door, and her husband was coming down the hall behind her. It was probably over in a matter of seconds."

"I'm with you, Tyler, and all the casings are by the front entrance," said Jamison as jabbed his thumb over his shoulder toward the front door. "The shooter probably never stepped but a couple of feet into the house. The casings are .223. It could have been the SIG 516. They sell a lot of them here in the States."

"Yeah, he fired a bunch of shots for sure. Mike looks like he's been hit at least a dozen times. Seems like every shot passed through him too. Hell, it was over for him in a hurry," said Tyler as he turned to leave. "The shooter was good too—every shot hit him in the upper body. Mike must have stood there for a few seconds. He might have seen his wife go down and was in shock. Just standing there taking the blows."

"Well, it's gruesome… Just like with Hasse, this guy didn't fuck around either," said Miles.

"No, sir, you're right. He was also very determined." Tyler turned to walk away. "Let's go tell Russ and Preston what we saw on the surveillance recording."

When the Rangers exited the house, Russ and Preston were talking to Chief Burns and Sheriff Klein in the front yard. Coming up the drive was Collins. Preston stepped away to talk to SAC Collins, and then the two of them walked into the house. "Let us talk to you for a minute in private, Major," said Tyler as he looked at the two officers. They nodded in understanding and stepped away as the Rangers walked in the other direction to put some distance between them and the cops. When they were out of earshot of anyone else, they stopped and grouped up.

"What ya got, Tex?" asked Wilson.

"Well, sir, when we were on our way here, I looked at the Williams surveillance, and he wasn't at home this morning during the time of these murders. All the blood is dry, so it definitely happened hours ago," said Tyler. "Now, he did leave his house the night before, but he was gone."

"No shit… Hold on, I'm going to get Preston. I want him to hear this." Wilson went to the front door of the house and waited on Preston to exit. A few minutes later, he came back with Preston. Collins was still in the house. They looked up to see the forensic van pulling into the driveway. They all turned to walk farther away from the front drive. "Go on, Tex, tell Preston what you just told me."

"What is it, Davis?" asked Preston.

"Well, sir, you know I have surveillance on Eric Williams's home. We looked at the recording on the way here, and he wasn't at home this morning," said Tyler.

"When did he leave?" asked Preston.

"At six yesterday evening, and he got back home at six this evening," replied Tyler.

"Well, it's not a crime to leave your house, Davis, and he was gone for twenty-four hours. He could have an alibi as solid as stone," said Preston. Preston knew that Tyler thought the driver was Williams's wife. Russ had told him that Preston thought that was a reach.

"Well, sir, Miles brought up a good point. What if Williams went to his in-laws' last night and left early this morning to come here? That would cover their ass really well. The wife's parents could alibi them. Or maybe they left when the parents were asleep and they'd have no idea when they left," said Tyler, trying his best to sell Preston on the possibility, knowing that he wasn't really convinced of his own theory in the first place.

"Davis, I know that Williams has motive, but what about the car? Do you think Williams drove his car here? The car at Hasse's murder was a Vic. It's nowhere to be found," replied Preston, trying his best to sound patient. He knew that Tyler was an exceptional investigator, but all investigators made mistakes. "Listen, I'm not totally shooting you down here, but I learned from Sheriff Klein that several neighbors in this neighborhood have security cameras. We should be able to identify the car by tomorrow. If it's Williams's car, I'll make sure personally that you get the warrant you want so bad. But what if it's not? Or what if it's the white Crown Vic? Where does that leave us?"

"Yeah, I've thought about that... The Vic could be hidden somewhere," said Tyler.

"Well, they're doing a fucking good job of hiding it. The whole fucking state of Texas has been looking for it," said Preston, beginning to get frustrated with Tyler the bulldog. He knew Tyler didn't want to release the bone. Then again, that's what made him so good. "Look, I tell you what. It's Easter tomorrow. The forensic team is here. They need to do their job. Sheriff Klein is having his officers collect video from the neighbors. You men are done here for the night, so go back to Dallas, and when things shake out here tomorrow, we'll discuss it some more. At least by then there'll be something on the car. I'm going back to Austin in the morning. Russ and Collins are going to keep me up on all new evidence that comes forward, and Monday we're having another video conference. I'll have time to think about everything and we'll go from there. But we're sure not going to Eric Williams's house tonight and put him in handcuffs."

"With all due respect, sir, I'm not suggesting that," replied Tyler.

"I know you're not, Davis, and I'm not trying to sound curt. It's been a long week for all of us, especially after the Evan Ebel debacle. And now the McLellands. It's a shit pile," said Preston, with the last week's fatigue showing on his face. "And I know you're wanting to solve these crimes, and I appreciate your determination, but we've got to follow the evidence, so let's get some more and see where it takes us. We'll know so much more by Monday. Take your lovely girlfriend to Sunday Mass and y'all spend Easter with your families. I promise to think about the surveillance and everything that we've learned, and we'll see where we're at on Monday. It's all I've got right now."

"Works for me, sir. Talk to you on Monday," said Tyler, holding out his hand to Preston.

Preston took Tyler's hand. "Okay, Davis, enjoy your Easter. Tell Priscilla I'm sorry tonight was ruined for her and that I was happy to meet her. And that goes for all of you," he said, looking at Miles and Jamison. "You men relax tomorrow and put this out of your minds for twenty-four hours. Let us handle this for a day. I guarantee you we'll have a better handle on things by Monday."

"Thank you, sir," replied Miles.

"You do the same, Mr. Preston. Enjoy your time with family tomorrow," said Jamison. The three Rangers turned and walked back to Tyler's truck. It was not yet midnight. On the way back to Dallas, Jamison told Tyler to drop them off at his house in East Dallas; Miles was going to spend the night at his house. He said he would take Miles to get his car from Russ's house in the morning. That would put Tyler at home by 1:00 a.m. *That works for me*, thought Tyler. *Shaves at least an hour off the drive home.*

The three of them talked very little on the way back. They were exhausted from the last week, and now this. All three of them were shot, mentally and physically. They just wanted to get some sleep. Preston was right: let the big guns come up with a plan. Then they would run with it.

*****

Priscilla had texted Tyler and told him she was back at his house; Katie had brought her over. He knew she would be on the couch waiting for him. Sure enough, there she was when he came in the patio door, watching TV. She came over and gave him a big hug. "What's going on, Tyler? Why would someone kill his wife too? I just don't understand what's going on. It's all so...so...sinister. Katie didn't tell me exactly what happened until she brought me here. At the party she said something minor happened and y'all would be right back. I almost fell out of the car when she finally told me."

"I know, I don't understand it either," said Tyler, as he sat on the couch and pulled off his boots. "But I really don't want to talk about this right now. Would you make me a large hot tea with a couple of shots of Jameson in it and bring it to bed while I get in the shower, please, ma'am?"

"Of course. You go on. I'll be there in a few minutes."

Tyler was determined to take Priscilla to Mass in the morning, especially with it being Easter Sunday. He was going to take this hot shower and drink the toddy and try his damnedest to sleep. You have to be mentally tough for your families and loved ones. Rangers had to roll with it or it would eat 'em up.

When he came out of the bathroom, Priscilla was lying in bed like she was asleep. Only his reading light was on, attached to the headboard. The hot tea was on his nightstand. He slipped into bed and slowly drank his tea in the quiet. Then tried his best to drift off to sleep.

Tyler did fall into a deep sleep. Priscilla got up at eight the next morning and had no intention of waking him. If they made Mass, fine; if not, that was fine too. She cooked a breakfast of chorizo and egg burritos with cheese. She put them in the oven to warm. He awoke at ten and assured her they were going to Mass. They had breakfast and headed off for downtown Dallas. "Do you think it might be your suspect?" asked Priscilla on the drive.

"It's possible. He wasn't home at the time of the murders. But as Preston pointed out, it's not against the law to leave your house, and he did leave the night before, so he could have gone anywhere," answered Tyler. "Then the old saying goes, you can't hunt deer in your living room. You have to go hunting in the woods. So I know my suspect could have been at the McLellands'. He sure as hell wasn't home. I just need evidence to put him there."

"Don't you worry, Tyler. After Mass I'm going to have the Father say a special prayer for you," said Priscilla, smiling at him with the unwavering certainty of a believer. "You'll get your warrant, you'll see."

That would work for Tyler. That would work big-time.

It was a beautiful service, standing room only. Sure enough, there was Priscilla in line to speak with the priest after the service. He would stand at the cathedral's entrance to greet and pray with the parishioners. Being Easter, the line was quite long. Tyler stood in the church courtyard and patiently waited on her. After some time, maybe half an hour, he looked up to see her talking with the priest. She spoke to him for a few minutes. Tyler was out of earshot. Eventually the two of them bowed their heads in prayer. Priscilla gently embraced him. As they separated, he held her at arm's length by the shoulders, looking her in the face. He was telling her something, and from his expression and demeanor, he seemed to be assuring her. This was all very cool with Tyler; he could use all the help he could get.

Priscilla spotted Tyler in the courtyard sitting on a concrete bench by the wrought iron fence. As she approached, her eyes seemed to glow; they looked like kaleidoscopes. She was on a natural high. She took his hand and led him across the street to the street vendors selling cups of sweet corn, tacos, and Mexican soft drinks made with real sugar. With food and drink in hand they walked the block up from the church to a small park to eat. Tyler broke the comfortable silence. "Seemed like you and the Father had an intense conversation."

"Oh, we did. He was very concerned about what I told him," she replied. "Very concerned. I'm expecting a miracle."

"Oh yeah? You are, huh?"

"Yes, I am, and the Father is too," she said with a laugh. "He told me God would punish the wicked. He took me by the shoulders and said to go with God in peace. I could feel the spirit surging through my body. Tyler, it was a feeling of tranquility. I have a good feeling for you. The tide is going to turn very soon. I just know it, I do. Very soon." With that, she took his hand and squeezed, then she turned back to eating her cup of sweet corn.

CHAPTER 28

HERE GOES, THOUGHT TYLER, TURNING off his alarm on Monday morning. Preston told him that evidence garnered on Sunday should identify the car used in the McLellands' murder. Tyler had not watched any of the news stations on Sunday night. He was going into this meeting cold. After taking Priscilla home last night, he returned home to relax in preparation for today's meeting. Easter Sunday had been about his leaving the investigation alone for twenty-four hours, as per Preston's instructions. He had concentrated on having a good time with his girlfriend the day before, and that was the extent of it. His kids had spent Easter with their mother, whom Tyler had been divorced from for over ten years, and Priscilla's daughter had flown to El Paso to spend Easter with her dad and brother. So the day had been about just the two of them. Now it was back to business.

Tyler made a special point to get to DPS headquarters well before eight o'clock. When he pulled into the parking lot, he saw that everyone had the same idea; it was full of his coworkers' cars. The McLelland murders had the Rangers curious about what was next on the agenda.

When he entered the conference room, the only Ranger who hadn't yet arrived was Joe Vasquez, and he walked in just two minutes behind Tyler. In fact, he had not yet taken a seat; he was pouring coffee and getting doughnuts and fruit when Joe entered the room. When Tyler sat down, he saw that the video feed was on with all the Austin brass in attendance, including Preston. This was unusual because he normally made his entrance right at 8:00 a.m. Even Major

199

Wilson was sitting in his chair at the head of the conference table. As soon as Vasquez took a seat, Preston got right to the point.

"Morning, gentlemen. I'm glad to see everyone showed up early. I have much to tell you, so with all of you present, I'll get right to it. The car used in the murder of the McLellands was the white Crown Vic."

"Son of a bitch," said Steve Jamison. He had been assigned to locate the car and had turned up nothing. Everyone there knew it wasn't for his lack of trying. But they knew he was disappointed, especially since it had been used again in the McLellands' murder.

"I'm sure you're dismayed, Jamison, but there were many others besides you who searched for it. It was just not to be," said Preston in an attempt to console him. "Whoever these people are, they're smart. It hasn't been easy at any point in this investigation." Preston leaned forward and peered directly into the camera. "The next thing I'm going to tell you men is of much more interest to us than the getaway car, much more interesting." Preston paused for the briefest of seconds. He had everyone's attention. "Yesterday someone sent a message through Crime Stoppers asking the Kaufman police, and I quote, 'Do we have your full attention now?'" Preston leaned back in his chair to watch the reaction of the Rangers.

If he was looking for shock value, he got it. Every Ranger seated at the table turned to look at one another in disbelief. Their minds were working in unison, each thinking, *What the fuck?*

"Sir, Crime Stopper communications can't be traced. That could have come from anyone...even a prankster," said Miles to Preston and everyone present. "There's no way of tracing it."

"Miles, you are absolutely correct. So we've taken what we know about these cases and given this additional information to the FBI profiler working the case at Quantico. He believes with this communication coming so soon after the McLelland murders, the perp was exhilarated to boast about his recent kill. The profiler believes if it had come, say, two weeks later, it was more likely to be a prankster. He feels strongly that it was sent by one of the killers."

"That's some sick shit..." said Vasquez.

"Now this is where it gets really interesting. All of you know that Davis has a video surveillance set up to watch Eric Williams's home," said Preston, and Tyler could feel his stomach tighten up. "Well, he was able to document that the Williamses left their home on Friday evening at 6:00 p.m. I say the Williamses, but it could have been just one of them. Unfortunately, it wasn't that detailed of footage to see inside the car at dusk. At this time we're assuming that it was both of them, Eric and his wife, Kim. The McLellands were murdered when the Williamses were not at home. All of us here in Austin have watched the recording. We were very busy, as I promised Mr. Davis we would be. Jason Chime sent us the video yesterday evening. Major Wilson had him come into the lab yesterday and download the video feed for us. Eric Williams left his home on Friday and did not return until twenty-four hours later, on Saturday evening. Gentlemen, this tells us that he had the opportunity."

All the Rangers turned to look at Tyler, including Major Wilson, who gave him a slight smile. Tyler just sat there waiting to see what else Preston was going to say. He felt like he was going to burst with anticipation.

"So where does this information take us? Well, according to the FBI profiler in Virginia, it takes us to a very solid suspect—one Eric Lyle Williams," said Preston, with a look of satisfaction on his face.

There was a discernable change at the conference table. The Rangers began to shift in their seats, turning toward Tyler, and nodding and looking from one to another as though maybe things were starting to finally shake out on these cases.

"All right, men, let me have your attention. There's more," said Preston, holding up his hand with a small wry grin on his face. He also knew that things just might take a turn for the better. "Now...do we have a shitload of evidence against Eric Williams? No, we don't. It's all circumstantial. And not strong circumstantial evidence at that. But that being said, you men are going to run with it. Tyler 'Tex' Davis, you have a search warrant being granted by Judge Raymond Johnson of the First District Court of Kaufman as we speak. He's been informed of what DPS has, what FBI has, as well as what the Forney police have. He had documents faxed to his office early this morning. He was fine with granting the warrant. Now you men go find the missing evidence we need on Eric Williams."

The whole conference room at DPS headquarters broke into a spontaneous verbal eruption. They were cheering.

"Hold on, men…hold on," said Preston, in an attempt to calm his Rangers down. The men turned their attention back to the screen. Tyler looked at the monitor displaying the Austin brass with a big smile on his face. "There is an FBI forensic van on its way to the Kaufman courthouse. It's to wait for you there until you arrive. There will also be two FBI agents with them, but the warrant will be issued to the Texas Department of Public Safety. Lieutenant Davis will head up the search of Williams's home. The time is now, gentlemen. If we're wrong, we're wrong. But after what happened Saturday morning, no one has the patience to wait any longer. If Williams is involved, we believe you men will find what we're missing. Congratulations, Davis. Go find what we need. All of us here in Austin believe if Williams is our man, you and the forensic team will discover the evidence. Good luck."

It was over just like that. Major Reed stepped forward and shut off the feed from Austin, and the screen went blank. The brass knew that the Rangers were more than ready to get to work; there was nothing more to say. It was time to get to work. Major Wilson turned to look at Tyler and the rest of his men.

"I knew before you men arrived what Preston was going to tell you. I can't begin to tell you how long we covered this over and over yesterday. Congratulations, Tex. With that being said, we're not going in like Nazi storm troopers to Williams's house. Yes, you're meeting up with the FBI forensic team, and yes, you will have a warrant. However, before it's served, Tex and Vasquez will attempt to conduct an interview with the Williamses this morning. If they refuse to speak with Tex, the warrant will be served and the home will be searched, and they will be brought in under suspicion. If they agree to an interview, Tex and Vasquez will assess their answers to questions about their whereabouts for the twenty-four hours they were gone.

"If Tex feels they are lying, or their alibi is weak or deemed to be shaky, the warrant will be served. If they have an alibi that is solid, the warrant will not be served. They must have someone other than their in-laws vouching for them. At this time, the belief is that their alibi will not carry water. Collins and Preston are not interested in a weak alibi. They are well beyond that. The FBI van will be located nearby to come immediately to the home. The time for waiting is over. We have two dead prosecutors and a wife murdered in Kaufman already. We can't afford for there to be a fourth. Get Jason on your way out. Take the SUVs. I believe you'll need three. Good luck, men. Let me know how it goes."

Wilson looked at Tyler before he left. They were both smiling; both were hopeful. This was make-or-break day, and they both knew it. The green light was what one hoped for, and it was on. Also the FBI was on board; it was their forensic team that was coming. They put a lot of faith in their profilers. But Tyler figured that yesterday Russ had gone to bat for him big-time. He knew that DPS brass along with FBI brass had spent many an hour deciding on which way to proceed; after this weekend, the waiting was done. And shit… what else better did anyone have after two months? They didn't, and two more people had died. Time wasn't of the essence—time was just flat out *right fucking now!*

*****

It was 10:15 a.m. when Tyler exited the Kaufman courthouse, warrant in hand. He thought how appropriate it was for the FBI and their forensic van to be parked on East Grove Street waiting for him. This was the street where Mark Hasse had been gunned down. Another crime scene that would forever be burned into his psyche. One of the FBI agents that was to accompany the Rangers to Williams's house was David Thompson. He had been the agent who looked over Mark Hasse's case files some two months earlier at the courthouse.

"Damn, Tyler, I remember when you called me into Hasse's secretary's office to look over the *Williams* case file. Shit, man, I blew you off. Then this morning I'm told by Collins to get my ass to Kaufman to meet up with DPS for a warrant being granted on Eric Williams's home. Then he tells me you're running the show. I felt like an idiot," said Thompson, looking a little sheepish. "He seems to think you're really onto something. Good job, man."

"That was so early in the investigation, David. You were right not to get tunnel vision. And to be honest with you, all I have right now on Williams is some rather piss-poor circumstantial evidence and a surveillance video of him not being at home when the McLellands were killed. Eric Williams is a very smart man. I've interviewed him one-on-one. He's quirky as hell and a member of Mensa. I'm a little nervous—confident in my ability but nervous. We're going to have to work like one-armed fiddle players to nail this son of a bitch. And he'll want to fuck with us. It will be like a game to him. I'm feeling like I did before a big football game, butterflies rumbling around in my stomach." Tyler looked from Thompson to the forensic team. "But we need to get rolling, so introduce me to your forensic team."

Thompson made the introductions all around between the Texas Rangers and the FBI team. There were two young women on the forensic team. One was a cute African American woman, Kadedra Perkins, and the other an attractive thin brunette, Sarah Lincoln. Tyler didn't think either one of them was much past her midtwenties. The two men making up the team were a little older, Bob Skills and David Moon. Moon was the senior support staff member. David Thompson and Agent Allen Harvey were in charge of the team. Tyler had them and his coworkers gather around him to map out the day's procedure.

"As you are all aware, the warrant for the Williamses' home was issued to DPS. I'll be heading up the search. Now saying that, I know we're all equally invested. I want the forensic team to work with Mr. Jason Chime here only as far as letting him photograph evidence," said Tyler, turning and pointing to Jason just in case his name had been mixed up in the introductions. "All evidence bagged and removed from the house will be your team, David, with this exception—that it is something I feel can be used at the scene to have the Williamses implicate themselves in the homicides. If you find something that you feel needs an explanation from the suspects, please take me aside and bring it to my attention. This suspect is at a genius IQ level. He will have covered his tracks beyond our imagination. I'm hopeful that he has overlooked just one thing. I'm very confident we will not find much as far as evidence goes. We are looking for the obscure. Now of course we are taking computers and cell phones, but besides the common evidence, it will be a tough row to hoe. Does anyone have any questions?"

No one said a word.

"I want y'all to know that there is a very slight chance that this warrant will not be served today. I and Lieutenant Vasquez here will go to the Williamses' home to interview them about their whereabouts from Friday evening until Saturday evening. If they tell us they went to Fort Worth to a hotel and danced the night away and had breakfast at the hotel Saturday morning from seven to eight o'clock, these are things we can verify. It will—and I repeat—will take something like that to call off this search. Any sketchy alibi will result in the search being carried out. If they refuse to talk to me and Ranger Vasquez, the search will be carried out. You will follow us to the Williamses' neighborhood and wait for our call. I will have you wait a few blocks away at a park. Does anyone have any questions?"

Again there were no questions. This wasn't their first rodeo.

"Okay, let's roll."

Tyler and Joe got into the lead Escalade and led the convoy to the park about half a mile from the Williamses' residence. The drive took some ten minutes or thereabouts. Together there were five vehicles following one another—the three Ranger SUVs, the FBI sedan with Thompson and Harvey, and the forensic team van. Once the others stopped along the street beside the park, Tyler and Joe drove to the Williamses' home. They knocked on the door and rang the doorbell. Eric Williams answered the door with his wife behind him. "You again… What is it you want now?" Eric asked in a sarcastic tone.

"I would like a minute of your time, Eric," Tyler said very calmly.

"Not this time. Get off my porch." Eric tried to close the door in the Rangers' faces.

Tyler quite forcefully stopped the door and pushed it back a foot. "Mr. Williams, I can make this as easy or as hard as you want it to be. As you know, there has been another murder in Kaufman. I know for a fact that you were not at home during the homicide. I am willing for you to let me in to tell me about where you were. If you don't talk to me now, I'm going to arrest you and your wife for suspicion of murder and take you both to the Kaufman police station for questioning. Then you can refuse to speak to anyone besides your attorney. It's up to you. Do it here or down at the station," said Tyler with a much different tone to his voice. "You have ten seconds to decide."

Eric Williams glared at Tyler with a look that could kill. Behind him, his wife was tugging on his shirt. "Let them in, Eric! I don't want to go to the police station! Let them in!" cried Kim Williams. Eric could tell by looking at Tyler that he needed to make a decision…and like right now. He stepped back from the doorway.

"All right, come in…but this is a bunch of bullshit," seethed Eric as he went and plopped himself down on the same sofa he had sat in when Tyler interviewed him the first time. Kim also took the same place she had sat in. They stared at the Rangers as they entered the house. Joe and Tyler sat on the chairs across from them.

"This is Lieutenant Joe Vasquez," said Tyler.

"I don't give a shit who he is," said Eric Williams. His face was beet red with anger.

"I'm going to say this very calmly, Eric, and I suggest you listen and listen good. How you spend the next several days will depend on it. You need to compose yourself and talk to us. The alternative is what I said at the door. If your attitude remains uncooperative, you both are leaving in handcuffs. And if you resist in any manner, I'll personally put my knee on your face after I throw you to the ground," said Tyler in a voice that conveyed just how damn serious he was.

"Eric, just talk to the men and stop acting like that," said Kim, pleading with her husband.

In an instant Eric Williams's demeanor changed. He smiled to himself and leaned back in his chair. "Fine, Davis…fine. What do you want to know?" asked Eric in a very calm voice. It was eerie how quickly he composed himself.

Tyler exchanged glances with Velasquez. Just a moment ago, they were seconds away from putting handcuffs on Eric. Neither one of them believed he would calm down that fast. "Well, Eric, we know that you left your house at six on Friday evening until Saturday evening at six. Where did you go?" asked Tyler.

"I went to my in-laws' house here in Kaufman. My wife was with me, ask her," said Eric, almost sneering.

"Is that right, Kim?" asked Tyler.

"Yes, it is. And when we left their house Saturday afternoon, we went to a friend's house to have steaks and celebrate Easter." She was obviously glad to not be on the way to the Kaufman jail.

Joe got out a pad and pen. "What time did you get to this friend's house, and who were they?" asked Joe.

"We got there about one o'clock Saturday afternoon and stayed until almost six. You can check with them. Their names are Ralph and Maggie Drake. I can give you their number," said Kim, spitting it out as fast as she could.

"So you stayed over at, what, your parents' home until then?" asked Joe.

With this question, Kim turned and looked at her husband. "Yeah, that's where we were until we left to visit the Drakes," replied Eric.

"So Kim...you were both at your parents' all night and all morning until you went to visit these friends, and they'll verify this if we have someone over there asking them that right now?" asked Joe very calmly, but with more than a hint of disbelief discernible in his voice.

With this question, she shot a look at Eric with panic on her face. He turned and gave her a stern look. She looked at Joe. "There are police at my parents' house right now? Asking questions?" she asked, visibly upset.

"Hell no, there's not, Kim," said Eric with disgust in his voice. "They're just trying to upset you. Shut up. Yeah, to answer your question, we were there all morning until we left to visit our friends and eat out in their backyard cookout. Call and ask them."

Joe looked at Eric for a good fifteen seconds without saying a word. "I'm going to ask her again, Mr. Williams. You sit there and shut your mouth and let her answer and don't say a word. I'm only going to ask you once." Joe slowly turned to Kim. "If someone was asking your parents right now if you and your husband were there all Saturday morning, they would verify this, is that correct, Kim?"

She shot another look at Eric and lowered her head. "Look, you've got her upset. I didn't have anything to do with Mike McLelland's murder, if that's what you think," said Eric, trying not to sound upset. He felt like he was on his way to jail if he raised his voice again.

"Enough of this bullshit," said Tyler. He pulled the warrant out of his jacket pocket. "Eric, I don't feel like you and your wife have been truthful in answering our questions. We are investigating the murder of Mike and Cynthia McLelland. I have a search warrant for these premises. Now again, I warn you that if you interfere with the search of your home, you will be escorted to jail and the home will be searched without you being present. What'll it be? You on that sofa or at the Kaufman jail?"

Eric just glared at him. "Fine, serve your warrant, but don't ask me or my wife another question. I'm calling my attorney." He stood up.

"That's fine, Eric. Use the landline over there. Watch them, Joe, while I call the team," said Tyler as he walked to the front door. When he got outside, he called Miles.

"What you got, Tyler?" asked Miles when he answered.

"Think we have a bird that wants to sing. Just need to separate it from the cat," said Tyler, chuckling into the phone. "Y'all come on. There's work to do here."

CHAPTER 29

Tyler waited outside in the front yard for the Rangers and FBI team to arrive. When the forensic van pulled up, Kadedra and Sarah began to put up the crime tape around the premises right away. The others followed Tyler to the front door and entered the living room, with the exception of the FBI agents. This was a DPS warrant; the agents were there to back up the forensic team. Eric and Kim were seated on the sofa as when Tyler had left. Joe was standing by the sofa. Eric literally jumped up from his seat when all of them walked in.

"What the fuck is this?" he asked, with an incredulous look on his face.

"We're searching your home. I gave you the warrant. It's that one there in your hot little hand." Tyler smiled.

"I thought it was just going to be you two assholes looking around," said Eric, obviously pissed.

"No, sir, and if you curse me one more time, I'll have you wait in one of our cars and this might take a while," replied Tyler.

"This is bullshit. I don't know what you expect to find. I had nothing to do with these murders," said Eric as he sat back down.

"Then you have nothing to worry about," said Tyler as the forensic team began to spread out to the different rooms. "Where are your cell phones?"

"What do you need our phones for?" asked Eric.

"Stop acting like a dumbass, Williams," said Vasquez. He was starting to lose his patience. "You more than anyone knows how this works. Just answer the question."

"Mine is in my purse on the dining room table," volunteered Kim. "Eric's is on the nightstand in the bedroom." The front door opened, and Kadedra and Sarah entered the room.

"Kadedra, you'll find Mrs. Williams's cell phone there in the dining room in her purse. Go and make sure Eric's is in the bedroom," said Tyler. "Let me know if it's not there."

"Yes, sir," she replied.

"Sarah, you, Jason, Rich, and Jamison go to the garage and inspect their cars. Back them out in the driveway if there's no room to work. Where are your car keys?" asked Tyler, looking at Kim.

"In my purse. The key ring has keys to both cars."

"That makes no sense," said Eric, laughing. "Everyone who's followed this case knows that the car used was a Crown Vic. We don't drive a Crown Vic." He was smiling at Tyler like a parent would to a child saying something silly.

"Thank you for that input, Eric," replied Tyler. "We're just here to waste time."

Bob Skills came into the living room. "Mr. Davis, there's something back here I'd like you to see." Tyler followed him into the master bedroom. Bob walked into the bathroom and opened the medicine cabinet. "Look at all this opioid medication prescribed to Kim Williams," said Bob, holding out several bottles with his gloved hand. "There's oxy, Percocet, Vicodin, and anxiety medications."

"Shit...she seems to have a Dr. Feel Good working with her," said Tyler. "All right, lay them out here on the counter. I want Jason to get a photo of this." As he stepped into the hallway, David Moon motioned for him to come into the spare bedroom. He pointed to a gun safe in the corner.

"We need to look in there, Mr. Davis."

"Yes, we do... Let me have a pair of latex gloves." David Moon went to his forensic equipment box sitting on the floor and handed Tyler the gloves. Tyler put them in his jacket pocket and walked back into the living room.

"Miles, go get Jason in the garage." Tyler turned to Eric. "I need the combination to your safe."

"What do you expect to find? The murder weapon?" laughed Eric.

"Actually, that's the last thing I expect to find. But I'm going to look inside it anyway. What's the combo?" Eric hesitated just to fuck with Tyler. "We can have it taken down and opened, Eric. Make it light on yourself." Jason Chime came in from the garage. "Jason, go see Bob Skills in the master bedroom." He turned back to Eric. "The combination?"

Glaring at Tyler, he said, "Twenty-six...seventy-seven...twenty-five...seventy-two. It should be easy enough for you. It's a touch pad."

"Eric, stop being like that...I don't want to go to jail," said Kim, sounding exasperated. She also appeared to be very nervous, rubbing her hands together incessantly.

"You should listen to your wife," said Joe Vasquez.

"I'll be right back," said Tyler as he left to go open the safe. He put on the latex gloves as he walked down the hallway. He punched the numbers Eric had given him on the safe's keypad and heard the door's bolt disengage as he turned the handle. The safe held a couple of shotguns. One was a 16-gauge double-barrel; the other was a Remington pump 12 gauge. On the top shelf were boxes of ammo, shotgun shells. On a shelf to the right was a file folder held closed with an elastic strap. Tyler sat on the bed and began to look through the papers. He laid them out on the bed as he went through them. He came across insurance documents, receipts for automobile purchases, bank statements, letters of distinguished service from the Texas Guard. Tyler saw nothing of real interest until he got to the last file slot. He opened up a folded piece of paper, taking a second look after setting it aside.

It was for a hunting lease here in Kaufman County. According to the agreement, Eric Williams leased seventy-five acres from a Mr. Willard. It stated that Eric leased the land for a year at a time; included was the sum Mr. Willard was paid. The lease ran through the end of this year; the signatures of both men were at the bottom of the page. At the top of the page was the name and phone number of Mr. Willard. Tyler put the other papers back in the file, returning it to the safe. He closed the safe door and walked outside to the front yard. Sitting on the front steps were FBI agents Thompson and Harvey. They were letting the forensic team do its job inside.

"How's it going in there?" asked Harvey.

"Nothing of significance as of yet," replied Tyler. "Excuse me, I need to make a phone call." He walked to the Escalade he had driven to the Williamses' and sat in the front seat. He pulled the lease agreement from his coat pocket and punched in Mr. Willard's number. It rang three times.

"Hello," came a gruff voice.

"Is this Mr. Willard?"

"Yes, it is…who wants to know?" came the same gruff tone. Mr. Willard sounded like an older East Texas good ol' boy. He had the rough drawl down pat.

"Mr. Willard, I'm Tyler Davis with the Texas Department of Public Safety. I'm calling you regarding some land you lease to Eric Williams."

There was a noticeable silence on the other end of the line. Finally Mr. Willard spoke.

"Yeah…so…what about it?" Mr. Willard's tone changed just enough for Tyler to notice.

"Well, sir, I came across the signed agreement during a search of Eric's home. I was wondering if you could tell me a little something about the property," asked Tyler. Again there was a prolonged silence. He knew the wheels were turning inside Mr. Willard's head. This had evidently taken him by surprise, especially the part about searching Williams's home.

"Not much to tell you. The land has been in my family for years. Eric goes out there to dove hunt and shoot his guns. He pays me five hundred dollars a year. What's the big deal? It's all perfectly legal in Texas," answered Willard, raising his voice just enough to sound defensive.

"That is, Mr. Willard, perfectly legal," said Tyler, trying to reassure him in case he was getting paranoid. "Let me ask you this—are there any structures on the property?" Tyler was hoping against hope, waiting for an answer, his eyes closed unconsciously.

"Yes, there is. It's nothing to speak of. There's an old barn on the place. My father built it when I was a boy. My brother and I helped him build it. We were twelve and thirteen. That was a long time ago."

Tyler opened his eyes and let the words roll through his mind. This next question to Mr. Willard was very important for Tyler. He let it roll. "Mr. Willard, would you meet me out at your property this afternoon and let me have a look in that barn?" Tyler could feel his heart pounding in his chest.

"You say you're a, what…a Texas Ranger?" asked Mr. Willard, sounding a little unsure as to how he should answer. There was more than a hint of skepticism in his voice. "Can you show me a badge if I agree to meet you?"

"Yes, sir, I'm a Texas Ranger. And I have a shield." Tyler could barely contain his emotions. He wondered if it showed in his voice.

"Yeah, I can meet you there but there's nothing to see. Just an empty old barn and some fields with a stock tank. Don't know what you're expecting to find."

"I appreciate that, Mr. Willard. According to this lease, your land is off of Farm Road 255. What is the junction?"

"It's at 255 and County Road 390. I can meet you there in say an hour. My property is just a mile up from the County Road. I'll bring the key."

Tyler looked at his watch. Eleven o'clock. "That's fine, Mr. Willard. Should put us there at noon. Do you have a cell phone you can bring so we can hook up, no problem?"

"Talking on it now. I'll carry it along. I'll be there at noon… What did you say your name was again?"

"Davis, Tyler Davis."

CHAPTER 30

Tᴠʟᴇʀ ᴇɴᴛᴇʀᴇᴅ ᴛʜᴇ GPS ᴄᴏᴏʀᴅɪɴᴀᴛᴇs into his smartphone for County Road 390 and Farm Road 255. Estimated time of travel was thirty-five minutes. He went inside the Williamses' house and had Joe Vasquez follow him back outside; Tyler wanted to speak to him in private. He left Miles inside to babysit Eric and Kim. He didn't want them to know what he had found inside the safe. It was just a hunch, but Tyler felt it was just the kind of thing Eric would overlook. After all, it was just a land lease agreement; very innocuous, actually. Tens of thousands of these were signed each year in Texas. Virtually all land in Texas was privately owned. Landowners made a hefty profit each year leasing out their land for hunting. It was big business in Texas.

When they were outside, Tyler handed Joe the lease agreement. As he was reading it over, Tyler said, "Joe, I called Mr. Willard a few minutes ago. There's a barn on the property."

Joe looked up from the paper. "You're shitting me?"

"He's agreed to meet me there in an hour and allow me to inspect the property. If I find something, I'm going to have the forensic team come out there. Tell Thompson and the others only if I call you. I don't want to put the cart before the horse. As of now it's only a hunch."

"Yeah, but you're thinking what I'm thinking," said Joe, sounding more than a little fired up.

"I'm almost too excited to think about it," replied Tyler. "But yeah…sure I am. It's just the kind of thing Williams would overlook."

"Damn, Tyler, I'm excited for you. And you're right, these leases are a dime a dozen in Texas. He probably never gave it a second thought," said Joe, looking back over the paper. "Where was it? In the safe?"

"Yeah, in a paper file folder. It was lumped in with insurance documents and shit. I almost overlooked it myself. I sat it aside on the bed. Then it hit me." Tyler looked up to see the Rubys crossing the street, walking toward the crime tape out in the front yard. "I'll call you in an hour if I find anything."

"Good luck, my man… I hope it works out." Joe gave Tyler's shoulder a squeeze and a light "go get 'em" punch in his chest before returning to the house.

Tyler walked to greet the Rubys standing just outside the crime tape. He lifted it and stepped into the street to talk with them. "Hello, Kent, Martha." He shook their hands. The two of them had big smiles on their faces.

"Seems as though your surveillance paid off," said Kent.

"Yes, it did, Kent, as far as knowing that the Williamses' weren't home when the McLellands were murdered. Then again, leaving one's home is not a crime. Not having a solid alibi was the catalyst for us being here today. For that I have both of you to thank." Tyler easily returned their smiles.

"Oooh…it was our pleasure." Martha beamed. "Have y'all turned up anything?"

"I'm not at liberty to discuss that with you, Martha, sorry. But if we do, it'll be on the news. Let me thank you again." He took both of their hands and hugged Martha. "I'm not trying to cut y'all off, but I have some place I have to be in half an hour. I'll get back with you about getting my equipment out of your house."

"Don't let us keep you, Tyler," said Kent. "We were glad to help. It's been exciting, especially looking out and seeing the FBI forensic van outside."

"You both should be very proud. Y'all were a very important asset to this investigation." After walking a few feet away, Tyler stopped and turned to them. "Watch the news." He waved and walked to the Escalade. Kent put his arm around Martha, and she reciprocated as they crossed the street to their home.

Thank God for the Rubys, thought Tyler when he got behind the wheel of the SUV. Hell yeah, they should've been pumped to see the FBI van out in front of Williams's house, especially after the McLellands were murdered. Someone might have gotten a search warrant anyway because Kaufman was ready for something to break. As in *right fucking now*. But with DPS having the surveillance, he knew that Preston and Wilson wanted to be granted the warrant. It was by far the most compelling evidence anyone had from Saturday morning.

The FBI would have to relent under the circumstances. It was all good; everyone was in this together. If Eric Williams was found to be tied to these murders, it was a feather in everyone's cap. They had all worked hard on this case for two months. But Kent and Martha…they had been the difference makers, thought Tyler. God bless their hearts. What had the priest told Priscilla after Mass yesterday? The Lord shall punish the wicked. If the wicked be Eric and Kim Williams, let him get to punishing.

I'll be glad to do my part and help him along all I can, laughed Tyler to himself. He fired up the Escalade and put it in gear, taking off up the street to meet with Mr. Willard.

*****

Just as Tyler imagined, Mr. Willard was a country gentleman. He had a cigar stump in his mouth and wore a pair of light-tan Carhartt coveralls over a white T-shirt. He had the look of the men who frequented his father's gun store in Palestine when Tyler was just a boy. Mr. Willard's hair was almost solid white—no, it was white; there wasn't enough black there to change squat. Mr. Willard looked to be in his middle seventies. He pulled up to the designated junction driving a brand-new cherry-red Ford F150 pickup truck. He might not be styling in his choice of clothes, but he had the ride down, thought Tyler. And he wasn't alone. Sitting next to him was a woman whom Tyler assumed to be Mrs. Willard. She was about his age with the same white hair. She wore it short with curls all along the neckline.

Tyler exited his car when Mr. Willard pulled up. Willard did the same; the woman stayed seated in the Ford. Holding up his shield with his left hand, he extended his right to greet Mr. Willard. The old man took his hand in a firm grip. "Pleasure meeting you, sir. I want to thank you for meeting with me," said Tyler as he returned Mr. Willard's strong grip. "Is that your wife there in the truck with you?"

Mr. Willard glanced at the badge before he spoke. "No, young man, that there is my sister. She's visiting from Waco. My wife is under the weather. She didn't feel like coming." Tyler could tell by his demeanor that he felt something big might be up. He just didn't know what it could be. "My property is just down the road there a piece. I'm fine with showing it to you. I know this has something to do with Eric, but I don't have the faintest what it could be about," said Mr. Willard as he rubbed the stubble on his chin. "My family has known the Williamses for decades. My father was friends with his father. They're some of the finest people you could know. Now I do know he comes off, oh…a little high-strung, so to speak. But he's served his country in the Texas Guard, and before he got fucked out of his law license, he served this county for years as a justice of the peace. And did it with distinction. My wife thinks the world of Kim. All this mess has played havoc with her health. Just doesn't seem fair to us. So I don't see how you looking over my land is going to amount to anything."

"When was the last time you were out here, Mr. Willard?"

"Not since I leased it to Eric. Had no reason to come out here. Got the property willed to my son. When they throw dirt on me, he can do with it as he pleases. Till then I'm just hanging on to it because my father left it to me. Too old to bother dove hunting anymore, and my son lives in Dripping Springs. He's a dentist, has a practice there in Austin. He bought some land in the hill country and had it high-fenced. Brought in some exotics. I hunt with him now every year. Got me a blackbuck last year. Have him hanging on my wall. Prettiest thing you've ever seen."

"Well, sir, I don't know if I'll find anything on your property, but as you know there have been three murders here in Kaufman, and Eric came on our radar due to his court case. I've been assigned by my Major to investigate him. It's just routine. We have to eliminate everyone who has motive. I know he's a family friend, but he is of interest to DPS. With his leasing land from you, I need to look it over. Now you can refuse, but then I'll be back with a warrant."

"No…no sense in all that, I understand. Enough jawing, let's go to the gate and get this over with." Mr. Willard turned and walked back to his truck. Tyler followed him up the gravel road, stopping behind him as he unlocked the gate and drove through, parking so as to allow Tyler to pull up beside him. Tyler couldn't see a barn. He pushed the button to roll down the passenger window.

"Where's the barn, Mr. Willard?"

"It's at the back of the property. It can't be seen from the road. Follow me."

There was a faint path in the grass leading across the field. It had been driven on just enough to make it out. Within a couple of minutes, Tyler could see the barn. It was quite large, big enough to hold all the hay this land could produce, thought Tyler as they got closer. The barn had two large double doors that were closed and padlocked. *Oh shit…*he was thinking. *If that's Eric Williams's lock, I don't have a warrant.* Mr. Willard was going to have to open those doors. When Tyler stopped in front of the barn, Mr. Willard was already out of his truck and walking toward the locked barn doors. He reached up and pulled on the lock with his bare hand. The lock looked brand-new; it was made of shiny brushed brass.

"Do you have a key for that lock, Mr. Willard?"

Without answering, Mr. Willard reach up again, but this time tugged several times on the lock. He let go, standing there staring at the lock. He was surprised to find his barn locked, figured Tyler. "No…no…I don't have a key."

"Is there another way in?"

"There's a loft door in the back, but this is the only door at ground level. Damn…why's it locked?" Mr. Willard was asking himself.

Tyler walked up and stood just a couple of feet from him. "Mr. Willard, I'm going to ask you something very important. I don't want to cut that lock off if it's not you who put it there, but it's your barn. Will you allow me to pry off the hinge and enter your barn?"

Again Mr. Willard rubbed the stubble on his chin. He reached up, taking the cigar stump from his mouth, and turned to look at Tyler. "What do you expect to find in this barn, young man?" asked Mr. Willard as he turned to look again at the lock, putting the cigar stump back in his mouth. He lowered his head and stared at the ground waiting for Tyler's answer.

"Mr. Willard, I think there just might be a late model Crown Vic in there."

He stood there staring at the ground. He began to slowly shake his head back and forth. Was he saying no? wondered Tyler.

"I can't imagine Eric would do such a thing… Let me get my crowbar, Mr. Davis." With his broad shoulders slumped, he walked to the bed of his truck, reaching for a crowbar. His sister was still sitting in his truck watching the men. The lock might have been new, but the lock hinge was old; Mr. Willard popped it off with his first try. Each man took a door and they opened them up. A couple of pigeons flew out the doors, and the two men gazed into the dark, cavernous barn. Tyler could see a string of single bulbs stretching from just above the barn doors to the back of the barn, probably attached to the loft. The single row of lights were about six feet apart.

"Does the barn still have working electricity?" asked Tyler as he let his eyes adjust to the light coming into the barn from the doorway. The barn was a long rectangle, and the back section where the loft was located was still very much pitch-black. *How the fuck did those pigeons get in here?* wondered Tyler. The barn was like a tomb. No sunlight was entering from anywhere but the entranceway. The barn was built with overlapping slats.

Mr. Willard had yet to answer Tyler's question about the electricity. He was just standing there staring into the back of the barn. Everyone in Kaufman knew that the police were looking for a white Crown Vic in both the Hasse and McLelland murders. If Tyler was correct and the car was here in the barn, as he told Mr. Willard he suspected, it would directly implicate his longtime family friend Eric Williams. Tyler knew when the old man found the barn locked he was taken aback.

Without saying a word, Mr. Willard walked to his right and flipped a switch next to the barn door. Five of the eight bulbs on the strand overhead came on. The lights were low wattage, maybe sixties. Tyler squinted. *Shit, are they only forty watts*, he wondered. As his eyes began to adjust to the low light, he could just make it out, barely visible under the loft: a tarp covering what looked to be a car. Two tires were exposed, for the tarp didn't go all the way to the ground. Mr. Willard turned to look at him. "I'll wait for you in the truck," he said in a voice that came out more like a croak as he turned to exit the barn.

Tyler didn't hear a word he said. Well, maybe the words reached his eardrums, but they didn't register in his mind. He began to walk to the back of the barn. With each step, he could see that much better as his eyes began to adjust to the dim light. When he reached the car, he took hold of the tarp with both hands, pulling as he walked backward. There it was, with the front grille facing him. A light-cream Crown Vic. His heart was beating so hard he was dizzy. He turned around and began to walk toward the barn doors. The light filtering in was angelic. *This must be what people see when they have a near-death experience*, thought Tyler. It was beautiful.

As he stepped into the sunlight, he could feel the warm rays on his face. He had never felt more alive. He looked at Mr. Willard and his sister sitting in his truck. Mr. Willard got out of the truck and walked over to Tyler. He stood there next to him, not saying a word. Tyler took his phone out of his pocket and pushed "Russ" on his contact list. It was second, right after "Girlfriend."

"Yeah, Tex…have y'all found anything?" asked Russ.

"Russ, I found the Crown Vic," said Tyler. He felt like he was in a dream.

"What? You found the Crown Vic at his house?" asked Russ in total disbelief.

"No… It's in a barn on land he leases here in Kaufman County. I need you to contact Judge Johnson and have him grant a warrant on property belonging to Mr. …What's your first name, Mr. Willard?" The lease only had the initials H.M.

"Henry." Mr. Willard's voice was still coming out as a weak croak.

"On a Mr. Henry M. Willard. Located on Farm Road 255 in Kaufman County."

"Great fucking job, Tex! You did it…you nailed the bastard! How in the hell did you find it?" Russ's voice was so excited it almost pulsed through the phone.

"Found a land lease agreement while looking in his safe. Called the owner of the land, and he met me out here. I found it in the barn. The landowner is standing here with me now."

"Damn, Tex, you had Williams pegged from the start. I listened to so much shit about him not being worth considering. I knew to give you the benefit of the doubt. No one else had a fucking thing. It's a goddamn shame about the McLellands. Would have liked to have had something sooner," said Wilson, sounding somber thinking about what could have been.

"Yeah, I thought about that too, Russ. We gotta let that go, have to play by the rules. This is America. I could have been wrong. Let it roll, or it'll drive us crazy."

"I know, Tex…but it's still a damn shame, especially Mrs. McLelland. She didn't have a damn thing to do with any of this shit."

"I hear you, Russ…I hear you."

"I'm calling in the warrant. Have Miles pick it up. Then I'm calling Preston and giving him the good news. After that, I'm on my way there. What are the coordinates?"

"County Road 390 and Farm Road 255. Follow the gravel road about a mile. The gate is on the left. I'm calling the forensic team over here. They won't find anything at their house. It'll all be here."

"I know that's right, Tex. Again, good fucking job. You're a genius," gushed Wilson.

"Russ."

"Yeah, Tex."

"I want to put the handcuffs on them."

"Shit, Tex…that goes without saying. Have Vasquez stay at the house. Leave as soon as the forensic team shows up."

"Okay, Russ, thanks." The line went dead. Tyler pushed Vasquez's number.

"Yeah, Tyler."

"Joe, have the team pack up now and come out here to County Road 390 and Farm Road 255. The Major is calling in a warrant now. Have Miles pick it up. You stay and babysit. I should be back there in just over an hour."

"So it was there, huh?"

"Yeah, Joe, it's here."

"Good job, man."

"Thanks, Joe." Tyler put the phone in his pocket, looking at Mr. Willard. "You heard what's coming. You want to be here? You don't have to stay if you don't want to."

"No…no, I don't. I'm wanting to go home. Y'all lock the gate when you leave." He was getting his voice back. He sounded almost like his old gruff self.

"Will do, Mr. Willard, and thank you."

Mr. Willard turned and got in his truck and pulled away. His sister never did get out of the passenger seat. Tyler watched as his taillights disappeared down the grass road. He turned to go into the barn for one more look. When he reached the front grille, he extended his left hand, touching the wheel well, his fingers on the metal. He slowly began to walk around the car as if asking, *Are you real?* When he had made the full circle around the car, he dropped his hand and walked to the barn's entrance, going to the SUV. He took a seat, leaving the door open, putting a pinch of snuff between his gums. He turned on the radio to KHYI, the Range, and turned up the volume.

A couple of minutes later, Brett Dillon played Chris Knight's hit song "Framed." *I was framed*, went the song, *even if I did gun him down.*

CHAPTER 31

IT TOOK LESS THAN AN hour for the Texas Rangers, FBI agents, and their forensic team to show up at Mr. Willard's barn. Rossman called Tyler when he arrived at the 390 and 255 junction. Tyler told him to come up the farm road for a mile and look for the open gate, and then follow the flattened grass road to the barn. Tyler heard them enter the gate before he saw them, but soon enough spotted the grille flashers on the Escalade leading the way. Behind the Rangers were Thompson and Harvey in their sedan, followed by the van. Tyler was standing at the rear of his SUV as they pulled up and parked. After they exited the vehicles, all of them gathered around Tyler to get the skinny on just what had transpired out here at the old barn.

"At the back of the barn under the hayloft is a soft-cream Crown Vic that everyone has been searching for, for the last two months. I didn't try the doors, so I have no idea whether it's locked. If it is, let's wait for the warrant. In the meantime, David, you and your team can set up lighting. It's dark as hell in there. Kadedra, call and have one of your tow trucks come to the scene. We'll want this thing hauled out of here sometime tonight. You have the coordinates?"

"Yes, sir, Mr. Davis."

"Where's Jamison?" asked Tyler.

"He went to the courthouse with Miles to pick up the warrant," replied Rossman.

"Okay, fine. Now in the meantime, search the whole barn. There are old hay bales that could be hiding anything. It was too dark for me to even bother looking around. If you need more light, pull your cars up to the barn door and turn on your headlights. It's going to get dark in a couple of hours. I suspect y'all will find some very interesting evidence once you start looking around. I would like to stick around, but I have an arrest to make." Tyler had a big grin.

"I know you do, Tyler. Way to go, man," said Agent Thompson. Everyone was joining in with the congratulations and smiles.

"All right, get after it. There's a gold mine in there," said Tyler, laughing along with the group. Everyone was happy to be here; nothing of significance had turned up at the Williamses' house. Now there was sure to be a trove of evidence just inside the barn doors. The FBI agents walked into the barn as the forensic team began to unload their lighting equipment and supply bags. Jacobs, Rossman, and Chime stood there with Tyler to ask him a few questions before he left.

"How did you find it out here, Tyler?" asked Jason.

"Joe didn't tell y'all?" asked Tyler.

"No…he stayed in the living room with the Williams the whole time. I don't think he was going to let either one of them out of his sight for a second," answered Jacobs. "I don't think he likes Eric too much. He kept staring at him."

"Yeah, Joe knows what's up. He's not going to let Eric pull something stupid like shoot him, that's for damn sure. He had them both sit right there in the sofa, didn't he?" asked Tyler.

"Hell yeah, and when Mrs. Williams said she needed to use the bathroom, he had Sarah go in the guest bathroom with her and Rossman here stand outside the door with the door half open. And this was after the bathroom was searched top to bottom for weapons," said Jason, laughing.

"I don't blame him. After I saw what happened to the McLellands, I wouldn't let either one of them out of my sight either," replied Tyler, looking at each man with the been-there-done-that look. "Let me tell y'all how I found this place and then I'm outta here.

"I searched the safe in the back bedroom and came upon a land lease agreement Williams has with a Mr. Willard here in Kaufman. I called him and asked him if there was a building on his land. He told me there was a barn on the place. He agreed to meet me. The rest is history. I just knew in my gut Williams was hiding the car somewhere."

"Damn, Tyler, way to go," said Rossman. "I'm not knocking the forensic team, but had they searched the safe it probably would have been overlooked."

"Oh yeah, I thought about that more than once while I was waiting for y'all to get here. Remember this morning I said to look for something obscure. It was a lucky break. I have a priest and my girlfriend to thank for that," laughed Tyler.

"What…?" asked Jacobs.

"Never mind, I'll tell you later."

"One last thing, and you get out of here…it's funny as hell," said Jason.

"Okay, hurry up, I've got people to put in jail."

"When you called Joe to have us pack up and come out here, he calls us into the living room where he's got the evil eye on Eric and Kim. He jots down the coordinates on a piece of paper and tells us to meet you here. Well, Williams sees us leaving and starts laughing. He starts talking about how he knew we wouldn't find shit because he's innocent, and on and on he goes. So Joe just sits there not saying a thing. Well, I'm the last one out the door and Williams asks him why he's not leaving with the rest of us. Joe calmly looks at Eric and tells him he's waiting on you to return. The look on Eric's face when he knew he was going to be left alone in that house with Joe…oh my god, Tyler, it was so funny. I thought Eric was going to shit himself. He didn't say a damn thing after that. He sat there with his mouth shut," said Jason, laughing.

"That was a story worth waiting for," laughed Tyler. "Yeah, boy, I'd have liked to have seen that little weasel's face. I bet he hasn't said a word since y'all left. All right, I'm out of here. Rich, jump in your car and follow me to the gate. I want you to wait for Miles and Jamison."

Tyler pulled up at the gate with Rich right behind him and went to his window. "Back up and leave the entrance clear. Keep your grille flashers on and the car parked here. You catch a ride back to the barn with Miles when he shows up with the warrant. Wilson is on his way here, and it'll probably be dark by the time he arrives. There's a tow truck and probably Collins and who knows who on their way out here. This gate needs to be seen."

"You got it, Tyler. I wish I could be the fly on the wall when you arrest Williams. The look on his face when you tell him where you've been…oh shit, what I would give to see that!"

"Yeah, I've been thinking about this for a while now. Must admit to you, Rich, when Clements was killed and then two days later Ebel was in Wise County having a shootout with our Troopers, I started to doubt I was on the right track. And what bothered me was I felt so sure. It was right there in my gut. But then when the days rolled by with no connection between them, my resolve began to return somewhat. Then the McLellands get whacked just over a week after Ebel, and I see on my video surveillance the Williams were not home…right there, it hit me."

"What did?" asked Rossman.

"Eric used that as his cover. He thought with Ebel being killed in Wise County, right here in Texas, and him being a known member of the 211 Crew, the hit on Mike would lead us to believe that it was another gang murder. I don't even know if Williams would have killed McLelland if Ebel hadn't been killed here in Texas. He thought that was his alibi. Who would have thunk it? What he overlooked was that there had been no link found between Hasse and Clements, and it was investigated thoroughly. So Preston and Russ were ready to move on someone, and I had the surveillance. Eric's a genius, but he has no common sense. He was his own worst enemy."

"Damn, Tyler, you've thought this through. No wonder the Major thinks so much of you."

"I was just trying to put two and two together. If Wilson put you on Williams's ass, you'd have figured it out too. Hey, I'm out of here."

Tyler made a right on the farm road, coming to a stop at the junction of County Road 390. Just as he was about to turn for the drive to Williams's house, he saw the grille flashers coming toward him. It was Miles and Jamison with the warrant. They pulled up and stopped next to him, rolling down the window, holding out the warrant. "Good job, men," said Tyler, as he flashed the thumbs-up. "You can't miss 'em, boys. Just up the road a piece, look for the flasher." Waving the warrant in his hand and smiling at Tyler, Miles took off up the gravel road.

*****

As Tyler pulled up in front of the Williamses' house, he noticed that the crime scene tape was still up around the perimeter of the yard. There were two media trucks parked across the street. When he got out of the Escalade, the reporters and cameramen came at him asking for an interview. He waved them off and then heard the helicopter overhead. One of the Dallas news stations, figured Tyler. He walked into the living room. Sitting there on the sofa, just where he left them, were Eric and Kim. Sitting there in the chair was Joe. He stood up when Tyler walked in. "Sit down, Joe. I want to talk to Eric here before we leave."

"Well, you can just leave now, Davis, we don't have anything to say to you," said Eric with a sneer. "You served the warrant, and your team found jack shit. You need to leave us alone. My attorney will be here any minute, and this is going to court on harassment charges. We aren't answering any more questions."

"Fine, Eric...fine. I'll do the talking, and you can just listen. The quicker you shut up, the sooner we'll be out of here."

"You don't seem to understand, Davis. It's over. Your forensic team left. Quit fucking with us. Got it?" Eric was glaring at Tyler, thinking he held all the cards.

"All right, all right, I got it. Just humor me for a minute and we're leaving."

"Let him talk, Eric, so he'll leave," said Kim. She gave him a pleading look.

"Okay, five minutes, and then get the hell out of my house," said Eric as he sat back with a glare.

"Thank you, I appreciate that. Do you know where I've been?"

"I *will* answer that question. I don't give a flying fuck," replied Eric.

"Maybe your wife is curious." Tyler turned and looked at Kim. "I had a visit with a Mr. Henry Willard."

"Oh, Eric…" cried Kim. She put her hand up to cover her mouth.

"Shut the fuck up, Kim," said Eric as he shot her a look that could kill.

"Close your trap, Eric, or I'll put a sock in it," said Joe. "You're trying my patience."

The color began to drain out of Eric's face, and his wife began to whimper.

"Yes, indeed. Mr. Willard and I had a nice long talk. That's why I've been gone so long. He showed me around his property on Farm Road 255."

"No, Eric…no," cried Kim. She began to sob with her head bowed down. Tears were dropping onto her lap.

"Keep your mouth shut, Eric," said Joe.

Very calmly Eric said, "Well, if you were out there without a search warrant, that's against the law. Not that there's anything for you to find." He was making a real effort to sound confident.

With Kim Williams sobbing in the background, Tyler continued. "Oh, I know. We both know the law. It's just that I still work for law enforcement, and you don't anymore. And when I said *we* would leave this house, I was planning on taking you along. The forensic team that left here is at Mr. Willards's barn with, I might add, a search warrant I had my Major call in." A huge cry came from Kim. It was more like a moan. Eric just sat there stone-faced. "Do you remember when you sat in that very spot and said you were glad to see I was on this case because maybe I could solve it? You said Mike McLelland sure as hell wasn't smart enough… Well, sir, you made damn sure of that, didn't you? Plus you got your wish. I was on the case."

Kim was bawling now. How could someone cry so long, wondered Tyler.

"Another thing I want to get off my chest, Eric. When I came to your house and interviewed you and your wife over two weeks ago, you bought the bullshit story I told you about never suspecting you. Well, I've had your house under surveillance for almost two months. Just days after Mark was killed. You've been my main suspect all along. Mr. M...E...N...S...A...member. Where the fuck is your common sense?"

"Fuck you..." Eric managed to choke it out.

"Oh, someone here is going to get fucked all right. It's just not going to be me. Just a couple of more things before we haul your ass off, Mr. Mental Giant. You thought killing McLelland soon after Ebel was killed would throw us off, didn't you? You figured we would for sure think it was a gang doing these murders because Ebel was a 211 Crew member and he was killed in Texas. In fact, you tried to convince me of that, remember? I knew you were full of shit. Answer me this—would you have killed Mike if Ebel hadn't been killed here in Texas? I don't think so. You thought you were so much smarter than us."

Kim was still sitting there boo-hooing. Eric was just staring holes through Tyler.

"Well, dumbass, we searched and searched to put Hasse, Clements, and Ebel together. No one, and I mean no one, could find a link. Not DPS, FBI, Kaufman, or Colorado police. Can't you read? Don't you watch the news? What the fuck were you thinking? You made it easy after you killed the McLellands. You became the prime suspect, especially when you contacted the Kaufman police through Crime Stoppers. Now that was a real stroke of genius. Just couldn't help yourself, could you? Had to toot your own horn. Look at me, look at me. Well, sir, a lot of really smart men with 'genius' common sense sat around on Easter Sunday and looked at you all right. They are the men who gave me the green light to sit right here in your home and 'look at you.' And what really pisses me off is your killing Cynthia McLelland. You're the really smart fucker... Why did you do that? She was just married to someone you hated. I know why. You did it because it made it easier for you. It would have been much harder for you to get him alone and not be seen. So fuck it...kill her too, right? When you are executed, Eric, I guarantee I'll be there watching. You sorry son of a—"

There was a knock at the door. "That's my lawyer. Let him in," said Eric.

"Sit there and shut up," said Joe.

Tyler went to the front door and saw an older couple standing on the porch. He recognized them as Kim Williams's parents. "Officer, can I please see my daughter?" asked Kim's father.

"Daddy," cried Kim from the living room, jumping up from her seat.

"Do as you were told, Mrs. Williams. Sit your ass back down and shut up," said Joe Vasquez from the living room.

The front door was adjacent to the home's front entrance. There was a partition wall blocking the view from the porch directly into the living room. The couple looked worried. Tyler stepped out on the porch. "You two need to follow me back out to the crime tape," said Tyler as he brushed past them and turned, waiting for them to follow. "Y'all had no business crossing the tape. I could arrest you both."

With them walking close behind him, Tyler stopped to hold the tape up for them to duck under by the street. There were a few curious onlookers nearby, and the reporters began to approach them. Tyler looked up at the reporters and said in a loud voice, "Please stand back, I need to speak to these people in private. Don't make me ask you again!" The reporters stopped and walked back across the street to their trucks. The neighbors walked several feet away.

"Can our daughter come out and speak to us?" asked Kim's father. "We demand to know what's going on."

"Sorry, I can't do that right now," replied Tyler. "I'm going to bring them both out in a few minutes. I'll allow you to speak with your daughter then." The helicopter was still overhead and made it hard to hear. It had gotten closer when they had walked across the lawn. "Now the two of you stay behind this tape. If either of you cross it again, I'll take you to jail."

Tyler heard Kim's mother say, "Oh dear" as he turned to walk back to the house. When he reached the front stoop, he turned to see the reporters walking over to Kim's parents, still standing where he left them. Another media truck pulled up across the street. Tyler went back into the house. He took a seat back in the chair. "Now where were we? Oh yeah… Joe, let's handcuff their sorry asses."

Both Joe and Tyler reached for their cuffs, with Tyler putting his cuffs on Eric.

"Why are you arresting my wife?" asked Eric, looking indignant.

"We're arresting you both for the murders of Mike and Cynthia McLelland, and for the murder of Mark Hasse. I do know you pulled the trigger, Eric, and I think we'll eventually prove your wife was an accessory by driving the getaway car. Read 'em their rights, Joe."

Kim Williams never stopped crying since Tyler had mentioned Henry Willard.

Joe began the Miranda spiel: "You have the right to remain silent. Anything you say can and will be used against you in a court of law. You have the right to an attorney. If you can't afford one, one will be provided to you. Do you understand?" Neither of them answered.

Tyler turned to Joe. "Take Eric out to the car. I'm going to have Kim here compose herself. I told her parents they could speak to her before we took her downtown. Tell them to come up to the porch and wait for me to let them in. I'll be out in a few minutes." Tyler was doing this because Kim's parents were elderly and, hell, he could wait a few more minutes before escorting them to jail.

"Okay." Joe turned, taking Eric by the arm. "Let's go, you sorry asshole."

Tyler looked at Kim, and she was already trying to stop crying after hearing what Tyler had said. "I'm not going to take the handcuffs off. You don't deserve that. Your parents are going to see you under worse conditions before this is all over. Now I will go get a washcloth and wipe your face if you'd like."

"Yes…please," she managed to squeak out.

"Sit back down there and don't move. I'll let your parents inside in a moment." Tyler walked into the bathroom and let the water run until it got warm and wetted a cloth. When he returned to the living room, she had stopped crying. He wiped her face with the cloth and returned it to the bathroom. He came back and asked her, "Are you ready?" Kim nodded her head. Tyler walked to the front door and opened it. Kim's parents were standing at the front steps. He stood back and motioned for them to enter. "You can sit there on the chairs," said Tyler. "Don't go to her." The older couple did as they were instructed.

Kim's mother spoke first, looking from her daughter to Tyler. "What in the world is going on? Why is my daughter handcuffed?"

"Don't ask me, ask her. I'm sure she'll be happy to tell you about it," said Tyler.

"What's going on here, Kim?" asked her mother.

She looked at her parents through bloodshot eyes. Her face was all blotchy from crying. "They think Eric killed Mark Hasse and the McLellands."

"What does that have to do with you?" asked her father. "Why do they have you in handcuffs?"

Tyler could tell Kim was making a real effort not to start crying again. "This Texas Ranger thinks I drove the car for him." She did manage to get that out sounding somewhat composed.

"Oh, course you didn't do any such thing... You told him that, didn't you?" asked her mother. Kim didn't reply. Her mother asked again, "Well, you told him that wasn't so, right, Kim?"

Still no reply.

Her father stood up, glaring at Tyler. "This is ridiculous, mister...whoever you are."

"First of all, sit your ass down and lower your voice," said Tyler. "I'm going out of my way to let you speak to your daughter."

Kim's father sat back down in the chair.

"I'm Tyler Davis with the Texas Department of Public Safety," said Tyler, looking at both of Kim's parents. "And that's exactly what I'm doing right now, providing public safety. I think the two of you had better prepare yourselves for some very grim news over the next several days. I don't think this is going to turn out like you might hope."

"That's ridiculous! My daughter would have nothing to do with such a thing. No, sir, you wait and see," said Kim's father in exasperation.

"Whatever. Let's button this up. I'll let you give her a hug. It's hard to hug someone through bulletproof glass."

"What a horrible thing to say!" exclaimed Kim's mother.

"Oh, yeah…well, shooting people down in the street and murdering couples in their home isn't exactly what they're teaching in the Girl Scouts these days. Think about this when we leave here." Tyler looked at the couple sitting across from him. "If your son-in-law did this, and I'm sure you both know how mad he was about losing his law license, who would have driven the car for him? Was it one of you?" Both of their mouths literally dropped open at the question. "Well, who, then? Eric's brother lives in Fort Worth. We checked him out. He was at work at the time of the Hasse killing. I don't think the neighbors are in the 'help your neighbor commit murder' business. I'm not trying to be an asshole here. I'm trying to brace you for what I expect to be some very bad news. I suggest you prepare for the worst. I can't express this strongly enough."

Kim's mother turned and looked at her. "Kim…Kim, should we be worried?"

"Maybe…just a little bit," replied Kim with her chin on her chest.

"Oh my god, no…" cried her mother. Her father was looking at the floor; he seemed to be letting the severity of the situation settle in. Maybe he was thinking that his son-in-law could convince his daughter to drive a getaway car for him. Hell, he had to know the bastard better than Tyler did.

"Let's go, Kim," said Tyler as he stood, taking her by the arm. Her mother and father came over and gave her a hug, not saying another word. "Y'all need to walk straight to your car and leave," said Tyler. The older couple turned and walked out the front door. Tyler waited a minute to give them a chance to leave and not be photographed with their daughter being led out in handcuffs. As he walked out the door and crossed the lawn, the reporters and cameramen began to approach, asking for a statement. Ignoring their requests, Tyler opened the back door of his Escalade and placed Kim in the back seat next to her husband. Joe was sitting in the driver's seat. Tyler walked around the car and got in next to him.

Joe turned and looked at Tyler. "How did they take it?" he asked.

"Oh, you know, they were in denial at first. I don't know about the mother, but I think the old man got it. Hit it, Joe, let's roll."

Joe pushed the ignition button, and the Escalade roared to life. He hit the siren to back up the reporters and cameramen surrounding the car and began to slowly pull away from the curb. When he got to the end of the street, he turned off the siren. As he made the turn at the stop sign, Tyler reached into his jacket pocket and pulled out his phone. He pushed the name at the top of the contact list and waited for the answer.

CHAPTER 32

When Joe and Tyler pulled into the Kaufman police station, it was total chaos. There were people everywhere. The media was out front trying to get close for that special video footage, reporters were shouting questions, onlookers were yelling obscenities. Kaufman police were doing their best to get them all to move back across the street. The problem was there were just too many people. This arrest was big news in Kaufman, and it showed.

Chief Burns and Sheriff Allbright stood at the front entrance to the station as Joe and Tyler pulled up with their suspects. As they escorted them from the SUV into the station, the helicopter could be heard overhead; it had followed them from the house. Word had gotten out that the Crown Vic had been found. It was all procedural from here—get them inside and booked for first-degree murder.

When they were in the station's foyer, Chief Burns asked Tyler, "What do you want to do first here, Davis?"

"I'm going to take Mrs. Williams to interrogation room one. I want to speak to her alone." He turned to Joe. "Take Mr. Williams upstairs and see if you can get him to talk. If not, just book him."

There were Kaufman police everywhere inside the station. It seemed that no cops were out on patrol. Virtually all the attention was focused on Eric. Most of the officers followed Joe up the stairs, including Chief Burns and Sheriff Allbright. Taking Kim by the arm, Tyler led her to the interrogation room just around the corner. This was the same room he had questioned George Hamilton in some two months ago. The reason Tyler wanted to question her was because he thought she might agree to talk; he knew damn well that Eric would remain silent.

Once inside, Kim was told to take a seat at the table. Tyler stood at the table's edge. "Kim, will you talk with me without an attorney present?" She nodded her head yes.

Tyler walked behind Kim and had her stand; he removed her handcuffs. "Have a seat, Kim." Walking around to the opposite side of the table, he sat across from her. "I need for you to acknowledge verbally that you will speak to me without an attorney present. Everything you say to me is being recorded."

"Might as well. The car's been found. Eric and I both knew if it was located, we were done for."

"Good, that can only help you. Now tell me about it." There was a knock on the door. "Come in," boomed Tyler. In walked Officer Randall Hoskinson, of all people, with bottled water. Randy and Tyler just looked at each other. Neither spoke. He sat the water on the table and smiled at Tyler as he exited the room.

"Can you do something for me first, Mr. Davis?" asked Kim.

"If I can... What is it?"

"Can you send someone to get my pain medication from home? I need my medication," pleaded Kim.

"Hold on, I'll have that young officer go get it for you," said Tyler, getting up from his chair and stepping out into the hallway, closing the door behind him. He took a few steps away from the door, waiting a couple of minutes before reentering the room. He took his seat at the table. "He's on his way to get it for you now, Kim. In the meantime, you'll need to talk with me."

"Oh, thank you... Where would you like me to start?"

"Starting at the beginning would work for me."

"Well, after Eric's trial, he was angry—very angry. He felt Mark and Mike McLelland had conspired against him. He didn't think they liked him and that the whole theft case was personal. If he said it once, he said it a thousand times: 'trumped-up bunch of bullshit.' He wanted vengeance."

"Was it Mark he had it in for the most? Is that why he killed him first?"

"No, not exactly… He ran several ideas by me. Besides Mark and Mike, he wanted revenge on Glen Ashworth, another judge at the courthouse."

"I know Judge Ashworth. What was Eric's beef with him?"

"Eric said the testimony at his trial concerning his threatening a former girlfriend should not have been allowed by Ashworth. He was the trial judge. Eric told me it wasn't true, and I believed him." Kim began to rub her hands together. "He was another person Eric wanted to take out. He had something special in mind for him."

"Like what?" asked Tyler, wondering just where this was going.

"Eric made some napalm and bought a crossbow. He thought about shooting Glen with it during the Super Bowl, but he changed his mind."

"He made some napalm? How the hell did he do that?" asked Tyler, not believing what he was hearing.

"I don't know…" she said, looking at Tyler like he was an idiot for asking. "He's really smart. He was in the Texas Guard. Eric knows how to do all kinds of things like that. He showed it to me. It was in a mason jar. It's stored at the barn."

"So he was going to shoot Ashworth with the crossbow and then do what with the napalm?"

"Well, Ashworth only lives a few blocks from us. He was going to shoot him and cut him open, then pour the napalm in his stomach and set it off."

Tyler just sat silently for a moment. This guy was more fucked up than he imagined, and he imagined he was pretty well fucked up. "Okay, he changed his mind. So is that how Mark came to be the first victim?"

"Yes… He said he wanted shock value. He decided to kill Mark instead. He wanted to do it like the movie *Tombstone*. That's why he did it at the courthouse."

"So I was wrong this afternoon when I said he wouldn't have killed Mike if Eric Ebel hadn't been killed here in Texas?"

"No…you were right about him using that as a distraction, but he was dead set on killing all three of them. He was just waiting for the right opportunity. With Easter weekend and all the coverage about that man being killed in Wise County, and with him being associated with the 211 Crew, Eric said the time was perfect. We had even driven out to the McLellands home a few days before and taken pictures. Eric talked about it for a week."

"Go on…tell me about his plan for them."

"Well, we went over to my parents to visit and spend the night. We planned on getting up early while they were still asleep to slip out of the house, then drive out to the barn and get the Ford. Eric didn't want to chance one of our neighbors seeing us leave our house early in the morning. We left our car at my parents' and drove my mother's car to the barn. That way, our car was never gone from the night before in case someone noticed. It was parked in front of my parents' house the whole time. It was all part of having an alibi."

"Eric was really thinking this through, huh?"

"Oh, yes. Like I said, he's smart."

"All right, go on. What time was this?"

"It was early. We left my parents at four thirty and got to the barn a little after five. Eric put on his disguise and then we drove to the McLellands'."

"Oh yeah…he wore a disguise. What was it?"

"Eric dressed up like a tactical police officer. He wore black pants with a bulletproof vest that had 'Sheriff' on it, and goggles. He modeled it for me just days before the murders. He also had a helmet."

"He did what…? He modeled it for you?" asked Tyler, shaking his head in disbelief.

"Oh yeah, he pranced around the house like a runway model. He was excited, happy."

"Damn…that beats all… Okay, so you're at the McLellands'."

"So when we get to their house, it's still dark out. Well, not pitch-black. It's early dawn and it's stormy. There's lightning in the distance, and you could hear thunder. It was ominous…really." Kim looked up at Tyler and she had this strange look on her face. It was like she was there again, reliving it in real time. "So the house was dark, and Eric's plan was to go to the house and say there was a suspect in the vicinity to whoever came to the door. He felt like the way he was dressed, either one of them would open the door."

"I know Cynthia opened the door and he shot her right away. What about Mike?"

"He told me about shooting Cynthia first. He said he shot her twice when she opened the door. Then he shot Mike next. He didn't say where he was. He did say he shot Cynthia again in the head before he left because she was moaning. He came back to the car, and we left. Eric was only there for a minute or less. Then I drove to the barn to drop off the Ford, and from there we went back to my parents' to establish our alibi. They had gotten up before we got back. We told them we had to run to the 7-Eleven for coffee. They thought we were only gone for a few minutes. Three hours later, we went to our friends' house for the cookout. We had steaks and celebrated. Both of us were quite happy about how well it went."

Tyler was taken aback by how matter-of-factly she was telling the tale. All the tears and gnashing of teeth were history. Kim was calm now; it was just unemotional story time. At that moment, Tyler felt like he was right about another thing—it takes one to marry one.

"So Cynthia McLelland," he said, "was I right about her? Was she collateral damage? Did Eric kill her to get close to Mike?"

"Yes, that's right. Eric felt that was the only way. He had to go to their house, and he knew she would be there. He wanted Mike dead, so the wife didn't matter. As I said, he was mad. We both were."

"So tell me…what did Eric say when I left your house after our interview last month?"

"He thought there was no way you thought it was him. He believed everything you told him. He thought the focus was on the Aryan Brotherhood and that Colorado gang, and that we would get away with everything. He said you were just a stupid dog chasing its tail. I wasn't so sure. You seemed very professional to me. I felt like you were someone to be reckoned with, but I didn't say anything. I just followed along."

Damn, thought Tyler, *"just following along"? What was up with this woman?* Tyler felt like it was time to delve into the mind of Kim Williams. From the first time he met her, he knew there was something about her, some underlying reason she went along with Eric.

"Kim, I'd like you to tell me about you. Why would you go along with Eric on this? I know that both of you were angry, but what y'all did was sinister. The two of you could have left Kaufman and started over. Moved to Dallas or Fort Worth where his brother lives. Made new lives for yourselves. Eric has a good education. He could've consulted on court cases. Time has a way of healing wounds. You're both relatively young."

"Mr. Davis, I'm not making excuses, but I let him manipulate me." Saying this, she looked down at the floor before continuing. She looked back up at Tyler. "And I was easy to manipulate…I guess."

"How so?" He wanted to hear this, he knew something was up with her and he thought he knew exactly what it was.

Kim didn't answer right away. She sat there a moment just staring at her hands as she rubbed them together on the tabletop. Tyler waited patiently for her to answer. Finally she spoke. "I've been addicted to oxycontin and other pain medications for some time now. Years, actually. I've spent days just lying in bed. My desire to live a full life seemed to vanish. And when Eric lost his job, I was like putty, I suppose. I ceased to care."

There it was, just as he suspected when he saw all the prescription bottles at their house. He knew by her appearance something wasn't right with her. He knew it the first time he met her, but he didn't know what it was. Now he knew… A person doesn't change that much in a short period of time. Kim was still several years short of fifty. She and Tyler were roughly the same age.

"Didn't Eric try and help you? I'm sure he had to know you had a problem."

"He did complain to me about it before his trial. But afterward, he used it against me."

"How so?"

"He said he would flush my pills down the toilet if I didn't help him. After that, I went along with everything he concocted. I needed my medication, Mr. Davis. Then as the months passed, and the more he went on about it, I was on board completely. His joy was my joy. It kind of…gave me something to look forward to. Maybe I was brainwashed to some extent. I really don't know," she said, with a pathetic look on her face.

"Kim, I'm sorry to hear this… It's going to cost you the rest of your life. Even with you cooperating completely, I doubt you'll ever get out of prison. Maybe you'll avoid the death sentence at best." Tyler was thinking how none of this had to have happened. If only the two of them had licked their wounds and moved on, it all could have been so much different.

Her chin dropped to her chest as she responded. "I know…I know." Her voice was barely discernable. There was nothing left; Kim Williams was a shell.

"Stand up, Kim. It's time for you to be booked for your crimes." Taking her by the arm, Tyler led her into the hallway. Waiting outside was Sergeant Cox. "Sergeant, book Mrs. Williams here for the first-degree murders of Mark Hasse and the McLellands."

"All right, Davis," said Cox as he took Kim by the arm and walked her down the hallway. Two Kaufman police officers followed closely behind him.

Tyler walked out of the station to get some air. The helicopter was nowhere overhead, but the media was still out in full force. The Kaufman police had gained control, moving them back across the street. Tyler walked to the Escalade; sitting in the driver's seat, he closed his eyes, letting the last two months flow through his mind.

Damn…what a turn of events. You couldn't make this stuff up, he thought. He had gone from feeling confident to being adrift and back and forth from there. He was glad it was over, but he was not overjoyed. Too much tragedy had transpired. Too many people had died. Loved ones had lost family members… It was all such a shame.

The passenger door opened. It was Joe. Tyler turned. "How did it go with Williams?"

"As expected—he lawyered up," replied Joe. "You ready to roll? We have all day to talk about this tomorrow at headquarters."

"Oh, shit yeah, I'm more than ready." Joe reclined his seat all the way back and closed his eyes. Cranking up the Escalade, Tyler pulled out of the parking lot, driving past all the reporters and cameras. He pointed the car toward the highway and Big D.

EPILOGUE

Tyler never went back to the barn, but he did view the pictures Jason took of the evidence found there. Just as Kim had said, there was the uniform Eric had worn to the McLellands' home. Blood spatter belonging to Cynthia McLelland was found on the vest. Many firearms were located as well as an assortment of badges and more tactical gear worn by the police. Sure enough, there they were: jars of napalm. The evidence was overwhelming. What did Eric Williams do, knowing that there was a mountain of evidence against him? He pleaded not guilty.

The case went to trial some eight months after their arrest. Kim Williams filed for divorce, turned state's evidence, and testified against Eric. All the things she told Tyler during their interview at the Kaufman Police Station were repeated by her to the jury. It was heartbreaking for the families to hear. Kim was calm on the stand, telling the story with little emotion. She admitted to wanting to help Eric and that she was happy when the murders were carried out. It was all quite chilling. Eric Williams never took the stand in his own defense.

The jury found him guilty of murder, and he was sentenced to death. He now sits on death row in the Huntsville State Prison located in Huntsville, Texas, as prisoner number 01994758.

Kim Williams pleaded guilty and avoided a trial. She was sentenced to forty years for her role in the murders. It was more than likely she would serve all of her sentence due to the nature of her crime. Should she be released, she would be almost ninety years old.

Tyler was offered a promotion to major in the Texas Department of Public Safety, but he respectfully declined to continue to work in Company B in the Dallas headquarters. Major Wilson was offered a promotion to the Austin Divisional Headquarters as a captain, but he also declined to continue to work in north Texas. If Major Wilson had accepted the promotion, Tyler could have taken his job in Dallas. Wilson asked Tyler if he wanted the job. Tyler wasn't interested.

Tyler went back to the cathedral to thank the priest who had prayed for him. Finding the land lease agreement had seemed like a miracle. It could have been overlooked. Tyler didn't take the priest's prayer lightly, and he wanted him to know it, so he delivered the thanks in person.

Priscilla moved back to El Paso to help her family take care of her ailing father. She said she might move back to Dallas someday, but Tyler knew she loved it there, so he wasn't holding his breath. He had to roll with it.

Tyler went back to his cabin the next deer season but didn't see the cougar but did take a nice buck with his bow. He's still at the grind with his fellow Rangers and the Major, just waiting…waiting for his fellow man to make their choices.

ABOUT THE AUTHOR

Guy K. Griffin grew up in Texas and enlisted in the US Navy soon after high school, serving on the USS *Holland* (AS-32) moored in Holy Loch, Scotland. This submarine tender supplied American nuclear subs patrolling the North Atlantic in cooperation with our British allies. Upon completion of his military service, he worked as an industrial electrician for the government.

As for his lifelong love of reading, he credits his mother, who saw to it that he had special tutoring in reading after falling severely ill in early grade school. His tutor, a very kind retired schoolteacher, made this a remarkably pleasant experience. Since then, not only did his love of reading never wane, it motivated him to become a writer. For this, he thanks his mother, who gave him the greatest of gifts.

Mr. Griffin is now retired, living in the Dallas area. He lives with his dog and two cats, spending much of his time writing with a special interest in true crime.